STRESS
MANAGEMENT
From Basic Science to Better Practice

STRESS
MANAGEMENT

From Basic Science to Better Practice

WOLFGANG LINDEN

University of British Columbia

SAGE Publications
Thousand Oaks ▪ London ▪ New Delhi

For information:

Sage Publications, Inc.
2455 Teller Road
Thousand Oaks, California 91320
E-mail: order@sagepub.com

Sage Publications Ltd.
1 Oliver's Yard
55 City Road
London, EC1Y 1SP
United Kingdom

Sage Publications India Pvt. Ltd.
B-42, Panchsheel Enclave
Post Box 4109
New Delhi 110 017 India

Library of Congress Cataloging-in-Publication Data

Linden, Wolfgang, Dr.
Stress management: from basic science to better practice / Wolfgang Linden.— 1st ed.
   p. cm.
Includes bibliographical references and index.
ISBN 0-7619-2946-0 (pbk.)
   1. Stress management. I. Title.
RA785.L55 2005
616.9′8—dc22

                                        2004011006

Printed on acid-free paper in the United States of America.

05   06   07   08   09   10   9   8   7   6   5   4   3   2   1

Acquisitions Editor:	Jim Brace-Thompson
Editorial Assistant:	Karen Ehrmann
Production Editor:	Tracy Alpern
Copy Editor:	Kristin Bergstad
Typesetter:	C&M Digitals (P) Ltd.
Indexer:	Rachel Rice
Cover Designer:	Edgar Abarca

Contents

Preface

When in doubt, do both!

—Kay McPherson, 1995, political activist
(cited in Colombo, 2000)

Books are predictably judged by their factual content, but their impact is greatly affected by how well the author tells a story. In the world of science that story is often told in an impersonal, dispassionate tone. Nevertheless, a major book-writing project cannot be completed unless there is a passion about the material, something that indeed makes a living story out of possibly dry material. Prefaces to books, especially science books, allow an author to reveal some of the more personal experiences that led up to a given writing project. In the case of this book on stress management, the story probably began (one is never quite sure of these things) when, almost 20 years ago, an anonymous grant reviewer noted that I had not really explained what was meant by the statement "all patients will receive a stress management intervention to help cope with their arthritis pain." I can vividly recall my immediate and profound indignation that this reviewer did not know what stress management was. Fortunately, this initial, emotional knee jerk gave way to reflection and critical reading. I discovered that there was no unified and shared definition of stress management, no "gold standard." No wonder this reviewer wanted to hear details and see an elaborate treatment protocol!

Thereafter, I gradually refined my thinking, tested interventions, and accumulated clinical experience in providing stress management, mostly in groups. All along, I kept looking for written materials that offered a comprehensive, manualized approach to stress management that could be used, and to some degree adapted, to varying clinical populations, and then evaluated for its comparative effectiveness across different applications. A number of informative and practical books did emerge in these literature searches; they often described useful techniques, offered take-home exercises for patients, and provided tips for practitioners. However, it all remained piecemeal; nobody actually put it all together. No recognizable, shared, underlying model seemed to exist; no researchers became naturally emerging leaders in this field; and researchers and practitioners did not rally around or champion a particular approach.

Intriguingly, one of the reviewers for this book's prospectus commented that most of what I was going to write about had already appeared in some (fragmented) form or another over the past 30 years. One could take that as strong discouragement against even attempting this book project. Alas (using a little stress-reducing cognitive reframing), I saw it as a particularly motivating comment because it also implied that these many ideas and technique descriptions had not been critically reviewed or aggregated into a reasoned, comprehensive format. Apparently, such a critical and synthesizing discourse was badly needed, and according to this reviewer it was at least 30 years overdue. Hence the subtitle: From basic science to better practice.

A final piece in building the motivation for this book project arose from a literature search that I had encouraged two of my students (Lephuong Ong and Sandra Young) to do. I was hoping that together we would gather material and conduct a statistical meta-analysis on the effectiveness of stress management. Although we had no trouble finding a large number of controlled evaluations that were labeled "stress management" interventions, we were overwhelmed by the diversity of labels, techniques, combinations of techniques, broad areas of application, extensive range of outcome measures, uneven training of practitioners, and different delivery formats. Instead of attempting a gigantic meta-analysis, we decided to first write a brief review paper simply describing the "fuzzy" morphology of the field of stress management (Ong, Linden, & Young, 2004). This article stopped far short of trying to settle conceptual issues in this area of research and practice, largely because the scope of such a project could not be accommodated within the space confinements of a typical journal article. In this article's conclusion, we also called it premature to consider a comprehensive review of outcomes because we could not safely ascertain whether interventions were similar enough to allow meaningful categories for evaluation. After much review and discussion, we still felt like we were "left hanging," not knowing what the body of relevant research conveyed or where its boundaries were. Now, if one is as critical (if not cynical) about the status of stress management outcome research as we were, what then is the purpose of this book?

The book's subtitle, *From Basic Science to Better Practice*, conveys my conviction that the term *stress management* as typically used in the literature is so fuzzy, and so unevenly and poorly defined that it requires critical review with an open mind regarding either its possible abandonment or a major attempt at clarification and redefinition. This book is meant to engage in such a review and discourse. Even though the reader may find it hard to believe, when I began scrutinizing the literature I did not yet know what my conclusion was going to be. Would it become only a critical review that ended with a dismissive showing of where the field had gone irretrievably astray? Or would a proposal for a more constructive conceptualization emerge? In the end, this book is meant to be constructive, not just critical.

Along these lines, I first identify the roots of the stress management field and place the relevant basic research under a microscope, describing the linking pathways of stress and health (Chapter 1), critically analyzing the elements of the stress process and extracting supporting research for a rationale of stress management (Chapter 2), and finally describing various stress management techniques and their effectiveness (Chapter 3).

The literature that bears on understanding stress itself and stress management is so broad that full coverage would require a series of massive tomes. Some review of biological, sociological, epidemiological, organizational behavior, medical, and psychological literatures (Chapters 1 and 2) was required to create a foundation for this book, yet there is no doubt that this broad search strategy cannot do justice to every piece of relevant research. It is hoped, however, that at least the major themes brought forward by each of these disciplines are identified early in the book and then accurately reflected in Chapters 3 and 4. The construction part begins tenuously with the delineation of a comprehensive stress process model that also imposed a structure for Chapter 2; its utility is tested at the end of Chapter 2 when conclusions are drawn about what stress management should consist of. The book ends with a critical summary and numerous recommendations in Chapter 4.

While I had many helpers building the strengths of this book, I claim sole ownership of its flaws and weaknesses. I am indebted to Lephuong Ong and Sandra Young for having slugged their way through an intensive literature search on intervention studies, and want to thank Jocelyn Leclerc, Yvonne Erskine, Larissa Jackson, and Farnaz Barza, who spent many hours working Internet search engines and racing off to the library to find yet another article to include. I am especially grateful to Jim Brace-Thompson, my editor at Sage, who—from the beginning—believed in the potential of the project and wholeheartedly supported it. Thanks also to my dear friend and colleague, Bill Gerin, who acted as the psychology liaison for Sage. Also, I am thankful to the reviewers of the prospectus who set my head straight about the many efforts and tribulations required to get this writing job done; their feedback was invaluable (and, of course, they were right about the trials yet to come). The additional reviews obtained on the first complete draft of the book were also very thoughtful and diligent and added considerably to my workload! That notwithstanding, these reviewers have earned my gratitude because their input greatly helped me tell my story in a more lucid and persuasive fashion: Mark A. Lumley, Wayne State University; Karina W. Davidson, Columbia College of Physicians & Surgeons; Rick Harrington, University of Houston–Victoria; William R. Lovallo, University of Oklahoma Health Sciences Center and director, Behavioral Sciences Laboratory, VA Medical Centers, Oklahoma City; Paul Lehrer, UMDNJ–Robert W. Johnson Medical School; Richard J. Contrada, Rutgers University; David M. Young, Indiana University–Purdue University Fort Wayne; and David Fresco, Kent State University.

The best outcome I can reasonably expect is not that the field can be single-handedly defined and circumscribed with this one effort; that kind of success is highly unlikely. I rather hope that readers concur with the patterns I see, and that they find some appeal in the model presented here. If these same readers can get excited enough to challenge my work and to make efforts to improve it, then the investment will have been worthwhile.

On the whole, the book is meant to be presented in a neutral, arm's-length style, but the various conclusions and suggestions are largely subjective, maybe even opinionated. The examples and case stories given to illustrate a point often originate from my clinical work or simply reflect my own idiosyncratic worldview. Inevitably, the contents are a blend of knowledge developed and disseminated by many other researchers, and of my own clinical, research, and life experience. In consequence, parts of this book are clearly driven by personal opinion and experience, and this is meant to make the book unique and to add life. Other sections, in turn, are meant to be more objective, arm's-length perspectives on a topic. A particular area where that more-objective perspective was applied is the description and evaluation of intervention outcomes. How much each of these subjective and objective elements uniquely contributes to the final gestalt is difficult to say, but I firmly believe that both are needed. Also, it is only fair to inform the reader explicitly that I am a clinical psychologist by training and experience and that I may— unintentionally, I assure you—display ignorance about fields of stress research that are not proximal to my day-to-day work environment.

Wolfgang Linden

About the Author

Wolfgang Linden grew up in Germany and received his first academic degree (Diplom-Psychologe) from the University of Muenster in 1975. A year later, he began graduate studies at McGill University in Montreal and received his PhD in clinical psychology in 1981. Following a one-year position as Lecturer in Psychiatry at McGill University, he joined the Psychology Department at the University of British Columbia, Vancouver, where he is now Professor in the Clinical Psychology Program. His research interests span psychological factors in etiology, treatment, and rehabilitation related to cardiovascular disease and cancer, eating disorders, and the translation of research findings into clinical practice. He maintains a private practice and offers stress management workshops to companies, community groups, and outpatients.

1

Stress

Definitions and Pathways to Disease

Stress is essentially reflected by the rate of all wear and tear caused by life.

—Hans Selye, 1956

Scientific and Popular Definitions

It makes little sense to write about stress *management* (SM) unless there is clarity about the phenomenon that is to be managed. For this reason, a broad but by no means exhaustive review of the term *stress* and its importance for health is provided first. In this chapter, the meaning of the terms *stress* and *management* is explored, and research is described that reveals how they can be connected.

"Stress" has become so ubiquitous and so much a part of everyday language that, at first glance, there appears to be no need for a definition. Selye (1976), a pioneer of stress research, points out that "stress is a scientific concept which has suffered from the mixed blessing of being too well known and too little understood." Consistent with Selye's view, it is argued here that when concepts from basic science become popularized, there is potential for oversimplification or alteration of the term that may ultimately belie its origins and add to confusion.

When seeking definitions, the general populace does not read scientific journals. People are much more likely to refer to other "gold standards" of definition like *Webster's Dictionary*. Ideally, definitions contained therein are in full accord with scientists' definitions but just appear in a simpler or broader language. What, then, can one learn from consulting a dictionary?

Webster's dictionary (*Webster's Illustrated Encyclopedic Dictionary*, 1990) gives six definitions, ranging from a generic definition to more specific ones depending on areas of application. The first, most generic, one is: "Importance, significance, or emphasis placed on something." The second, third, and fourth deal with stress as a feature of spoken language and sound: "The degree of force with which a sound or syllable is spoken"; "The relative emphasis given a syllable or word in verse in accordance with a metric pattern"; and finally, "an accent" in music. The next definition relates stress to physics: "An applied force or system of forces that tend to strain or deform a body, measured by the force acting per unit area." Finally, a definition is given that is more psychological in nature: "A mentally or emotionally disruptive or disquieting influence, or alternatively, a state of tension or distress caused by such an influence." One can easily see differences in these many definitions such that only the definitions used for physics and psychology contain elements of an action and a result, a challenge and a response. The novelty of the term *stress* also provided a considerable challenge for translation into other languages; for example, there are no equivalent terms in French or German, and in the end it was largely decided to use the word *stress* in the same way across many different languages. Given that Selye (1976, p. 51) saw stress as the result of a process, he further felt a need to label the beginning of the process in a manner distinct from the outcome and coined the term *stressor* to refer to a causative agent, a trigger for this process.

A two-step sequence of "stress" is also reflected in definitions found in psychological textbooks. Girdano, Everly, and Dusek (1993, p. 7) state, "Stress is the body reacting. It is psychophysiological (mind-body) arousal that can fatigue body systems to the point of malfunction and disease." Hence, popular and scientific definitions see "stress" as a process in which external and internal stimuli, forces, or systems interact, where triggers activate a response system that may lead to exhaustion and vulnerability (Wheaton, 1996).

My definition of stress, as applied to stress management, is this:

> Stress is a mediational process in which stressors (or demands) trigger an attempt at adaptation or resolution that results in individual distress if the organism is unsuccessful in satisfying the demand. Stress responding occurs at physiological, behavioral, and cognitive levels. Stress is more than just acute subjective or physiological activation and has its potentially most deleterious health effects when it becomes chronic.

Before delving further into the history and basic research on the stress concept, it should be clarified that, consistent with my definition of stress, the emphasis is going to be on chronic stress and its health consequences rather than on a singular, traumatic kind of stress exposure. Exposure to a traumatic event, like witnessing or being subjected to violence, is a profound event with potentially grave and long-lasting psychological sequelae; in their most severe form, these sequelae qualify for posttraumatic stress disorder, which can be quite debilitating. Little is known about the long-term physical health consequences of traumatic stress (with the exception of early life exposure to trauma, discussed below) and the treatment techniques embraced by stress management (Ong, Linden, & Young, 2004) are not treatments of choice for posttraumatic stress disorder (Taylor, Lerner, Sherman, Sage, & McDowell, 2003).

Also of importance is the recent introduction of the term "acute stress disorder" (American Psychiatric Association [APA], 1994), which was meant to describe initial reaction to trauma that in turn predicts posttraumatic stress disorder. There is considerable debate whether science and clinical practice are well served by having two disorders that are so closely interlinked, and that are really distinct only in the time period required for their manifestation (2 days to 4 weeks relative to at least 1 month post trauma; Harvey & Bryant, 2002). Notwithstanding this debate, neither acute stress disorder nor posttraumatic stress disorder will receive much attention here.

How Can Stress Be Measured?

Having a clear definition of a construct is a useful and necessary precursor for its measurement. In the case of stress, which was defined as a multistep process, the answer to the question posed in the title of this section is anything but simple. The great majority of what has been written about the measurement of stress is really the measurement of the *stress response,* that is, the *result* of the stress process. Because stress responding can occur at behavioral, cognitive, and physiological levels, measures of stress responses at each level would ideally correlate highly with each other, meaning that they would be synchronous. Unfortunately they are often desynchronous, and some observations made in my laboratory and a brief anecdote may serve as illustrations of the relative desynchrony among various stress measures.

When exposing individuals to controlled laboratory stressors, we routinely request participants to provide a rating of the stressfulness of the experience, primarily to serve as a validation check. This method has been very effective in showing that a mild stressor like exposure to white noise receives a mean rating of 3 on a 10-point scale whereas an arithmetic challenge with interjected harassing feedback is likely to rate on average of 7 out of 10, thus validating the anticipated differences of the severity of the stressors. However, irrespective of the type of stressor used, and provided that a large sample was tested, some participants rated the exact same stressor 1 out of 10 whereas somebody else rated it 10 out of 10. What accounts for such whopping differences in perception? It is posited that these often greatly varying ratings of the same stimulus reflect a blend of (a) stable, natural response tendencies toward repressing or sensitizing to individually relevant affective information; (b) the subjective, idiosyncratic meaning of the stressor; (c) possible differences in the ability to perceive simultaneous physiological activation; and (d) possible mood priming via pleasant or unpleasant daily events that preceded participation in the research study.

A researcher who sees such great variability in the judgment of the exact same stressor develops great doubt about the comparability of subjective stress ratings across individuals, and develops a cautiousness that outsiders may not readily share. Along these lines, I had been approached by a TV reporter who was aggregating information from "experts" and the lay public about the presumably growing level of stress in the Canadian populace. The TV production team wanted to measure the absolute level of "stress" by conducting a representative telephone survey and using self-reported stress levels as the index of "real population stress." When I told the reporter that in my opinion this method of assessment was not an adequate way of measuring "population stress," he was quite surprised and asked for an explanation. The analogy I used was that measuring "stress" was a lot like measuring "winter." We all (especially we Canadians) know what winter is, but it is also clear that there is no single defining characteristic of "winter." That notwithstanding, people know and even agree on a number of features that jointly characterize winter, including below-freezing temperatures, reduced daylight, snowfall (or increased rain in some climate zones), a time epoch in the calendar ranging from December to March, and so forth. My position with this reporter was that the more of these features we measure, the more we capture the global phenomenon "winter," and that measuring "stress" is very much the same.

An attempt at applying this reporter's crude definition to a real-world problem may further serve to strengthen the point. If one accepted that self-reported stress by one individual was a fully satisfactory definition of stress, then workers' compensation boards and various insurance companies would likely go bankrupt as a consequence of the resulting number of "stress disability" claims they would have to pay out on. In a variety of jurisdictions, workers' compensation boards already have to deal with these issues and have categorically decided that subjective self-report is clearly not sufficient for a stress-related disability.

In principle, reliance on self-report of stress would make sense if there were a close correlation (with high sensitivity and specificity) of self-reported stress with the biological markers that are known to play a critical role in the process of activation, failure of recovery, and exhaustion. Unfortunately, the literature indicates that biological changes and self-reported stress, even under relatively transparent circumstances, are at best moderately correlated, as research on acute physiological reactivity in the laboratory shows. Even in well-controlled laboratory environments with reduced stimulus complexity, physiological and parallel mood changes rarely show correlations exceeding $r = .3$. Self-reported distress rarely explains more than 10% of the variance in physiological change (Linden, 1987). While disappointing, this is not really surprising because (a) there are few direct pathways between central nervous system activity and conscious awareness, (b) researchers have observed marked individual differences in ability and willingness to sense and report physiological changes (Pennebaker, 1982), and (c) people rely heavily on contextual clues for inferring physiological changes from mental representation of environmental events ("This is an important test and I know that I am ill-prepared, so whatever I feel must be 'stress' and my fast-beating heart confirms this"). At the level of sensation, there is inherently limited awareness of biological markers, ranging from complete inability to sense, for example, lipid changes or platelet aggregation in the blood, to a rather modest awareness of blood pressure or heart rate changes, to reasonably accurate knowledge of breathing rates or rising blood alcohol levels (although even in the latter cases false feedback studies show that only large changes are accurately perceived). Understanding the relationships between context use and accurate physiological sensing requires delving into basic psychological research that differentiates sensation from perception.

The problems that are endemic to people's relative inability to accurately sense stress-related biological changes, and to the unavoidable influence of context variables on self-reports of stress, are particularly worrisome when important decisions with long-term impact have to be made and objective indices are hard to come by (see the discussion above on the workers' compensation systems that process claims for stress-related disability).

Is there an answer to the question, "Can stress be measured?" In an absolute sense, the answer has to be emphatically "no." Given that stress is not a fixed state but a process with multiple phases and with interacting cognitive, behavioral, and physiological processes, we cannot readily index stress and should not even attempt to draw inferences from it from any single index, whether subjective or physiological. We can, however, aggregate information from self-reported distress, observe behavior, and determine physiological activation that is known to be relevant to the stress arousal and exhaustion process. Grossi and his collaborators (Grossi, Perski, Evengard, Blomkvist, & Orth-Gomer, 2003), for example, have compared people with self-reported high and low burnout and found a reasonably high level of parallel self-reported stress and physiological marker activity in neuroendocrine and immune systems. Self-reported stress levels were also sufficient to predict significantly greater mortality risk over 5 years in a cohort of 6,920; this effect held true even after controlling for sociodemographic and known cardiovascular risk factors (Rasul, Stansfield, Hart, Gillis, & Smith, 2004). No class of measurable phenomena that are correlates of stress (and certainly not any single index within each class) can be accepted as absolutely reflecting "stress"; any inference needs to involve understanding of the context and needs to establish the concordance of various stress markers. One can take, for example, cortisol and its precursor ACTH, which are widely considered to be good markers of the stress response. In addition to reflecting varying stress levels, they are also influenced by naturally occurring diurnal patterns, individual differences, and random fluctuations that prevent absolute inferencing of cortisol activity to mean "stress."

Nevertheless, I do believe that it is meaningful to study subjective reports of stress in the same individual over time (as is done in diary studies) and then relate them to parallel occurring objective events, given that the individual difference variables in stress reporting are presumably stable over time. This claim needs to be tempered, however, with the fact that reactive situations (like stress and pain reports in claimants for a disability) threaten the trustworthiness of subjective stress reporting.

A History of Models for Stress and Health

The decision to start with a chapter on the history of stress should not be taken to mean that an exhaustive review and discussion will follow; the intent here is to focus on those features of previous theorizing that have most prominently contributed to shaping this book and its objectives. Readers who want more in-depth reviews of theories and proposed biological pathways from stress to disease can seek out a large number of books and review articles. As such, there are many excellent undergraduate textbooks in health psychology that provide broad overviews, and for greater depth of facts and discussion, I recommend Lovallo's (1997) excellent discourse, *Stress and Health,* as well as McEwen's (1998), Ray's (2004), and Kelly, Hertzman, and Daniels's (1997) review articles.

These caveats notwithstanding, some background on major theories and empirical findings needs to be presented early in this text so that sound, empirically based psychophysiological rationales for stress management interventions can be offered, and so that my criticisms of extant thinking and writing on stress management can be solidly grounded.

What may appear to be modern approaches to understanding stress have roots in ancient views of health and disease that can be traced to beliefs and practices of Oriental (around 2600 B.C.) and Greek physicians (around 500 B.C.) who advocated moderation, avoidance of excess, and concepts of balance and harmony. The current practices of acupuncture, meditation, yoga, biofeedback, self-hypnosis, and Autogenic Training can be traced back to these ancient views of health as a state of good balance.

Cannon (1928) can be credited with describing a view of physiological balance that at once reconnects medicine with historical views of a healthy balance and also represents a sound approach to physiology that is actually measurable and quantifiable. His work underscored that the autonomous nervous system response to challenges needs to be understood as a dynamic interplay of sympathetic and parasympathetic activation in the autonomous nervous system. These two regulatory forces of the nervous system have opposing actions and both need to be strong and responsive to achieve or maintain health.

Selye's (1956) general adaptation syndrome can be seen as an elaboration of Cannon's work in that he showed conditions and pathways for nervous system activity to become unbalanced. The general adaptation syndrome describes stress as a potential 3-step sequence of events in which a challenge (like the appearance of an aggressor—step 1) precedes the body's activation of its innate coping abilities to deal with the challenge: fight, flee, or otherwise adapt (step 2). Frequently, the whole process of challenge and response ends right there because the challenge has been effectively met, and the constructive arousal that accompanied the stress resistance and that allowed active responding is no longer needed and can return to a physiological resting state. Consistent with Cannon's work, it can be seen that after initial sympathetic activation, the body's natural inhibitory systems "kick in" in the form of counterregulatory, de-arousing, parasympathetic activation. However, not all challenges are of time-limited nature and/or allow quick, decisive responding, and the body continues to resist, becoming by necessity exhausted at some point (step 3). This physiological exhaustion is considered to carry disease potential because the body is now weak and unable to resist. Interestingly, the term *exhaustion* found in Selye's work has been carried forward into other researchers' work and, for example, a Dutch research group has coined the term *vital exhaustion,* which they have shown as critically preceding myocardial infarction (Van Diest & Appels, 2002). Vital exhaustion describes a psychophysiological state of mental numbing that is related to perceived low self-efficacy (i.e., an awareness of one's own low level of effectiveness), inability to cope, and a subjective sense of low energy and fatigue, thus vividly describing a blend of biological and emotional features that aptly represents Selye's notion of exhaustion.

Selye's original work posited a whole-body response such that external challenges were held to lead to the same cascade of physiological responses. The typically occurring physiological changes in response to a challenge are well established and described in numerous textbooks. Figure 1.1 describes the paths and the sequence of activities in Selye's activation-exhaustion model (1976).

This coarse model of Selye's activation/exhaustion model leads to a series of questions that need answering if the full process is to be understood: (a) Which stimuli (or stimulus properties) activate the process? (b) What is the physiological chain of actions that mark an activation process? (c) Who, under what circumstances, adapts and who, under what circumstances, becomes exhausted? Satisfactory answers to these core questions ought to provide the stress management researcher with the critical knowledge needed to develop a sound rationale for interventions.

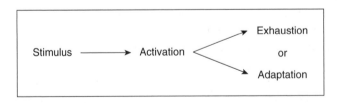

Figure 1.1   The Selye Model of Stress

Stress-triggering qualities of stimuli will not be discussed first (a detailed review is found at the beginning of Chapter 2). Instead, the physiological activation process is described first because it is central to the originality of Selye's work. Selye believed in response universality; that is, all stimuli above perception threshold are held to trigger similar physiological stress responses across different species and across situations. This presumably universal cascade of events (adapted from Sarafino, 2002) is as follows:

1. Environmental stimuli that are judged to be of subjective importance trigger cortical activation that sends chemical messengers to the hypothalamus, where

2. they stimulate the production of corticotrophic releasing factor (CRF) and other chemical messengers that, in turn, activate two distinct tracks of bodily reactions.

3. In the first track (also commonly referred to as the sympathetic adrenal medullary axis), these messengers feed information forward to the pituitary gland, which

4. changes the chemical structure of the messengers and releases adrenocorticotropic hormone (ACTH) into the bloodstream.

5. When ACTH reaches the adrenal glands, it initiates the production of cortisol, which, in turn, increases metabolic rate. Cortisol inhibits the function of phagocytes and lymphocytes in the immune system (i.e., it serves as a messenger for needed adaptations of the immune system).

6. On the second track (commonly referred to as the hypothalamic-pituitary axis), chemical messengers leave the hypothalamus and trigger electrochemical changes that advance as signals down the brain stem and the spinal cord toward the adrenal glands.

7. At the level of the adrenal gland, this activation leads to release of epinephrine, which supplies extra glucose to musculature and brain. Epinephrine also increases suppressor T-cells and decreases helper T-cells, thus revealing a second connective pathway of stress reactivity to immune function.

8. The adrenal glands also release norepinephrine, which then speeds up heart rate and increases cardiac output and blood pressure.

9. Ultimately these activities and their results are fed back to the hypothalamus, which serves as the "master controller" of this whole process.

This cascade of physiological responses to challenge involves intricate interplays and feedback loops of biochemical and electrophysiological processes that regulate autonomic nervous, endocrine, and immune system activity. Within the autonomic nervous system, activation of the sympathetic branch (via release of ACTH) prepares organs for the fight-or-flight response by dilating pupils and bronchi, increasing the rate and force of the heart's pumping action, constriction of blood vessels, secretion of epinephrine, and decreasing peristalsis. An important physiological control function is assigned to the parasympathetic branch of the autonomous nervous system that opposes these actions and is functionally designed to facilitate recovery. One can readily see that the teaching and learning of techniques to maximize parasympathetic system flexibility is of critical importance to physiological stress management.

This activation process, that is, the fight-or-flight response, does not carry within its definition any connotation of inherent maladaptiveness; if anything, the opposite is true as long as fight or flight is really necessary for survival. In the evolution of species, fight-or-flight responses are highly useful tools for survival because they maximize the availability of muscular energy, sensory acuity, and protection of tissues from injury. However, a critical and widely accepted feature of Selye's view of the activation response is that our biological systems cannot sustain this activation for a long period of time; all living creatures become exhausted if the fight-or-flight response does not lead to resolution of the challenge. The changed flow of blood during activation relative to rest can be used to show how initial adaptiveness of the activation process can turn into a long-term health threat. During rest, most of the body's blood volume circulates between the heart and the viscera so that needed nutrients and oxygen are available for organ function; that is, about 60% of blood flow during rest goes to the kidneys, skin, digestive system, and bones. During fight-or-flight responses, however, the bulk of the total blood volume is made available to the muscles and the brain, with only a fraction still being available to support visceral functions (in that case, only about 20% of the blood volume goes to skin, digestive system, kidneys, and bones; Astrand & Rodahl, 1970). Just as whole living beings cannot stay alive without nutrients or oxygen for an extended period of time, neither can individual organs. Recovery from the stress-induced blood redistribution to muscles and brain needs to occur relatively quickly if the organ tissues are not to suffer damage from lack of nutrients and oxygen. This relatively simplistic description of how activation can turn to exhaustion is quite suitable for explaining the stress-exhaustion process to patients who present with stress-related psychophysiological disorders.

Selye's idea of response universality has been challenged by subsequent models and research findings discussed in more detail below. What was initially a simple stimulus-response model was expanded to include genetic and early learning differences in responsivity as well as acute response modulation through behavioral and cognitive activity.

In order to understand how macro-level effects at the community level can affect cellular activity and vice versa, Brody has described a 17-layer system in which levels of influence for stress and health are organized on a continuum from mini to macro activity, from atom to molecule, to cell and tissue, to organs, systems, whole person, and finally community and society (Brody, 1973). He presumes that each level of activity influences the ones directly above and below so that ultimately a connection can be shown between molecular change and societal change. The direction of influence can be ascending and descending on this continuum.

A particularly influential model of stress and health is Levi's (1972) interactional model (Figure 1.2), which extends Selye's work by arguing that the magnitude of a stress response can be better predicted by understanding the stressor in the context of a person's predisposition, thus opening the door for a better understanding of individual differences in the stress response magnitude.

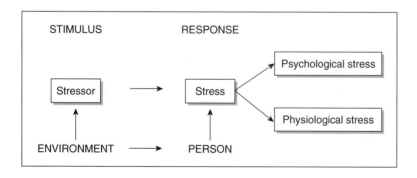

Figure 1.2   The Stress Diathesis Model

While useful for driving and organizing further research, Selye's and Levi's models are now considered simplistic by more cognitively oriented researchers. Before continuing to discuss more expansive models, it may be of use to organize existing models into categories. For the purpose of this book, the categorization structure proposed by Feuerstein, Labbe, and Kuczmierczyk (1986, p. 122) was adopted here; it differentiates the following four types of models: (1) response-based models, (2) stimulus-based models, (3) interactional models, and (4) information processing models.

Selye's model is considered a response-based model because it presumes that all stimuli trigger the same cascade of physiological responses and that the nature of the response (activation and resolution vs. activation and exhaustion) ultimately dictates the health outcome. Levi's model is more of an interaction model because it opens up the possibility that the response to a stimulus is not universal but affected by the type of stressor and the context, which, if understood, allows a prediction of the magnitude and likelihood of a subsequent stress response. The problem with simple response- and stimulus-based models is that they do not account for the great variation that people actually show under equally demanding conditions. Interactional and information processing models allow for the existence of feedback systems and presume a more cyclical nature of stress processes. In one such model (Cox & McKay, 1978), a critical element in determining the magnitude of a potential stress response is the cognitive appraisal of a demand situation in that stress is presumed to result when the perceived capability to cope does not meet the perceived demand. This "imbalance" is by definition "stress." Perceived ability to cope is in part determined by actual capability, and perceived demand is in part determined by actual demand. Discrepancies between actual and perceived demand and actual and perceived coping capability are further moderated by prior learning and personality differences. Cox and McKay further posit that individuals judge the adaptivity of their coping attempts and that information is fed back to the individual, who may then reevaluate the stressfulness of the situation, or the levels of (perceived and actual) demand and capability.

Information-processing models are fairly similar in that they focus on attention, appraisal, and memory processes. Hamilton (1980) sees perceived stress levels as the aggregated result of a stressor recognition and evaluation process that integrates the importance and meaning of the stressor, the amount of attention that the system allocates to it, and memories about past effective and noneffective coping experiences. According to Hamilton, stressors themselves can have three challenging qualities:

(1) anticipation of physical pain or danger, (2) threat of social isolation or rejection, and (3) stimulus complexity involving either concurrent response demands or novelty and complexity. More than one of these qualities may be present at the same time, and it is reasonable to predict that stressors are ultimately leading to greater stress responses if two or even three of these qualities are present simultaneously.

When trying to use models of stress to build an empirically grounded rationale for stress management, one needs to realize how application of various stress theories to different species also creates unique challenges and opportunities for studying stress-related disease etiology. Applying basic research findings from the animal model to human applications is particularly challenging for understanding attempts at prevention and intervention. This can be illustrated by relating stress models to plants, animals, and humans and by highlighting similarities and differences. Bernard (1961) makes the case for a reductionist approach to understanding survival of simple organisms like plants. These organisms are dependent on their environment to supply nutrients, water, light, and so forth, and if these "supplies" become exhausted, the organism dies. Yet even this reductionist perspective allows adaptation in that plants may evolve to thrive in more or less light, or varying degrees of water supply; ultimately, however, they are still supply-dependant. Animals, on the other hand, have mobility and can actively seek out supplies, and this search can lead to extreme efforts such as the annual migration of geese over thousands of miles, even from one hemisphere to the other, in order to obtain stable food supplies. This greater mobility translates into much greater activation potential of the organism, but that, in and of itself, also carries the potential for quicker physical exhaustion as can be seen, again, in the example of migratory birds who may not survive a lengthy migratory flight to their winter (or summer) location. In humans, there is the same principal dependence on environmental features as applies to all organisms (e.g., oxygen and nutrients), there also is mobility (fight or flight) as is seen in animals, and, in addition, humans possess cognition and mental representation that can serve as stress triggers (which will be discussed later in this book). Cognition is also a potential source of stress resolution. Without denying the possibility of thought processes and a degree of consciousness in animals, findings from tests of animal models offer little generalizability to human cognitions. Stress triggers for humans can range from very physical (like lack of air supply during an asthma attack, which is of course a factual challenge to survival of the organism), to very psychological and human-specific triggers, like a sudden fear response to the teacher's announcement of a pending test for which a student did not study, or a husband's sudden realization that he forgot to get a birthday gift for his wife. Hence, the gamut of potential stress triggers for humans is almost infinite, covering physical, objective challenges inherent in the environment at one end of the spectrum, as well as symbolic and learned challenges at the other end.

The most recent models of stress and health have challenged Cannon's (1935) relatively rigid notion that a homeostatic state is needed and desirable for survival, and have attempted to classify the types of challenges that do not merely trigger acute responses but also possess potential to become chronic stress triggers. Theorizing about ideally functioning physiological systems had initially focused on the idea that there are ideal values (reflecting homeostasis in the sense of Cannon) and elevated, that is, maladaptive, values (as is the case with blood pressure). However, this model implied a rather static definition of homeostasis and has been replaced by the recognition that living systems must adapt, change, and accommodate to changing circumstances to guarantee survival of a species. A system's ability to achieve long-term stability and health through ongoing adjustment change has been labeled allostasis (Sterling & Eyer, 1988). Allostasis presumes that physiological systems strive to remain within a healthy range of function that allows optimal responsivity to external challenges while maintaining their own control functions. The allostasis concept is not meant to be in contradiction to the homeostasis concept; rather it modifies the definition of homeostasis as a desired variability within a healthy range instead of a fixed static level. A good example of the danger of "excessive stability" in the physiological domain is the observed lack of variability in the intervals between heartbeats that precede sudden cardiac death (Kamarck & Jennings, 1991). Similarly, the immune system works at its best when responding to immune challenges, and it is argued that repeated challenges can strengthen the system's ability for future adaptive responding; this principle is, of course, the well-known rationale for vaccinations. The same can be stated for the value of physical exercise, which, when applied in moderation, serves as a stress buffer because it enhances the body's ability to adjust, to respond quickly to challenges. At a psychological level, parents, for example, must adjust their expectations about reasonable rights and responsibilities for their growing children; as the children mature, curfews and allowances may need to be adjusted upward, and increasing levels of responsibility can be expected in return. Failing to make such adjustments is almost guaranteed to create family strain and prevent desired maturation.

The extent of challenges or demands on a system is, then, referred to as the allostatic load, which at some point may exceed a given system's ability to cope. McEwen (1998) describes four types of situations in which the nature of the challenge and the resulting allostatic load may exceed the body's capacity to respond and therefore lead to damage. The first such scenario is the frequent repetition of exposure to a stimulus with no time for recovery before the next stressor is represented. Figure 1.3 displays this "repeated hits" scenario.

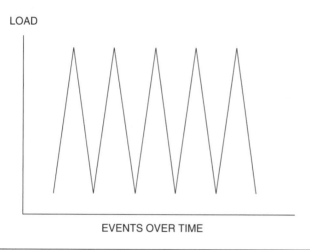

LOAD

EVENTS OVER TIME

Figure 1.3   Repeated Hits Model

A real-world scenario that represents this type of situation would be emergency room staff in a busy city hospital where recent personnel cuts have led to serious understaffing that requires frequent overtime work. Anybody watching an episode of *E.R.* on television will see this scenario come to life! The potential for quick burnout and exhaustion in this environment is readily apparent.

A second type of allostatic overload is also characterized by repeated stressor appearance but differs in that some individuals fail to show adaptation that others are capable of. An example would be adjustment (or the lack thereof) to living close to a fire station; some people may develop the capacity of sleeping through repeated siren noise in the night whereas others simply fall farther and farther into sleep deprivation. This scenario is displayed in Figure 1.4.

A third type of stressor situation with high "overload potential" is one where badly needed recovery is delayed or fails to happen. This type of situation (displayed in Figure 1.5) arises, for example, through chronic work stress or in response to interpersonal conflict, as diary studies of marital interactions (DeLongis, Folkman, & Lazarus, 1988) and interpersonal

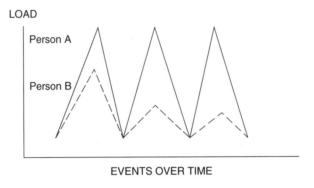

Figure 1.4   Lack of Adaptation Model

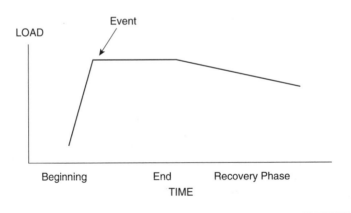

Figure 1.5   Lack of Recovery Model

laboratory stressor studies (Earle, Linden, & Weinberg, 1999; Linden, Rutledge, & Con, 1998) have shown. Such scenarios are not particularly rare, as Frankenhaeuser (1991) has shown in her psychophysiological evaluations of working mothers. These women showed understandable stress responses to heavy demands at the workplace, and the return home provided no reprieve either (as was shown by tracking stress hormone release) because there still were housework and other family responsibilities waiting for them.

A fourth situation is not displayed graphically because it involves multiple, complex, interacting systems; here the inadequate response of one allostatic system triggers a compensatory response in other systems. An example of this nature provided by McEwen (1998) describes stress hormone activity. If cortisol secretion in response to a challenge does not occur, then inflammatory cytokines are released that make animals (and presumably humans alike) susceptible to autoimmune disturbances.

The addition of the allostatic load concept to stress research represents an expansion, refinement, and evolution of Selye's concept of the adaptation syndrome but does not contradict its basic premises. With the addition of research on allostasis, there now is a richer, better-documented picture of how to differentiate normal from pathological stress responding, and extensive descriptions exist of various critical situations as well as a rich body of studies on the physiological pathways and their interactions for understanding the linkage of stress to disease outcomes. Interestingly, neither Selye's original work nor the expansion model arising from the allostasis concept deals with how the stimuli themselves come into existence, whether or not they deserve attention, and whether they can be eliminated or manipulated. These stress models do not address the question of potential modifiability of the stimuli themselves. The inherent message is that stressors exist and that physiological systems (and the people who are governed by these systems) must respond; that is, people are not seen as creators or shapers of their own environment, they are simply considered to be reactors.

Understanding Stress Responsivity

Individual Differences in Stress Responding and Their Origins

As any astute reader of scientific articles on stress reactivity will quickly find out (especially when reviewing tables of results in stress reactivity studies), people's responses to the exact same stimulus vary greatly. In my laboratory, we have obtained such evidence in numerous controlled studies where participants were exposed to contrived stressors (like physical exertion, mental arithmetic, simulated public speeches, or affect provocation). It is normal and typical that under the exact same stimulus condition one can see an average increase of 10 beats in heart rate and maybe an *average* of 10-mmHg (millimeters of mercury) increase of systolic and diastolic blood pressure (SBP and DBP, respectively) in a healthy sample. Yet one not-infrequently observed extreme in response variability can be an actual *drop* in heart rate and blood pressure (of −5 points) under acute stress (relative to resting baseline). At the other extreme, heart rate increases of +50 beats/minute, SBP increases of +40 mmHg and DBP increases of +30 mmHg are also often observed in the most responsive research participants, who, incidentally, may not show any signs of cardiovascular disease at the time. Understanding the reasons for this remarkable variability in subjective and in cardiovascular stress responsivity may hold important clues for changing reactivity, and it may provide information for what to build into the rationales for stress management.

For this reason, the current section is devoted to a description of the wide range of variables that are known to mediate and moderate stress reactivity. The reader should note that (similar to the above section on stress-disease pathways) this section can serve only as an illustration and not an exhaustive review of all prior research on stress reactivity. For more detail, the reader can consult Lovallo's (1997) book, or a special issue of *Psychosomatic Medicine* where the status quo of the cardiovascular reactivity concept was placed under a magnifying glass (Kamarck & Lovallo, 2003; Linden, Gerin, & Davidson, 2003; Schwarz et al., 2003; Treiber et al., 2003). In the following pages, known classes (or types) of moderating and mediating factors are described, and many examples are given of how they interact to buffer against stress consequences or how they may act to worsen stress responses.

Genetic Predispositions

On the surface, it makes sense that SM researchers and practitioners are knowledgeable about but not overly interested in genetic predispositions for exaggerated stress responses because genetics are not open to modification; however, the same argument also underlines the importance of modifying those risk factors that are actually open to change. When one is known to be at risk, the subjective importance of modifying what is open to change ought to increase. Especially individuals with a genetic predisposition for stress-related diseases ought to have a keen interest in changing modifiable risk factors. Ewart (1991), for example, has presented a persuasive pathway model of how genetics and environment interact in the etiology of hypertension. He presents evidence that hostility aggravates the frequency and intensity of stress activation and that hostility is at least in part transmitted within families. This observation is supported by data on intra-class coefficients for siblings' personalities; among monozygotic twins the heritability coefficient for personality is estimated as .50; this decreases to .25 for dizygotic twins, and drops to .05 for adopted siblings. In sum, it is well established that family history of hypertension increases risk of the disease, and it is paired with typically heightened reactivity to stress. Personality, which is also partly genetic, has been shown to predict physical disease (Booth-Kewley & Friedman, 1987), and some personality features like hostility are predictive of greater stress responses.

Early Learning

In addition to genetic predispositions for differential stress reactivity, there is growing evidence that exposure to traumatic events early in life can serve a similar predispositional role that leaves some individuals more susceptible to long-term stress effects. Kendler and his colleagues (2000), for example, have investigated life event stress exposure and its predictive power for development of major depression and generalized anxiety disorder. They assessed life events that included dimensions of loss, humiliation, entrapment, and danger in a sample of 7,322 male and female twins and determined depression and anxiety prevalence. Not only did life events indeed predict prevalence of affective disturbance, but distinguishable event dimensions had specific consequences in that loss alone was not very predictive of long-term affect, but loss paired with humiliation was particularly predisposing for depression whereas loss and danger experiences jointly were more likely to lead to elevated anxiety.

The Kendler et al. study is one of many that provide compelling epidemiological evidence that adverse experience during childhood increases the likelihood of alcohol and drug dependence, eating disorders, affective disorders, posttraumatic stress disorder, and suicidal behavior (for a review see Surtees et al., 2003). Although epidemiological work can provide only "surface" descriptions of relationships, other researchers have extended this work by studying biological pathways, using animal models that center around maternal separation and abandonment stress (Caldji et al., 2001; Meaney et al., 1996). These researchers have shown consistent magnifying effects of early stress exposure on the nature of the hypothalamic-pituitary-adrenal axis response to stress. Similar impact of early stress exposure on cell-mediated immunity and subsequent survival has also been shown in rhesus monkeys (Lewis, Gluck, Petitto, Hensley, & Ozer, 2000), MRI technology has permitted showing how early trauma affects brain morphology in humans (DeBellis, 2001), and an autopsy study of Japanese children has confirmed adverse early trauma sequelae in terms of compromised immune function (Fukunaga et al., 1992). Using health care use as an index of the cost of stress, Biggs, Aziz, Tomenson, and Creed (2003) have also demonstrated that childhood adversity was an independent predictor of health care use in functional gastrointestinal disorders.

Personality

A connection of personality (i.e., enduring patterns of behavior) and disease may come about via different, typically indirect pathways. One such influence pathway sees certain personality types as translating into response predispositions that ultimately affect physiological regulatory systems (Schwartz et al., 2003). Another potential pathway is via stable individual differences in magnitude and frequency of stress responses (details follow in a later section), and a third one is via the influence that personality has on influencing other risk factors for disease.

Small but significant, simple linear relationships of personality predictors of blood pressure exist and have been found for trait anger/hostility, anxiety, depression, and defensiveness (Rutledge & Hogan, 2002). Rutledge and Hogan conducted a meta-analysis of studies that measured personality features and that also studied blood pressure change with follow-ups of 1 year or longer (averaging 8.4 years). Significant r values between .07 and .09 were observed for anger, depression, anxiety, and defensiveness, with defensiveness being the least often studied but overall strongest predictor.

Finally, there is evidence for linkages of personality factors to tonic physiological indices, which themselves are disease predictors. Using ambulatory blood pressure monitoring, Linden and his collaborators (Linden, Chambers, Maurice, & Lenz, 1993) showed that low social support in women, and high hostility and defensiveness in men, were associated with elevated levels of blood pressure even after the statistical effects of traditional risk factor effects had been partialled out. They also observed that high social support was negatively correlated with hostility, thus indicating a link between a personality factor and a stress-buffering feature. Further, in a randomized, controlled clinical trial of psychotherapy for hypertension, those patients with the greatest hostility reductions and those with improvements in use of constructive anger expression behavior showed the greatest blood pressure reductions during treatment (Linden, Lenz, & Con, 2001).

Miller and his collaborators (Miller, Cohen, Rabin, Skoner, & Doyle, 1999) assessed major dimensions of personality and tonic cardiovascular, neuroendocrine, and immunological parameters in 276 healthy adults. While neuroticism was generally unrelated to any physiological function, low extraversion was associated with higher blood pressure, epinephrine and norepinephrine, and natural killer cell activity. Low agreeableness (which is conceptually similar to hostility) was positively related to higher systolic and diastolic blood pressure and epinephrine. The magnitude of personality and physiology intercorrelation was small, accounting for no more than 7% of the variance. Interestingly, health practices that are presumed to represent one possible path for stress leading to disease did not mediate the association between physiology and personality.

Miller et al.'s findings map well onto results of Denollet and his collaborators (Denollet, Sys, & Brutsaert, 1995; Denollet et al., 1996), who have shown that a novel personality construct (coined "Type D," and consisting of social introversion and emotional inhibition) is highly predictive of cardiac death in cardiac patient populations. When the Type D construct was used to predict acute reactivity in the laboratory, the overall Type D construct did not predict cardiovascular reactivity per se (Habra, Linden, Andersen, & Weinberg, 2003). However, the two subfactors of Type D were independently predictive of differential cardiac and endocrine reactivity in a harassing laboratory paradigm; this was particularly true in men (Habra et al., 2003).

While most of the attention in the personality-disease literature has been given to indices of affective distress (i.e., anxiety, depression, anger/hostility), there is also a growing literature referred to as the "positive psychology" movement that attempts to identify psychological traits that buffer and protect from stress consequences (Lutgendorf, Vitaliano, Tripp-Reimer, Harvey, & Lubaroff, 1999). Some of that attention has been directed at the construct of sense of coherence (Antonovsky, 1979) and cannot be written off as simply being the opposite of negative affect.

Sense of coherence (SOC) is akin to possessing a meaning, a sense of purpose, a positive spiritual strength. In a sample of older adults who were about to relocate, SOC played a significant mediational role in buffering against the stress of relocation that was indexed by natural killer (NK) cell activity (Lutgendorf et al., 1999). This study compared healthy older adults about to move with a matched control group that was not moving, and found that poorest NK activity was seen in "movers" with a low sense of coherence. Fournier, de Ridder, and Bensing (1999) have studied the role of optimism in coping with multiple sclerosis; these researchers found optimism incorporated three distinct subfactors, namely outcome expectancies, efficacy expectancies, and unrealistic thinking. Unrealistic thinking was clearly related to mobility restrictions and was considered maladaptive; outcome and efficacy expectancies explained depression but were unrelated to mobility. The presence of optimism and social support were independent predictors of good physical outcomes in cardiac patients during their rehabilitation phase (Shen, McCreary, & Myers, 2004).

In sum, there is a growing literature that supports personality factors explaining small amounts of variance in predictor models of acute stress reactivity and in the etiology of stress-related diseases. Both stress-increasing and stress-buffering personality features have been identified. Although such linear independent contributions of personality to stress-related health indices have been established, current theoretical models place more emphasis on interactive models such that personality may exacerbate responses to acute stress and maintain chronic stress. Personality plays a more potent role in disease development when it is seen as a response predisposition that has its full effect when it is paired with the presence of environmental triggers that activate its hyperarousal propensities.

Stressor Exposure and Stress Reactivity as Predictors for Disease

The relationships between various stress response system markers, types of stressors, and response mediators and moderators have been extensively studied (for a review see Lovallo, 1997), and only summaries can be provided here. The trend in this literature is to move away from simple, direct cause-and-effect models and study multiple interacting systems and their short- and long-term adaptations. There is little doubt that complex models map much better onto the observed data on biological pathways and that, as a by-product, it becomes ever more challenging for researchers to advance the field because the best studies are the ones that broadly capture multiple response systems, predispositional factors, and consider both short- and long-term psychological and physiological adaptation.

The cascade of physiological events in response to a stressor described above includes activation of a multifaceted cardiac and hemodynamic response cluster that, however, would not likely be of any health consequence if recovery following activation was swift and complete (Linden, Earle, Gerin, & Christenfeld, 1997; McEwan & Stellar, 1993). Hence it was necessary for stress researchers to show how short-term activation can lead to long-term changes that are deleterious in nature.

A full understanding of pathways for stress leading to disease requires that researchers show how existing, adaptive self-regulatory systems change (or get "corrupted") by stress. A good example of a regulatory system that is critically affected by chronic stress, and that shows compensatory and ultimately harmful "adaptation," is the baroreceptor control system for blood pressure regulation. Baroreceptors are pressure sensors found in the walls of blood vessels that serve a critical role in the feedback system of brain-heart interactions. When pressure rises in response to a demand, the increased blood pressure is detected by the baroreceptors, which inform higher cortical centers that a fight-flight response has taken place. If the brain interprets a stress response as no longer needed, it reduces cardiac activation and the baroreceptors contribute by feeding information back to the brain that the down-regulation process is, at some point, complete. In essence, this system functions like a thermostat in a home, telling the "controller" that the heat activation can be stopped because a heat comfort level (or threshold) has been reached. Such systems have a set point that the regulatory systems are trying to maintain. However, if the demand becomes chronic and no brain signal for recovery is activated, then the baroreceptors react by actually changing the set point or threshold so that now a higher baseline or tonic level is considered the desired target. It is critically important to note that such set points are relatively stable but not absolutely resistant to change and resetting. Both animal (Dworkin, Filewich, Miller, & Craigmyle, 1979) and human studies (Elbert, Pietrowsky, Kessler, Lutzenberger, & Birbaumer, 1985) have provided supportive evidence for a resetting phenomenon that raises target levels and ultimately maintains higher blood pressure levels; that is, an upshift in tonic blood pressure occurs when no signals of stress resolution are fed back to cortical control centers.

Critical individual difference factors that mark higher risk for stress reactivity are familial history of hypertension, greater exposure to acute stressors, a propensity to show exaggerated acute responses to acute stressors, and a lessened ability to recover quickly (Linden et al., 1997; Roy, Kirschbaum, & Steptoe, 2001; Schwartz et al., 2003; Stewart & France, 2001; Treiber et al., 2003). Folkow (1982) has shown that individuals with a positive family history of hypertension have higher vascular resistance that, when activated, enhances cardiac responsivity to a stressor (Light, 1987). It is important to note that both initial reactivity to a stressor and recovery speed are individual difference factors that are relatively stable dispositions over time (Burleson et al., 2003; Frankish & Linden, 1996; Rutledge, Linden, & Paul, 2000), thus granting the candidate potential to play a significant role in pathogenesis.

Frequency and magnitude of acute stress responding is exaggerated and recovery from acute stress is slower in hostile individuals (Earle et al., 1999; Suls & Wan, 1993) and in defensive individuals (Rutledge & Linden, 2003); this finding is particularly true for men. A defensive personality style predicted blood pressure change over 3 years in a sample of 125 research participants, as did initial blood pressure hyperreactivity; when both variables were entered into a mediational model, it could be shown that individuals with high defensiveness *and* high initial reactivity also showed the relatively greatest blood pressure change over time (Rutledge & Linden, 2003). Similarly, the additive effects of three risk predictors (i.e., family history of hypertension, initial hyperreactivity to stress, and acutely high stress levels) represented a much greater odds ratio for hypertension development than either predictor alone, or than a combination of two predictors (Light et al., 1999).

The importance of personality style as a mediating factor in stress effects can be seen in a prospective study of 166 young adults who were studied over a 2-year period (Twisk, Snel, Kemper, & van Mechelen, 1999). The researchers tracked changes in daily hassles, life events, and behavioral and biological risk factors and assessed how changes were interlinked. The results showed that increases in daily hassles were predictive of a worsening lipid profile, decreased physical activity, and increased smoking behavior. All of these connections were particularly strong in participants with a "rigid" personality style.

A particularly useful model of the synergistic results of acute stress effects when superimposed on chronic strain is the study of caregivers to elderly Alzheimer's patients (Vitaliano, Zhang, & Scanlan, 2003). Caregiving itself is considered a chronic stressor, and the additional effects of vulnerabilities and resources on preclinical and clinical disease states can be studied in this model. A graphical display of the factors involved in this path model may facilitate the explanation of critical interrelationships. While most concepts in this model are self-explanatory, the term *metabolic syndrome* should be more clearly specified here. It refers to an intercorrelated cluster of risk factors that include elevated glucose levels, lipid levels, insulin activity, and obesity risk inherent in genetics and sedentary lifestyle. Although the sheer number of arrows in this pathway model (see Figure 1.6) gives the appearance of "conceptual clutter," the complex interactions suggested in Vitaliano et al.'s model are well justified in light of the evidence on risk factor interactions.

A review of the intricate relationships and relative contributing weights of these predictors for disease has been undertaken in a major review (Vitaliano et al., 2003) where it is shown that the presumed chronic stress of caregiving alone is not a sufficient predictor for disease. Chronic stress, however, accentuates and sets the stage for many risk aggregations. Caregivers of chronically ill patients, for example, are more likely to have poor health habits that contribute to metabolic syndrome. One can also expand or redraw this model by thinking of disease itself can as a "chronic stress platform" that accentuates more disease (Vitaliano et al., 2003). Given the typically advanced age of many caregivers, they themselves may be ill, and caregiver samples can be subdivided into those with and without history of heart disease or cancer. Caregivers who themselves were ill had worse health habits than had those without heart disease, for example, and they also reported fewer uplifting life events (Vitaliano et al., 2003). Suggestive evidence for one discrete pathway linking acute and chronic stress effects in caregivers comes from von Kaenel, Dimsdale, Patterson, and Grant's work (2003) on blood coagulation. Caregivers with high additional life stressors (assessed via structured interviews) showed poorer hemostatic function than did caregivers with the same level of caregiving demand and other medical risk factors but without the acute stressor exposure.

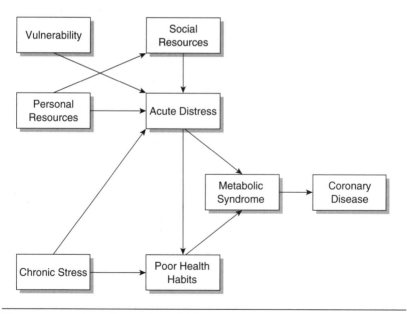

Figure 1.6   A Mediational Model for the Role of the Metabolic Syndrome

Another interesting model of study for synergistic effects of high stress exposure and other risk factors is that of job strain. Job strain (defined as being in a high-demand and low-control job) was found to cluster with negative affect, reduced levels of social support, and a preponderance of negative sentiments towards coworkers (Williams et al., 1997). Similarly, high job stress seen in firefighters has been shown to negatively affect their overall stress responsivity and lead to greater alcohol consumption (Murphy, Beaton, Pike, & Johnson, 1999), thus showing an indirect pathway for stressor exposure to lead to negative health outcomes.

The study of stress reactivity has been of great interest because controlled stress provocations are considered to provide a window into real-life stress and its consequences (Linden et al., 2003). Although stress reactivity research has flourished (especially in the cardiovascular arena), there is growing but still imperfect evidence for its predictive power in cardiovascular disease etiology (Schwartz et al., 2003). The predominant models of reactivity research have been challenged as representing too small a window because they pay little attention to recovery (Linden et al., 1997) despite many promising studies that elucidate the critical role that recovery plays in understanding how stress can lead to disease.

Epidemiological as well as acute provocation studies provide intriguing insights. In one of the largest studies on lifestyle changes to date, researchers have also studied the health effects of vacation as a type of planned recovery (Gump & Matthews, 2000). A sample of 12,338 patients who had completed a lifestyle program was followed for 9 years and the effects of holidays on mortality and morbidity were studied. The researchers reported a roughly 30% reduction in cardiac mortality and morbidity for those who took regular annual vacations.

Sleep is also worth studying in the recovery context given that is considered a primordial element in the body's "program" to seek low activation states and to facilitate recuperation from fatigue. Research on sleep is hampered by the difficulty of measuring sleep quality because reliance on self-reported data is problematic and acquisition of hard data by studying large numbers of individuals in sleep laboratories is often prohibitively expensive. The result is a general lack of trustworthy data. Fortunately, more reliable findings have become available in the form of a prospective study with 185 healthy older adults who provided sleep-lab data and whose mortality rates were then studied during a mean follow-up length of 12.8 years (Dew et al., 2003). Defining sleep quality via use of EEG data, these researchers showed a 2.13:1 mortality risk ratio for those with long sleep latencies (i.e., an index of poor sleep quality) after controlling for coexisting medical burden.

Elevated risk (1.94:1) was similarly apparent for lower sleep efficiency. In the same vein, Akerstedt et al. (2004), in a sample of 5,720 healthy employed men and women, have shown that disturbed sleep was a stronger predictor of fatigue than workload or lack of exercise.

Evidence Linking Stress and Stress-Related Risk Factors to Specific Disease Pathways

The previous sections were partially designed to describe linkages of single stress-related factors, in direct influence models, to disease etiology and to health maintenance at large. This effort revealed limited evidence for direct influence models; in its stead, most of the previous sections ended with demonstrations of how individual difference factors in stress responding relate to one another and how their aggregation and interactions augment health risks. Although previous sections focused on descriptions of generic pathways from stress to disease, the following section is designed to provide more specific evidence for the usefulness of the complex pathway models to describe *specific* disease outcomes and its unique predictor sets.

A 3-year prospective cohort study of 10,432 Australian women revealed that perceived stress was an independent predictor of new diagnosis of symptomatic coronary heart disease even if traditional risk factors had been accounted for. The associated risk (odds ratio [OR]) was 2.4:1, which exceeded the risk ratios observed for other risk factors. Note that an odds ratio (OR) of 2.4:1 means that an individual who carries a certain risk is 2.4 times more likely to develop the disease than one without the risk factor present. Perceived time pressure was not a significant predictor, whereas lack of social support (OR 1.4:1), body mass index (OR 1.9:1), poor nutrition (OR 2.1:1), diabetes (OR 1.9:1), and hypertension (OR 1.7:1) were. Alcohol intake and a physically active lifestyle, on the other hand, served as protective factors (ORs 0.4:1 and 0.6:1, respectively).

Also, Eaker, Pinsky, and Castelli (1992) reported outcomes from a 20-year follow-up of 749 healthy women from the Framingham study. Low education, high perceived tension, and no vacations predicted MI or cardiac death after controlling for age, smoking, blood pressure (BP), diabetes, gender, cholesterol, and obesity. Although a study like Eaker et al.'s cannot tell us what the pathway to disease was, there was strong experimental support that at least part of the influence of stress on health is via the influence that subjective stress has on unhealthy behaviors. Based on a survey of 12,000 individuals in 26 different worksites, Ng and Jeffrey (2003) reported that self-reported high stress was consistently linked (for men and women alike) with higher-fat diets, less frequent exercise, increased smoking, and greater number of relapses from being an ex-smoker.

Support for the needed demonstration of pathways can also be derived from controlled investigations of cardiac dysfunction under mental stress showing reduced supply of blood to the heart (Jiang et al., 1996; Krantz et al., 1999; Rozanski et al., 1988), reduced ability of blood to clot (Grignani et al., 1992), dysfunction in blood vessel walls (Ghiadoni et al., 2000), and reduced blood flow at sites with atherosclerotic plaque deposits (Yeung et al., 1991). Recent evidence on the linkage between inflammatory processes, stress, and cardiovascular disease has been diligently reviewed by Black and Garbutt (2002) and suggests a complex but empirically well-documented pathway from stress to cardiovascular disease via causation and/or aggravation of inflammatory processes. These authors argue that the inflammatory process is contained within the acute stress response, and—up to a point—stress responding is described as adaptive within the definitions of the fight-or-flight response. Hence, any psychological intervention that may reduce inflammation brought on by chronic stress also has considerable potential for preventing cardiovascular disease.

An additional pathway for linking cardiovascular health outcomes to psychological factors has been described in a series of programmatic studies that link specific cardiovascular changes to loneliness (Cacioppo et al., 2002). Cacioppo and his collaborators showed greater age-related blood pressure changes and poorer sleep in lonely than nonlonely older adults.

Evidence also links stress to immune dysfunction. Cohen et al. (1998) inoculated 300 volunteers with the common cold virus and monitored them for symptoms of illness. Participants who reported exposure to stressors lasting more than 1 month developed colds at a two to three times greater rate than those with low stress. Similarly, it has been demonstrated that stress negatively affects duration and intensity of illnesses such as herpes, hepatitis B, meningitis C, and human immunodeficiency virus (Cohen, Miller, & Rabin, 2001; Herbert & Cohen, 1993; Kemeny, Cohen, Zegans, & Conant, 1989). Social stress appears to play a distinctive vulnerability role in outbreaks of latent herpes viruses (Padgett, Sheridan, Berntson, Candelora, & Glaser, 1998). Owen and Steptoe (2003) tested the relationship of acute mental stress, immune and cardiovascular function in 211 middle-aged adults. Independent of other risk factors, high heart rate reactivity was associated with plasma interleukin 6 and tumor necrosis alpha whereas heart rate variability (an index of the heart's ability to adjust to varying needs) was not associated with immune function. Given that differences on absolute levels of heart rate had different effects than variations in heart rate variability, Owen and Steptoe concluded that individual differences in sympathetically driven cardiac stress responses are associated with compromised immune function, hence giving support to the rationale that stress management should target sympathetic arousal reduction.

While research on cardiovascular adjustments to acute, contrived stressors suggests that initial hyperreactivity is a useful predictor of long-term hypertension development (Treiber et al., 2003), the lab reactivity paradigm is not as useful for the study of acute stress and immune function. Segerstrom and Miller (2004) culled data from 300 studies and concluded that exposure to brief, contrived stressors was typically associated with adaptive up-regulation of immune function, in particular for natural killer cell activity. Only chronic stressors were associated with suppression of both cellular and humoral measures of the immune system. These findings suggest that time-limited stressor exposure may actually serve to strengthen immune function and entail a vaccination-type effect.

Interestingly, it is not necessary to document quantifiable, salient environmental stress triggers to show a link with disease vulnerability; mere perception of high stress was associated with lowered antibody production after vaccination (Burns, Drayson, Ring, & Carroll, 2002).

Despite limited evidence for the reliability of stress self-report due to contextual factors and individual differences (for more detail see section titled "'Take-Home Messages' That Are Pertinent to Stress Management," below), self-reported, perceived stress is consistently related to certain stimulus environments and has been shown to associate with other risk factors. Perceived stress (a) is higher in some occupations than others (low decision control, high demand), which themselves carry differential risks for disease (Williams et al., 1997); (b) is higher in low socioeconomic strata; (c) is associated with greater consumption of tobacco, higher relapse in previous smokers, worse diets, reduced physical activity, and poorer sleep (Cartwright et al., 2003; Ng & Jeffrey, 2003); and (d) contributes to physical inactivity and poorer diet thus worsening lipid profiles and contributing to the metabolic syndrome.

Research on cancer progression has shown mixed evidence for the role of stress but does elucidate a role for indirect linkages: Stressed cancer patients showed decreases in healthy behaviors and increases in unhealthy behaviors (like smoking), which in turn may affect cancer progression (Lacks & Morin, 1992). Another interesting development in immune research has been the discovery that not only does the brain regulate immune function, but the immune system itself triggers brain activity by alerting the brain to infection or injury by releasing a protein called pro-inflammatory cytokine (Maier & Watkins, 1998). This protein triggers a cascade of responses, including fever and listlessness, that in turn are held to serve an adaptive function by reducing energy output.

Earlier in this book there was mention of Selye's belief in the universality of a fight-or-flight response to challenge. This belief had to give way to the recognition that there are other possible types of responses. A particularly intriguing suggestion of a different response type is that of energy-preserving response (Maier & Watkins, 1998) that appeared to explain Kemeny and Gruenewald's (2000) results; these researchers have shown a cognitive equivalent to a proinflammatory cytokine activation in that HIV-positive men with rather optimistic outlooks developed AIDS symptoms less quickly than did those with negative though realistic aspirations.

While by no means exhaustive or comprehensive, the above discussion makes a strong case for the shared pathways of stress, genetics, and behavioral risk factors for physiological dysregulation and diseases of the cardiovascular, immune, and endocrine systems. One can readily see how stress reduction would affect other behavioral and biological risk factors and disease outcomes; these relationships can be made apparent by a more visual display. In Table 1.1, evidence is summarized about which risk factors predict which disease. Note that this table was selected for its illustrative value, not because it reflects the latest evidence. At the time of writing this book, the evidence has actually grown stronger.

Each x in the table signifies that, according to the Center for Disease Control (USDHHS, 1986), scientific evidence for a consistent link of risk to a specific disease outcome exists; it is striking how few cells in this table remain empty. What this table cannot show is how risk factors themselves are linked to one another and then cause synergistic effects on health. A great deal of information regarding clustering of risk factors was described above, and a particularly good demonstration of such clustering was provided above in Figure 1.6, which in turn is backed by statistical, meta-analytic review data (Vitaliano et al., 2003).

To summarize, a great deal of evidence links quantifiable stress (both self-report and physiological indices) to disease markers (Bunker et al., 2003). Although the term *disease marker* was consciously chosen to reflect imperfect evidence of causality, the available knowledge makes a strong case for a likely causal role of physiological exhaustion and lack of recovery in disease development.

Table 1.1   Diseases Potentially Brought On by Risk Factors

Risk Factor	*Disease*			
	Heart Disease	Stroke	Cancer	Diabetes
Tobacco	x	x	x	x
Alcohol			x	
Cholesterol	x	x	x	x
Hypertension	x	x		x
Diet	x	x	x	x
Obesity	x	x	x	x
Inactivity	x	x		x
Stress	x		x	x
Drug Use			x	x
Occupation	x		x	x

SOURCE: Adapted from the U.S. Department of Health and Human Services, 1986.

"Take-Home Messages" That Are Pertinent to Stress Management

Stress is well understood at the subjective, experiential level; it is simply part of modern life (if one is allowed to use such a platitude). Yet it is difficult to define operationally and then to measure because it is a process and not a state. This review of the literature revealed that the field has steadily evolved by expanding and elaborating early models, and has revealed much consistency in the observation of powerful and complex, interconnected pathways for stress-disease linkages, showing mutual influences of the nervous, endocrine, and immune systems. Studies of short-term as well as long-term exposure to stress, in animals and humans, confirm the critical role of chronic stress in disease development even though many of these pathways remain insufficiently understood (Kelly et al., 1997; Lovallo, 1997). Both self-reported stress levels and physiological markers possess usefulness in showing stress disease linkages, especially in repeated measures designs.

Early models like Selye's have in good part held up to scrutiny, and more recent models have typically expanded on earlier thinking rather than invalidating it. One notable exception to the claimed veracity of early models is the criticism leveled against Selye's belief that stress responses are ubiquitous, "whole system" responses in which all physiological response components operate in synchrony. One could wish that he had been right, because that would make the measurement of stress a lot easier! However, as knowledge of nervous system function has expanded, Selye's belief in a whole system response has required modification.

At least partly consistent with the general adaptation syndrome is the later subdivision of the nervous system responses into activities along a sympathetic-adrenal axis versus activation of a hypothalamic-pituitary-adrenocortical axis (HPA), but the presumption that both are always operating in parallel and are of equal importance to disease development is no longer held to be true (Dienstbier, 1989). The work of Frankenhaeuser (1991), Haynes, Gannon, Oromoto, O'Brien, and Brandt (1991), and Linden et al. (1997) make a strong case that physiological arousal of the sympathetic axis is not likely disease-contributing unless it is paired with substantial activation of the HPA axis and/or unless physiological recovery is delayed. This also implies that researchers interested in studying stress-disease linkages need to include measures of sympathetic activation (e.g., electrodermal activity) as well as HPA activation (e.g., cortisol) and use study protocols that are of sufficient length to permit adequate study of poststressor recovery. Cortisol changes relative to resting baseline, for example, may be demonstrable for as long as 1 hour poststressor even in what are clearly contrived, relative minor stressor exposure paradigms (Linden et al., 1998). Stress management should therefore target arousal reduction skills to facilitate *and* accelerate recovery, as well as teach skills to minimize initial reactivity that exceeds the biological/survival needs inherent in a given challenge.

In sum, at this time we have a much clearer sense of how diverse stress-related events and processes affect short- and long-term adjustments of the cardiovascular system (Kop, 1999), the immune system (Cohen et al., 1998; Sklar & Anisman, 1981), and the endocrine system (Dienstbier, 1989; Frankenhaeuser, 1991). On the whole, there is weak, at best mixed, evidence that mere exposure to stressors is a sufficient trigger for disease, but there is overwhelming evidence in support of interaction models, such that predispositions to hyperreactivity (e.g., via genetics, personality, prior exposure) paired with acute challenges lead to exaggerated responses, slow recovery, and sometimes exhaustion. The coexistence of these features in the same person contributes strongly to disease development. In support of this now dominant line of thinking, there is rapidly growing knowledge of how physiological systems interact, and there is a solid understanding of how stress can affect disease, possibly in a causal manner.

Knowing the effects of stress on multiple, pivotal regulatory physiological functions, it can no longer surprise that stress can affect many different disease processes. Even if not clearly demonstrated to be causal, it can at least be shown how maintenance and exacerbation of health problems can occur under high chronic stress (Lovallo, 1997; Segerstrom & Miller, 2004). This knowledge can and has been applied to diseases of the immune system (e.g., cancer, AIDS, lupus, multiple sclerosis, common colds), endocrine dysfunctions (e.g., diabetes), and cardiovascular health (e.g., high blood pressure, myocardial infarction, sudden cardiac death). As such, stress has been shown to be important to almost all causes of mortality and chronic disease processes.

Stress plays a critical role in understanding the impact of early trauma responses on disease susceptibility. The magnitude of acute stress responses and speed of recovery are also likely predictive of disease development, although the research base in this area is still weak. Outcomes are positively affected by the presence of buffers (physical fitness, presence of support, an optimistic outlook, a sense of meaning, enjoyable activities) and negatively influenced by the presence of chronic strain in everyday life, negative mood, defensiveness, anger/hostility, anxiety, and depression. There is evidence of gender differences in that men and women may not benefit equally from buffers like social support (i.e., women tend to benefit more) or be equally detrimentally affected by the presence of hostility and rumination (in this case, men are more likely affected). Similarly, reactivity to particular stressors may be gender- and population-specific.

In aggregation, this overview makes a convincing case that stress reduction (however brought about) has far-reaching beneficial consequences for physiological adaptation and health maintenance, and prevention of exhaustion. Stress reduction benefits achieved in one critical physiological system (e.g., the cardiovascular system) are likely to show generalized benefits for other systems (e.g., strengthening of immune function). Creation of stress buffers (i.e., forces or personality characteristics that protect against stress consequences) can also contribute to benefits across many physiological functions. This observation implies that research on stress reduction outcome can reveal benefits in physiological functions that were not even the primary target of intervention and measurement, and that broad, multisystem measurement is needed to uncover the full benefit of stress reduction efforts.

If stress management is taught to initially healthy individuals, then it is logically necessary to follow them for many, many years if researchers do not want to miss out on seeing initially nonexistent, then slowly accruing but potentially powerful benefits. Failing to see large immediate physiological benefits of stress management training applied to healthy individuals does not imply failure because healthy individuals will begin training at healthy levels of physiological function; detecting change is therefore difficult due to floor effects.

Not only do researchers need to consider long-term, parallel, interacting, and counterproductive effects in multiple regulatory systems, they should also differentiate potential health benefits in physiological *resting* functions from those reflected in differential *acute reactivity* to a challenge. This is a standard approach in studying immune system functionality and stress-health linkage (Glaser, Rabin, Chesney, Cohen, & Natelson, 1999) and provides unique opportunities to study outcomes. Lastly, documented immediate stress reduction does not necessarily lead to long-term benefits, and the researcher has a mandate to demonstrate lasting effects.

Given that the experience of stress has objective and subjective components, and that pertinent physiological systems are interconnected and interdependent, researchers can and should consider a wide range of potential measurement targets. For example, Miller and Cohen (2001) conducted a meta-analysis of the effects of psychological treatments on immune function (for results, see Chapter 3) and reported that the various studies had evaluated no fewer than 15 different markers of immune health! Similarly, adaptive cardiac functions can be subdivided into resting measures as well as reactivity indices and may be represented in more than a dozen endpoints, including systolic and diastolic blood pressure, pulse pressure, pulse-transit time, blood volume pulse, peripheral resistance, baroreceptor activity, time- and frequency-modulated aspects of heart rate variability, and so forth. In addition, subjective distress reports can be obtained from research participants, and dozens of standardized scales are available to achieve this; they may include simple one-item rating scales, a variety of standardized stress coping tools, self-report of negative affect, and peer or clinician ratings. Although the section on stress measurement was critical of self-report, this was not meant to discourage all self-report, given existing evidence of its predictive validity when studied within the same person. Finally, there are many behavioral expressions and consequences of high stress loads that can be tapped, ranging from acute changes in facial expressions of affect to return-to-work statistics or hospital emergency visits. Researchers in stress management are urged to broadly assess as many pertinent outcomes as possible. While this expectation greatly complicates the life of the researcher and drives up the cost of research, it also enhances the opportunity to show extensive, generalized benefits of "hard" outcomes that can convince consumers and policymakers of the value of psychological intervention (Linden & Wen, 1990).

2

Elements of the Stress Process and Implications for Stress Management

I wish you love at home, happiness in your work, and success with your stress.

—Peter G. Hanson, physician and
author, *Stress for Success*, 1989

The founder of modern stress research, Hans Selye, spent a lifetime trying to better understand the biology of stress and published hundreds of scientific papers and dozens of books on his findings. As stress concepts developed and matured, he took a much broader perspective that moved stress research from an initial, purely experimental science to a popular concept, to human applications, and to the integration of stress biology with a philosophy of life. In the seminal *The Stress of Life,* Selye (1956, p. 368) advises that the best way of handling and preventing unnecessary stress is to "[f]ight for the highest attainable aim but never put up resistance in vain." He bluntly states that stress is not altogether avoidable because that would mean avoiding life; instead the art is to strike a balance between knowing what is changeable and developing skills to implement change, and knowing when to withdraw, avoid, or look for creative, novel solutions to life's challenges. Using available psychological knowledge about human adaptation, this second chapter attempts to crystallize the needed skills for achieving such a balance. This objective also sets the stage, and creates the foundation, for empirically driven and widely applicable stress management strategies. It begins with the delineation of a proposed model that lies at the heart of this book and that determined its sequencing and its content.

A Model of the Stress Process, Its
Major Components, and Moderating Variables

Aggregation of knowledge from basic research on the physiology and psychology of stress and coping leads to a model that describes a multistep, sequenced approach with three basic components or steps: (1) stressor, (2) initial response (or coping), and (3) failing successful initial coping, a lasting physiological stress response (Figure 2.1). All steps in the process are influenced by known predispositions and coexisting buffers. The term *buffer* is used to describe environmental or personality characteristics that, when present, have been shown to protect against exaggerated acute arousal and to facilitate recovery. Although some of these features (e.g., physical fitness) may serve as mediators in a stress-disease pathway, the term *buffer* is used and preferred here because its use does not require the more stringent proof needed for claims of true mediation; on the other hand, calling a characteristic a buffer does not prevent it from serving a mediational function.

The remainder of this chapter is devoted to presenting research that supports the model and its components, and the proposed interactions or influence pathways that are indicated with arrows.

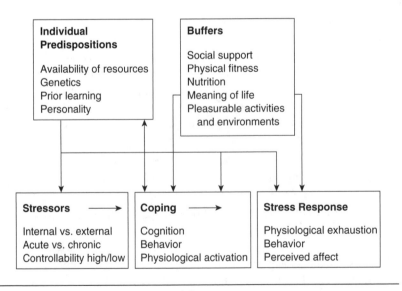

Figure 2.1   A Stress Process Model

The proposed stress process model attempts to clarify the sequential, process nature of stress, differentiating stressors from initial responses (coping efforts), and from a (possibly, but not necessarily) ensuing stress response. Individual predispositions are seen as correlated with, contributing to, and/or even shaping stressors themselves, such that people with high incomes have more control over stressors, possess a wider range of coping options, and are potentially at lower risk of developing stress responses (Gallo & Matthews, 2003). This negative effect of limited resources is worsened with a pattern of psychological adversity that is characterized by high job strain and low support (Steptoe & Marmot, 2003). While there is no apparent role for buffers to affect the stressors themselves, they are posited to play roles in the nature of coping and its results on the stress response. For example, we know that physically fit individuals recover more quickly from stressor exposure. These brief descriptions serve only to illustrate the basic principles of the model; the rest of this chapter delineates how these variables are interrelated and it sets the stage for developing comprehensive protocols for stress management.

Stressors and Stressor Properties of Relevance for Stress Management

Selye's original notion of a multistep sequence (or process) model presents a simple but useful description of the stress concept that shaped a part of the model in Figure 2.1. The existence of stressors or stimuli is the first step in this process; any sequence of events requires a trigger, a starting point. There are great individual differences in whether or not— and, if so, how strongly—different individuals respond to the same stimulus. These moderating variables were reviewed in Chapter 1 and will be referred to throughout. Notwithstanding the existence of moderator variables, if there is no trigger, there is no activation, no stress response. In order to be consistent with this time sequence, various existing stress management techniques will therefore be examined in the next chapter with regard to how they deal with inherent properties of the stimuli themselves.

An important question in this chapter is whether or not there are universal features of what makes certain stimuli "stressors"; that is, they carry a high propensity for subsequent stress responses. Do some stressors trigger stress responses more universally than others? If the answer is yes, then what characterizes these stimuli? Another important question for building rationales and components of efficient stress management is whether the stimuli themselves, if recurrent, can be identified and possibly modified. If the latter is possible, then it might be more opportunistic and smarter to teach skills of stimulus recognition and manipulation first than to start with teaching better coping skills. The logic here is akin to the idea that it is better to teach people how to fish than to give them food directly.

Fortunately, there is a rich body of experimental studies (animal and human) as well as epidemiological data that inform us about critical features of stimuli themselves. Animal models have been extensively tested and laid the foundation for further corroboration that the knowledge about the nature of persistent stressors themselves can allow prediction of poor long-term health outcomes.

A popular and useful animal model of stress and stress buffering has been the shock avoidance paradigm studied in great depth by Weiss (1971a, 1971b). Rats were placed in cages and exposed to electrical shock that (depending on the experiment) was either preceded by a signal or not, allowed avoidance learning by activating a lever that terminated the stressor, and even included testing of false beliefs using the so-called yoked-control paradigm. In a yoked-control paradigm, animals initially learn that they can stop electric shocks by lever touching, but at some point the feedback is made noncontingent and presumed control beliefs now fail to produce the previously effective avoidance behaviors. The independent variable in some studies was experimentally induced ulcers that could be reliably linked to the shock paradigm. Weiss showed that the resulting ulcers (indexed by the length of measured lesions) were dramatically attenuated (a) if a signal preceded the shock exposure, or (b) if control opportunities were contingent and learnable. By far the worst outcome was seen when animals had learned that pressing a lever was initially effective at preventing shocks but that was then made noncontingent. One can readily see that this type of response learning might be applicable to humans. Controllability and predictability appear to reduce stress as long as they actually work, whereas being taught that one has control when that later turns out to be a false belief is bound to translate into many repeated and ultimately exhaustive efforts at control that fail (Weiss, 1972).

One poorly understood but fascinating approach to linking stressor qualities to disease (or death) outcomes is via the study of traumatic events and sudden cardiac death. Engel (1971) analyzed a string of case studies and found that sudden cardiac death that was not explainable by a medical crisis was typically precipitated by a sudden catastrophic loss, often with public humiliation tied to it. Similarly, death records show that sudden cardiac deaths (not linkable to earthquake-induced injuries) were five times more likely on the day of an earthquake (Leor, Poole, & Kloner, 1996).

The conclusions one can draw from the stress research tested in animals can be used to understand and classify the degree of stress typically faced by people in different occupations. High-stress occupations are those with a lot of deadlines and time pressures (e.g., accounting), low control (conveyor belt workers), serious responsibilities (air traffic controllers), shift work (nurses), and needs for solving crisis situations (police officers, emergency room staff). Environmental conditions that may contribute to stress are often backed by both human and animal studies and include conditions like noise, crowding, captivity, relocation, and travel requiring adjustment and acculturation.

Selye's perspective on inherently stressful occupations has received ample backing from sociological and epidemiological investigations of workplace stress that concurs that occupations with low control and high demand (e.g., conveyor-belt jobs) are perceived as the most demanding and least rewarding (Karasek & Theorell, 1990; Siegrist, 1996). Not surprisingly, these types of occupations also have unusually high absentee rates (Karasek & Theorell, 1990). The description of low-control and high-demand jobs has been refined with the introduction of a reward–effort imbalance model such that certain jobs (especially those of the blue-collar type) are held to offer low reward (in forms of salary, prestige, or opportunity for advancement) while exerting high physical demands. The subjective job dissatisfaction ratings that accompany reward–effort imbalance jobs have been clearly linked to synchronous poor health outcomes (and high absenteeism). High decision authority in nurses strongly predicted high social support and high autonomy; that is, it represents a set of conditions where work stress is relatively low even if the job itself may be characterized as high demand (Tummers, Landeweerd, & van Merode, 2002). Kivimaki and collaborators (2002) reported prospective data on 812 employees who were followed over 25 years. After adjusting for age and sex, employees with high job strain (defined as high demand–low reward) showed a 2.2-fold cardiovascular mortality risk when compared with peers with low job strain.

Smith and Sulsky (1995) determined across three workplace samples which stressors were particularly salient to the workplace and which coping strategies were typically used in response to the recognition of the stressors' idiosyncratic importance. This approach is an application of

Lazarus and Folkman's (1984) stress coping model, which differentiates primary ("Is this challenge relevant for me?") from secondary ("How should I cope in this situation?") appraisal. Smith and Sulsky also measured outcomes of varying coping attempts; this latter information will be discussed later in the section on coping style outcomes. The samples included employees in a community college ($N = 160$, faculty, administrators, and support staff), blue-collar workers in a metal factory ($N = 65$), and a very large ($N = 432$) sample of employees in a number of different companies, including workers from all strata of the power hierarchy. Presence of job stressors was assessed using a standardized scale that tapped 11 dimensions: lack of feedback, lack of participation, lack of achievement, lack of competence of supervision, lack of interpersonal skills of the supervisor, lack of competency of others, lack of interpersonal skills of others, red tape, time pressure, job insecurity, physical demands, and strangers. Measurement of coping behaviors was based on endorsement of the three coping styles of control, escape, and symptom management; and the assessed coping outcomes were job satisfaction, global job stress, and self-reported health. Across the three samples, people-oriented stressors (i.e., lack of competence of supervisors and coworkers, and lack of social skills by those of these groups) were listed as the most frequent and most aggravating stressors, accounting for 24% of all stressor nominations.

Another interesting perspective arises from a representative survey of Americans about the types of psychological problems that made them seek professional help. The hands-down winner and most frequently cited reason for beginning psychotherapy is relationship issues. This emphasis on interpersonal stressors is consistent with evidence from diary studies of the effects of stress on mood where social stressors like marital disagreements were shown to have the most lasting negative impact on mood (DeLongis, Folkman, & Lazarus, 1988). While people's moods recovered quickly from stressors like time pressure or work overload, there was little recovery from social stressors. At an experimental level, the same phenomenon has been observed for cardiovascular and endocrine recovery from acute lab stress (Earle, Linden, & Weinberg, 1999); stressors that involved negatively toned social interactions were consistently associated with slow physiological recovery. Similarly, social stress has been shown to be detrimental to immune function. Dopp, Miller, Myers, and Fahey (2000) brought 41 nondistressed couples into the laboratory for a discussion of marital issues (15 minutes in length). Blood pressure and heart rate were assessed and blood was drawn for immune assays. Couples responded to the conflict task with cardiovascular arousal and parallel immune system weakening.

In the previous sections, evidence was presented for critical qualities of stimuli that will likely magnify stress responses and that appear to affect almost all living creatures. In the human literature, unresolved inter-personal conflicts appear to hold great stress potential as demonstrated in lab, field, and workplace studies. The animal literature also adds issues of unpredictability, chronicity, and lacking control. It is gratifying to see the consistency with which findings from the animal literature reappear in human studies, and how features of short-term triggers that have negative physiological effects can also be seen in chronic stress studies. To summa-rize, the most critical features of stimuli appear to be predictability, actual control, and belief systems about ability and need for control. At a more intimate level, interpersonal stressors marking workplace interactions or home life have particularly great potential for creating chronic strain.

Predictable occurrence of stressors leads to lessened stress responses, and there are numerous reasons why that makes sense. First, one can pre-pare for predictable stressors and either seek to avoid them altogether (e.g., by listening to car radio reports of traffic jams and choosing an alternate route to work), or have a ready coping response (e.g., letting people know via cell phone that one will be late for a meeting). Second, predictable stres-sors no longer startle as much (e.g., the neighbor's car has an oversensitive alarm that goes off three or four times per week in the middle of the night; and while still disrupting sleep, it is no longer taken seriously, and people readily fall asleep again after having uttered a few expletive comments about the neighbor himself and assigning the alarm no meaning).

The notion of control can be applied to SM in different ways. Effective control may result when people have a wide repertoire of tools needed to respond to a challenge: for example, the "big boss" requests that a cum-bersome report be ready in 48 hours, and one has the good fortune of lead-ing a team with competent members to whom one can delegate at least some of the required work. Control can also reflect the ability to have long-term impact on the reoccurrence of stressors; an example would be having suffi-cient amounts of money to permit scrapping an old, unreliable clunker of a car and buying a new reliable one. At least for the length of the new car's warranty period, there will be fewer car troubles and the probability of transportation problems as a stressor is eliminated or at least greatly reduced.

The literature on control in the coping process concludes that a search for the controllability of stressors should consider four distinct styles of potential control: behavioral, cognitive, decisional, and informational. Behavioral control is exemplified by opportunities to make choices among different behaviors (e.g., a driver stuck in a traffic jam chooses to switch from an all-news station with the usually gory stories of crime, war, and corrupt politicians to a radio station that plays calming classical music). Cognitive control refers to an interpretation process of stressors as either a threat or a challenge, as well as opportunities to make choices about which stimulus features will receive attention (e.g., beginning discomfort during a root canal procedure can be countered with a decision to try a distracting visual image of a pending vacation on a tropical beach). Decisional control opportunities specific to a given stressor may affect coping choices (e.g., a stressed-out computer consultant accepts a salaried job with regular hours). Lastly, informational control may be applicable in a situation where lacking knowledge about the nature of a stressor (e.g., the unknown pending sensations anticipated for minor surgery on the next day) can be remedied by learning about the procedural steps and generally known discomfort for this type of surgery via an Internet search for relevant information. Note that the concept of control as discussed for stimulus manipulations is closely linked to actual coping as discussed in the next section. Seeking to comprehend what types of control one may have over a given stressor fits under the section of understanding the nature of stressors themselves (step 1), whereas acting upon this knowledge becomes coping (step 2 in the model).

Discussing issues of stimulus controllability gives the impression that controllability of stressors is factual, objective, and relatively easy to determine. With respect to control, one needs to consider objective controllability as well as individual beliefs about the degree that environments can be controlled. Unfortunately, the concept of beliefs about control can reflect long-standing, maladaptive personality patterns, in which case it is more difficult to identify and change; that is, depressed individuals may falsely believe that they are helpless, and aggressive alpha males may think that the road belongs to them and that a mere honk of the horn will make the driver in front move over to let them by. Nevertheless, common sense supports the research finding that it is extremely demanding and likely exhausting to try to control something that one has no effective control over. This experience is told over and over again to marital therapists who hear complaints of continuous failure from spouses trying to change one another's personality to the one they wished they had married.

Of course, one sometimes cannot know whether efforts at resolution will pay off until a minimal amount of effort has been invested in finding out. An example may be the use of a marriage counselor to defuse smoldering anger in a marriage, only to find out that even after six sessions and a $900 bill, spouses are just as angry at each other as they ever were.

Unfortunately there are other, not necessarily frequent, instances in the real world where we have been taught that control features exist but well-intended attempts to make them work actually fail. A good example is the judicial system. It is an essential part of the lore of "civilized society" that people are protected by the law; however, it is posited that that belief may turn out to be a "yoked-control" situation. One example is the woman who finds out that a restraining order made by a judge to keep a stalker away cannot be effectively executed. Another scenario is that of somebody trying to retrieve $3,000 from a recalcitrant debtor; using the small claims court system will likely cost as much in expenses as was owed in the first place. Anybody testing real-world systems that are designed to protect and to give control (like the legal system or a harassment complaints office) may find out quickly that control can be an illusory belief and that a drastic adjustment of beliefs and expectations is needed to minimize stress responses.

In addition to the concepts of control and predictability that have been extensively researched, another stimulus feature of importance is the modifiability of stressful environments themselves; one needs to understand the origin of the stimulus. Some stimuli are independent, external, to the person (e.g., the neighbor playing his stereo very loudly); others are mostly internally generated or exaggerated (e.g., the stress experienced by firmly expecting oneself to get all A grades on the next set of tests).

The concepts of predictability, control, and stimulus origin can be used to describe and characterize stimulus situations, to create a taxonomy of stimuli. If one were to dichotomize each concept crudely into high/low predictability, high/low control, and external/internal stimulus origin, eight (i.e., $2 \times 2 \times 2$) possible scenarios arise, each with its own implications about what can and cannot be done in response. This proposed taxonomy is meant to help explain how one can approach a discussion of stressors; it can be a useful vehicle in stress management group sessions for the purpose of mapping out these stressor types and discussing their implications. While clearly simplistic, it nevertheless possesses heuristic value for clinical situations and can become a tool in teaching problem-solving skills.

The concept of high/low predictability can also be described as acute (= unpredictable) or chronic (= predictable). Admittedly, predictability (i.e., the acute vs. chronic distinction) and control are not naturally dichotomous but rather continuous in nature; similarly, what is described here as an internal stimulus (e.g., a personally held belief) may at some point in the person's history have been modeled and nurtured by others (like parents or teachers) and requires some trigger to become activated. Nevertheless, for the purpose of illustration a gross categorization may be useful. The categories, pertinent stimulus examples, and potential solutions are as follows:

External Stimulus/Acute Stress/Low Control

Example: Working in the World Trade Center in New York on September 11, 2001, and facing a terrorist attack.

What can be done about such a situation? The people working in the World Trade Center at that time had absolutely no forewarning, the attack was swift, and no attempt at acute problem solving was about to divert the planes' course. All people could do was to try the fastest and safest means of escape.

External Stimulus/Acute Stress/High Control

Example: Your 2-year-old car suddenly breaks down but fortunately it is under warranty; the dealer has to fix it and provide a loaner vehicle while you wait.

What can be done about such a situation? The answer is in good part built into the scenario's description. If the means are available, it is an efficient form of stressor manipulation to purchase a car that is relatively new and has a good warranty system. The event itself is not likely foreseeable but, at least to some degree, following the prescribed maintenance may help prevent breakdowns. Hence, the solution here is to call the dealer and request a loaner car while waiting for repair completion.

External Stimulus/Chronic Stress/Low Control

Example 1: A woman is the single child of an aging parent with Alzheimer's disease, works full-time, has three children at home, and there is no money to provide an alternate caregiver to the aging parent. To add stress, let's presume this parent is belligerent and irritable.

Example 2: Living in chronically war-torn countries like Israel/ Palestine, Afghanistan, or Rwanda.

What can be done about such situations? Both types of situations are very real and affect millions of people in this world. Neither is held to be easily fixable. The average citizen has little immediate power to stop civil war, and even the cited middle-aged mother of three has limited resources for immediate stress reduction. It is doubtful that she has poor coping skills given that she previously managed to juggle a full-time job and look after her children. It is not terribly likely, either, that the parent with Alzheimer's disease only appears to be belligerent because of the woman's irrational beliefs. The best one can possibly offer her is to identify additional resources, delegate tasks to her children or spouse, and seek forms of respite care in the community. People in war-torn countries often choose flight, and seek refugee status as a solution while knowing that this is not a panacea and requires difficult adjustments and further economic losses.

External Stimulus/Chronic Stress/High Control

Example 1: There is a daily traffic jam getting onto a particular bridge on the way to work (note that the notion of high control is of course true only if the individual has flexible work hours or alternative traffic routes are possible).

Example 2: A professor reminds her students that in the coming week they will be taking the midterm test and that they will need to be familiar with Chapters 8 through 11 of their textbook. This announcement is an immediate stress trigger for the students.

What can be done about such situations? Both of these examples represent much more trivial and transient forms of stress than the previous examples, but they are also prevalent and, in aggregated form, can represent a substantial stress burden. In both instances, recognition of the stressor's qualities also facilitates action plans like better travel planning, acquisition of time management or study skills. Stressor recognition may also elicit a desire to work with others to form carpools or study groups (either of which might also add coincidental social support).

Internal Stimulus/Acute Stress/Low Control

Example: One suddenly develops a major toothache, has no painkillers handy, and is not physically close to any dentist's office. Note that "major" toothache was chosen as a stimulus because pain research tells us that mental or behavioral distraction, which is otherwise a "portable" tool, does not work for major, invasive pain sensations.

What can be done about such a situation? The nature of this stressor does not permit categorical avoidance (except for the contribution that regular preventive dental care can provide) nor is it open to a quick fix. Nevertheless, it is useful to believe that a dentist can help, and then to get to the dentist's office as quickly as possible.

(Continued)

(Continued)

Internal Stimulus/Acute Stress/High Control

Example: An individual feels a sudden migraine coming on and knows that he has enough painkillers left to get him through the attack (let's ignore for the time being the debate about whether there are distinct external triggers for migraines, like weather changes).

What can be done about such a situation? It is the very nature of behavioral treatments for a migraine that they include teaching to recognize early signs of an oncoming migraine and acquisition of a repertoire of coping behaviors. Possessing the belief system that one does have a good repertoire of coping behaviors may itself serve as a stress-reducing belief system that in turn may reduce the probability of migraine attacks or make them more tolerable when they do occur.

Internal Stimulus/Chronic Stress/Low Control

Example 1: A severely crack-cocaine–addicted homeless person has come off her high and urgently needs another fix, but her dealer is out of stock. She does not know another supplier and is out of money.

What can be done about such a situation? In the short run, the answer is nothing. This woman will suffer from her urge for a fix until the urge is met. She may commit a crime to acquire the money needed to buy a fresh supply and ask around for other dealers. Of course, none of these is a desirable solution. In the long run, theft may land her in prison (which, incidentally, may bring her closer to treatment). The chronicity of the drug addiction is more likely due to longstanding problems like histories of family abuse, school failure, and poverty; attempts to treat just this one person make limited sense. At a larger, more contextual level, availability of individual help may even serve as an alibi for not seeking action against the societal root causes of substance abuse.

Example 2: A woman with pronounced borderline personality disorder is angry and distressed at her poverty, resulting from her inability to hold a job, and the frequent abuse she receives from her equally dysfunctional boyfriend.

What can be done about such a situation? The answer has to be similar to the one given for the crack-cocaine addict. There is no quick fix on the horizon. The problem is pervasive and insidious; the very nature of borderline personality disorder will prevent her from recognizing the problem for what it is, considering the need for professional help, and developing the needed trusting, collaborative therapeutic alliance required for change.

Internal Stimulus/Chronic Stress/High Control

The claimed utility of the $2 \times 2 \times 2$ factorial model of stressors is difficult to apply to this particular situation. It is posited that this type of scenario is rare or nonexistent because (a) if it is chronic, then it is predictable; and (b) if it is also internal and under high control, individuals who find themselves in this type of situation will quickly remedy or prevent it. In fact, it is the least likely combination of the three proposed critical stressor features to actually exist or persist.

In sum, analysis and reflection about the nature of the stressors themselves provide many clues about the question of stimulus controllability and the most promising first intervention. Much of this analysis can be undertaken without professional training or help, and common sense and life experience will carry a long way. Acquiring a clear sense of the stressor's properties appears to be a natural first step in managing stress; it represents a road map for action. Note also that problem-solving training as a coping skill will be described below and that stressor analysis is a core element, a first step, in problem-solving training (D'Zurillia & Goldfried, 1971). This further alerts to the fact that the proposed distinction of environment manipulation and coping is not a rigid, categorical distinction; skills training may be required to manipulate or remove stressors, but the kind of skill training needed depends on the nature of the stressors. If inaccurate job descriptions contribute to stress in the workplace, a worker may need strong assertion (and diplomacy) skills to raise the issue effectively with a supervisor. If a tendency toward procrastination increases stress levels as a deadline approaches, then time management skills may be helpful. In clinical practice, important clues about chronic stressors and hassles emerge from SM participants who keep a diary to record stressful daily events for a week (or more), and then review which stressors are repetitive, and possibly controllable, relative to the identified stressors that are rare and unpredictable. The benefit of diary keeping may be greatest if these diaries are also reviewed with a stress management trainer, a spouse, or a good friend who can provide some feedback. Repetitive, predictable stressors are obvious first choices for attempts to consider their modification and subsequent action plans. Frequently mentioned, repetitive stressors include workplace stress due to demand overload or role confusion, money problems, unresolved marital issues, and childcare issues (Ilfeld, 1980). Of these, people report to have the greatest number of choices for childcare issues and typically feel the least control over workplace stressors.

An important additional consideration relates to the target group for SM. When employees of a small company (or a small working unit of a larger corporation) participate in SM, an ecologically relevant, shared collection of prevailing stressors may be quickly identifiable; for example, fear of pending layoffs, grievances about seniority due to a recent take-over by another company, or repetitive harassing behavior by a supervisor. This stressor identification attempt would be much more difficult and lead to more idiosyncratic outcomes if SM participants had been recruited from all walks of life (as would be expected in a continuing education class offered by a community college, for example). Lastly, SM is often offered to distinct patient groups (with arthritis, diabetes, heart disease, for example) because each disease and its manifestations represent a distinct stressor that others do not have to deal with. The occurrence of anginal pain for cardiac patients is a prime example: It is disease-specific and is likely appraised as highly threatening. To a large degree, aggressive cardiologic treatment can eliminate the problem, and angina as a stressor is removed. In addition, many anginal pain reports are not indicative of a pending heart attack but are harmless; in these instances diligent education about symptom recognition and interpretation becomes a stressor manipulation (which incidentally also has built-in cognitive coping skill elements).

Predispositions

Earlier in this book, it was shown how predispositions magnify stress responses. Among them are genetics, which are currently beyond anybody's ability to control. Another important predisposition is socioeconomic status, which is theoretically open to change, but there is little clinicians can do in their offices to remedy poverty. There are many possible pathways for socioeconomic status to affect health (Gallo & Matthews, 2003). Among them are differences in education, knowledge, and access to health care; lacking a sense of control; and the resulting emotional and cognitive responses. These many possible explanations for the effects of socioeconomic status on health are not in competition with each other and are more likely to act in a synergistic fashion by reducing the resources of individuals at the lower end of the social stratum. It is also possible that stressed clients living in poverty are not aware of or skilled enough to access available resources like job training programs; this scenario would invite the teaching of problem-solving skills to access resources and thus reduce economic disadvantages.

More open to change via psychotherapy is the negative impact of early psychological trauma on current stress susceptibility. Unfortunately, however, such interventions tend to require long-term therapy, and few patients have the resources to access quality providers for this service. On the whole, negative predispositions often become deeply ingrained in a person's personality and attributional style, both of which are difficult to change, and this is a frustrating insight for sufferers themselves and for mental health practitioners. Nevertheless, if used skillfully, knowledge about greater susceptibility to stress in those with negative predispositions could be used to strengthen the motivation to make other modifications in the environment, or to teach coping skills in order to weaken the synergistic effects of predisposition and stressor exposure. A particularly challenging clinical example for this phenomenon is that of treating persons with borderline personality disorder, given that these individuals tend to have experienced trauma, rejection, and great instability during childhood. These patients will be hypersensitive to any change in relationships, readily feel rejected, and see all forms of interpersonal stress as extraordinarily threatening, with an ensuing escalade of dramatic outburst, unfair accusations, or suicide gestures.

Coping Skills: Cognitions and Behaviors

Step 2 in the stress sequence (see Figure 2.1) received the global label "Coping," and this term is used here in the broadest possible sense, not implying that any particular coping attempt is inherently adaptive. It recognizes that coping occurs at cognitive, behavioral, and physiological levels. The latter level, physiology, will receive minimal attention in this section because it would duplicate the description of physiological regulatory processes described in Chapter 1. Nevertheless, awareness of undesired physiological changes serves to initiate coping attempts and functions like a thermostat, triggering an end to effortful, and possibly exhausting, coping attempts until physiological arousal is reduced to a subjectively pleasant state (Pennebaker, 1982).

The literature on coping is immense (Skinner, Edge, Altman, & Sherwood, 2003; Somerfield & McCrae, 2000) and has grown at an explosive rate, to the point where some writers refer to it as the arguably most studied topic in psychology. Given this large scope, an exhaustive review of the basic research on coping is not possible here, but key concepts and findings need to be critically reviewed if the potential contribution of coping to SM is to be clarified. For the current purposes, answers to the following questions need to be extracted from this vast literature:

- What different types of coping exist? Does the field agree on these categories?
- Which theoretical models hold the most promise for helping SM researchers and trainers?
- What information from experimental coping research has utility for practical applications in SM?
- Have studies on coping and associated outcomes clarified what should be taught to whom, and how, for maximal effectiveness?

Coping Subtypes

Many of the theoretical roots of coping research can be traced back to Freud's writings on defense mechanisms and the work of subsequent psychodynamic theorists and researchers (e.g., Vaillant, 1977). Coping research is partly predicated on dissatisfaction with psychodynamic thinking, which sees defense mechanisms like displacement or regression as largely pathological, unconscious, and unintentional (Cremer, 2000). These qualities of defense mechanisms challenge attempts at empirical testing, render them difficult to translate into behavioral- or cognitively based training programs, and make them unattractive to researchers of normal personality and development. It is easy to contrast the differences of the coping literature with the key features of defense mechanisms by comparing the handling of the concepts of intentionality, awareness, and normality versus pathology (Cremer, 2000), but the resulting dichotomies may have been exaggerated in that most psychologists see consciousness and behavioral intentionality as continuous variables, not as all-or-nothing phenomena (Lazarus, 2000). Nevertheless, the difficulties associated with operationalizing psychodynamic terms into testable questions have contributed to the creation of coping research as a distinct body of work.

Notwithstanding the greater testability of coping concepts, key researchers in the field have been very critical of the value of much of the coping literature at large (Coyne & Racioppo, 2000; Somerfield & McCrae, 2000). The main criticisms have been excessive preoccupation with trait models of coping, inappropriate translation of prevailing interaction models into research protocols, and confusing research results that offer limited conclusions for clinical practice applications. The arising confusion is attributed in good measure to disagreements about consensual ways of defining and classifying different ways of coping (Skinner et al., 2003).

A large part of the coping literature focuses on coping preferences as a relatively stable predisposition, and sees it as an enduring trait, a personality style that can be measured via self-report questionnaires and that is presumed to be either adaptive or maladaptive. One cannot help but see this approach as analogous to the psychodynamic model that readily classified defense mechanisms as adaptive (sublimation, for example) or maladaptive (regression). Unfortunately, the theoretically based classification of psychodynamic defenses as adaptive versus maladaptive has largely defied empirical verification, and this in turn is largely attributable to the difficulty in accessing processes that are presumed to lie outside of consciousness. Similarly, testing trait models of coping has not been particularly helpful in identifying teachable coping skills because the models ignore differences in prior learning, individual goals, situational variations, and the need to match solutions to the nature of the problem (Coyne & Racioppo, 2000).

It is, however, still possible and even necessary to describe distinct coping styles as long as the search for distinguishable acute coping behaviors is not overloaded with the expectation that they will have to be generically classified as "good" or "bad," "adaptive" or "maladaptive," but where identification of subtypes is merely a tool in the study of person-by-situation interactions. Lazarus (2000) has not only been the key proponent of an interactional model but has also contributed to the identification of discernible coping subtypes. In the process of developing a measure of preferred coping styles, Lazarus and his collaborators have identified (via use of factor analysis) two distinct types of coping, henceforth referred to as problem-focused coping versus emotion-focused coping. Problem-focused coping embraces behaviors like taking charge of changing the environment or developing an action plan meant to lead to a factual solution, while emotion-focused coping represents attempts to process the affect associated with a threat or challenge. This discovery of two key approaches to coping is embedded in a cognitive process model that also assesses to what degree the stimulus possesses individually relevant threat propensities and whether or not the individual has the knowledge and skills to respond appropriately. Stress is the result of an appraisal process that sees the situation as threatening but the person's response capacities as insufficient to deal with the stressor (Cox & McKay, 1978).

Subsequent studies on coping subtypes have further subdivided problem-focused coping into confrontative coping versus planful problem solving (Folkman, Lazarus, Dunkel-Schetter, DeLongis, & Gruen, 1986). The development of another popular coping scale has led to expansion of the emotion-focused coping construct into a set of further subtypes, namely distancing, self-blame, avoidance, positive reappraisal, and support seeking (Folkman et al., 1986).

The latest addition to the fuzzy field of taxonomies for ways of coping is a massive review and critical discourse by Skinner and her colleagues (2003). These writers have reviewed 100 assessments of coping and have extracted a list of 400 different terms for ways of coping. When such diversity of terms emerges, psychological researchers usually hypothesize that the underlying number of truly different factors is much less, and that many seemingly unique terms use different words to describe the same underlying process or behavior. Using this type of extraction and simplification approach, Skinner et al. (2003) proposed a major overhaul of existing taxonomies and suggested that all existing taxonomies be replaced with their new proposed systems of organization. They proposed that the most logical organization reflects a $3 \times 2 \times 2$ factorial model that results in 12 families of coping styles. These families of coping can be organized into three overarching concerns that people seek to address; these concerns are considered to be broad, universal needs and goals that people have. One of these pivotal concerns is *relatedness* (including "social support," one's "place in a social structure," and "trust in others") and deals with coping efforts that result from our need for affiliation and love. A second concern is a sense of *competence* (including "mastery," "optimism," and "planning") and describes efforts people make to build and maintain positive self-esteem. A third concern focuses on *autonomy* (including such behaviors and thoughts as "compromising," "aggression," and "commitment to a plan of action"). Within each concern, coping can be organized around (or subdivided into) strategies that treat a stimulus as a *challenge* or a *threat* (e.g., "trusting" vs. "withdrawal" under *relatedness;* "optimism" vs. "despair" under *competence;* and "compromise" vs. "revenge"under *autonomy*). This distinction is of consequence for the affective valence of a situation in that threats imply a distressed affect that accompanies physiological fight-or-flight responses.

The next organizational factor is coping as it relates to the *self* or to the *context*. If the coping qualifies for an interpretation of challenge to *relatedness,* then a challenge to *self* may result in "shouldering" but a challenge to *context* may lead to "help-seeking." In the case of a perceived threat to *relatedness,* a threat to the *self* may lead to "pestering" whereas a threat to *context* may lead to "withdrawal." This model is displayed as Table 2.1.

Table 2.1 Skinner et al.'s Taxonomy of Coping

	RELATEDNESS		COMPETENCE		AUTONOMY	
CHALLENGES to	**SELF**	**CONTEXT**	**SELF**	**CONTEXT**	**SELF**	**CONTEXT**
	Self-reliance	Support-seeking	Problem solving	Information-seeking	Accommodation	Negotiation
	Shouldering Self-soothing Accept Responsibility Concern for others Protection Shielding Positive self-talk	Comfort-seeking Help-seeking Trust Appreciation	Strategizing Encouragement Determination Confidence Repair Mastery	Study Observe Interest Optimism Hope Prevention Planning	Cooperation Concession Committed Compliance Acceptance Commitment Conviction Endorsement	Compromise Blamelessness Taking other's perspective Decision making Goal setting Priority setting
THREATS to	**SELF**	**CONTEXT**	**SELF**	**CONTEXT**	**SELF**	**CONTEXT**
	Delegation	Isolation	Helplessness	Escape	Submission	Opposition
	Dependency Demanding Clinging Pestering Self-pity Whining Shame Abandonment Irritation	Withdrawal Freeze Loneliness Desolation Yearning Cutting off	Random attempts Flailing Falling down the stairs Self-doubt Discouragement Guilt Panic Confusion	Flight Avoidance Pessimism Despair Fear Procrastination	Perseveration Rigidity Unresponsiveness Self-blame Disgust Obsession Rumination Intrusive thoughts	Aggression Projection Blame others Venting Explosion Anger Reactance Revenge

Twelve families of coping organized around three concerns, two levels of distress (threat vs. challenge), and two targets of coping (self and context).

SOURCE: Skinner, E. A., Edge, K., Altman, J., & Sherwood, H. (2003). Searching for the structure of coping: A review and critique of category systems for classifying ways of coping. *Psychological Bulletin, 129*, 216–269. Copyright © 2003 by the American Psychological Association. Reprinted with permission.

This new taxonomy proposed by Skinner and her colleagues is appealing in its comprehensiveness and allows integration of a rich prior literature on ways of coping. Yet however promising it may be, the model and many of its terms are also so new that, predictably, no research is available that tests its utility. If one accepts the Skinner et al. model as the potentially most useful taxonomy, then all research findings on "which coping for which problem" that are described below suffer a major blow in that they will need to be interpreted as having arisen out of theoretical models that are now under intense scrutiny. Unfortunately, the recommendation of a needed paradigm shift in taxonomies of coping critically affects which trustworthy recommendations about "adaptive" coping can be drawn for the rationales and protocols of stress management. Further, Skinner et al.'s (2003) taxonomy may be appealing to coping researchers who are used to building and testing theoretical models, but its highly theoretical, conceptual nature does not readily lend itself to be communicated to participants in stress management programs, and it is not yet clear how this taxonomy may ultimately change the rationales and protocols for coping skills training in a stress management context.

Theoretical Models of Coping Efficacy

Because there is no solid empirical evidence for classifying psychodynamic defense mechanisms on a continuous scale of adaptiveness (Cremer, 2000; Lazarus, 2000), research on trait models of coping has been deftly criticized for being conceptually flawed and confusing in its findings (Coyne & Racioppo, 2000). These criticisms are partly methodological (e.g., overreliance on self-report) and partly based on a conceptual mismatch of theory to methodology given that the most popular and best-supported coping models favor a person × situation × needed coping style interaction (Somerfield & McCrae, 2000). Person-by-situation interactions, in turn, are best evaluated using within-person, longitudinal assessment strategies that attempt to represent the ipsative-normative model proposed by Lazarus (2000). This type of methodology has the advantage of eliminating the measurement error inherent in different people interpreting measures differently, and it makes fewer demands on people's ability to recall past emotion, thought, and behavior accurately (Tennen, Affleck, Armeli, & Carney, 2000). Such process studies have, for example, shown intricate effects of mood on subsequent attention in that depressed pain patients tend to perceive pain sensations as more intrusive than do nondepressed pain patients, which in turn augments their depressed mood and leads to withdrawal and inactivity; now they find their pain even more salient, thus creating a downward spiral of distress.

If the adaptiveness of particular coping behaviors is best shown within the same person via daily process studies, one can readily see that it will be challenging for such studies to provide generic suggestions for SM applications about the most adaptive coping styles for a group of trainees or patients. As a consequence, the application of coping skills training in SM would be easy if one could teach categorical truths ("avoidance is usually bad" or "action is good"), but benefits appear more likely to arise from a one-on-one teaching or therapy situation (trainer to trainee, therapist to patient) where adaptive coping skills training can be tailored to the particular individual's unique stimulus environment, preferences, and goals. While this individual tailoring is more laborious than teaching generically "adaptive" coping skills, there is little doubt in the minds of the field's leaders that application of an interactional model via individual tailoring is the only avenue of promise. Coyne and Racioppo (2000) even went so far as to call for a flat-out moratorium on any work using self-report–based, trait-based models of coping.

Which Coping for Which Problem? Empirical Evidence

The previous section described theoretical models of coping, and suggestions for what's adaptive (or not) were based on reasoning; they are speculative, and not necessarily based on data. To make matters worse, the latest attempt at bringing order into this perpetually changing field by Skinner and her colleagues (2003; see previous discussion) raises grave doubts that determining the efficacy of particular traitlike ways of coping can ever be useful given the absence of a consensual taxonomy of coping. Nevertheless, empirical tests of predictions based on earlier categorizations have been undertaken by many researchers, and a substantial body of research has accumulated over the past few decades.

In the workplace, outcomes for three global coping styles (control, escape, symptom management) have been investigated by Latack (1986) and by Smith and Sulsky (1995). Latack concluded that escape and symptom management were related to negative outcomes whereas control coping was related to positive outcomes. The work of Smith and Sulsky expands on Latack's work by also studying coping-outcome linkages as possibly distinct for the three samples. This was in part driven by the observation across these varied samples that blue-collar workers reported more escape coping, lower job satisfaction, and more emotional and physical distress symptoms. Consistent with Latack's findings, control appeared to be adaptive, and escape and symptom management were revealed as nonadaptive. Interestingly, the relationships between coping preferences and outcomes were confounded by the nature of the sample such that the college employees were more satisfied and felt they had more control, and these differential findings support previous criticisms of coping trait models that were inherent in these studies.

Attempts at integrating results from various studies on coping and outcomes initially revealed effective matches of problem-focused coping to acute, controllable types of problems, and emotion-focused coping for chronic, uncontrollable situations (Feuerstein et al., 1986). However, "adaptiveness" is not a rigid, universal quality of a particular coping style as people may have different goals even under similar circumstances, and these goals define what success or adaptation is. In a marital dispute about where to go for a vacation, one spouse's primary goal might be to assert (or reassert) his or her power position in the relationship while the other one wants to go Hawaii at least once in this life instead of visiting family in the Midwest (again). In this case, the goals vary in that one partner seeks primarily a concrete, short-term goal whereas the other is more concerned with the issue of power and control in the relationship.

The concept of emotion-focused coping has been criticized for being too broad. It has aggregated quite diverse coping styles under one large umbrella concept even though some of these coping styles may actually have opposing effects; examples given are denial versus social support seeking (Stanton, Kirk, Cameron, & Danoff-Burg, 2000). When concepts with opposing effects are aggregated under one label, it is inherently questionable to use the broad label in studies of adaptiveness because effects may become washed out. In an attempt to clarify the emotion-focused coping construct, Stanton and her collaborators coined the term *emotional approach behavior* and developed and validated a corresponding measurement tool. Based on a series of validation studies, they concluded that coping through emotional processing tended to be associated with good adjustment but warned against lapsing back into trait models, and underlined the continuing need to test situation-by-style interactions. Stanton and her coworkers (Sigmon, Stanton, & Snyder, 1995; Stanton et al., 2000) also noted that emotional approach behavior was notably more useful for women than for men, that nonvolitional emotional processing can readily become harmful rumination, and that overly spontaneous emotion expression via outbursts may be destructive to social relationships.

Stanton et al.'s notion of emotional approach behavior can be extended into attempts at understanding day-to-day stressors that require relatively small adjustments. There is strong evidence that emotional tone in day-to-day living is powerfully shaped by the accumulation of small events that have a negative or a positive valence (i.e., hassles vs. uplifts); the aggregation of these small events may be more important to mood than is the distress that can be attributed to major life events and crises (DeLongis, Coyne, Dakof, Folkman, & Lazarus, 1982). On the one hand, major negative life events like injury, divorce, losing a job, or the death of a loved one are fortunately rare, and most people have the resilience and social support to recover from these rare events (Bonnano, 2004). On the other hand, the balance of hassles and uplifting events in a single day greatly determines the emotional tone of the moment (DeLongis et al., 1982). Some hassles are uncontrollable and unpredictable; for example, even on the identified best route to work, traffic jams will happen and cannot be controlled by the individual. Even expensive equipment will break down at the seemingly most inopportune time and require attention, and most readers can readily recollect many hours spent dealing with the consequences of a nasty virus creeping into their computer, or waiting for a photocopy repairperson to show up.

Other researchers have framed what is effectively coping research as investigations of self-regulation strategies for mood. The basic premise is that people possess an innate desire to seek or maintain a mood state that is sufficiently variable to keep life interesting but devoid of wild fluctuations (Carver & Scheier, 1981). This view of mood self-regulation is akin to the prevailing self-regulation systems of physiological activity (described in Chapter 1); the two are highly compatible, mapping onto one another. There are known individual differences in how much mood variation people are comfortable with (see an extensive literature on sensation seeking), but on the whole there appears to be a natural tendency to avoid tension and bad mood, and to raise energy levels (i.e., reduce the mood states that characterize stress and exhaustion). Much of this research has been empiricist in that representative population samples were asked in numerous large surveys what they typically do to enhance mood and how well these strategies work. Not surprisingly, such studies provided a wealth of information that needed organizing, and this is what Thayer, Newman, and McClain (1994) undertook in a series of four studies. These researchers identified numerous strategies that people reported using for mood regulation. No fewer than 32 different strategies were listed and then clustered into blocks of similar actions; the researchers used self-report to assess preferred choices and their outcomes, and related these to differences in demographic factors. Questions were initially subdivided so as to tap into potential differences of strategy to target reduction of nervousness, anxiety, or tension. Aggregated results suggested that the same strategies were used for all three affective states.

Factor analysis clustered strategies/methods into three factors (specific activities that fit these clusters are listed in parentheses):

1. Emotional expression, use of food and drugs (engage in emotional activity, eat something, drink alcohol, smoke, engage in nervous behavior, call/talk to someone, use drugs, listen to music)

2. Muscle release, cognitive control, and stress management (use relaxation techniques, control thoughts, use stress management techniques, take shower/bath)

3. Pleasant distraction (engage in hobby, go shopping, tend to chores, avoid beverages with caffeine, watch TV/movie, have sex, engage in religious/spiritual acts, read or write, exercise)

Half of all strategies used for mood regulation can be directly tied to physiological rationales for arousal reduction (examples are exercise, breathing, resting, or consumption of "uppers" or "downers"). Distraction was generally given high success ratings for changing of bad mood (except for watching TV), but few people reported extensive use of a wide range of these activities; that is, there were low base rates of actual utilization. Also highly rated for success were exercise, music, and social interaction. Women were more likely to use social interaction and eating to modulate mood, whereas men were more likely to use alcohol.

When mood states are explained as the result, or the balance, of hassles and uplifts, then each element of this equation can be independently considered as potentially open to change, and this view introduces a note of optimism into attempts of self-control over one's mood. Even if hassles prove uncontrollable, people can create their own uplifts at will and thus affect the balance of the equation (Folkman & Moskowitz, 2000). Planning an enjoyable evening with friends or extracting the latest jokes from colleagues are examples of such attempts at creating uplifts that are indeed controllable.

Given the many different labels used to describe coping and the many potential targets for coping attempts, it is very challenging to systematically review and draw conclusions about the effectiveness of different coping efforts for a variety of target problems. Nevertheless, Penley, Tomaka, and Wiebe (2002) have conducted a diligent meta-analysis on this question and have provided an informative, but by no means simple, set of conclusions. Note that this was not a review of therapy outcome studies in which people were taught coping skills and the effectiveness of this intervention was then assessed in a pre/post fashion. This review describes research studies that are cross-sectional in nature, where participants provide information about their coping behaviors and the effects of such coping efforts on physical or mental health measures. In consequence, there are limits to the generalizability of the findings in that suitability of clinical applications remains unknown and that findings cannot be taken as analogs to the outcome of controlled trials of coping interventions. A particular strength of the Penley et al. review is the separate analysis of findings based on studies where *researchers* selected stressors relative to those studies where *participants* had selected stressors. This distinction is important because the inherent weaknesses of coping self-report are magnified when the stressor is selected by the researcher, given that this approach prevents a test of the preferred person-by-situation interaction model. In the case of participant stressor selection, participants can choose a personally relevant stressor and then describe how they deal with it; this approach maps appropriately onto the ipsative-normative model proposed by Lazarus (2000).

The results of this meta-analysis are a mixed bag of some clear and relatively simple conclusions and many complex findings that at times contradict prevailing beliefs. Irrespective of outcome type, solution/action-oriented coping led to positive health outcomes. The relatively clearest take-home message is that avoidance, frequent social withdrawal, and wishful thinking are unlikely to be successful strategies under many circumstances, and confrontative coping (i.e., bluntly expressing one's feelings and blaming others) appeared frequently counterproductive for relationship issues. The failure to find consistent support for active problem solving was puzzling and quite unexpected. Even if Penley et al. (2002) did not find support for a beneficial outcome of constructive engagement with stressors, the categorization system for stressors proposed above and the suggested taxonomy of ways of coping (Skinner et al., 2003) jointly suggest that at least consideration of constructive engagement with stressors is a potentially useful strategy.

There is a good likelihood that the reader of this section on coping expected to find clear evidence backing the belief that having an opportunity for control and acting upon it is universally beneficial. Penley et al. (2002) failed to find empirical evidence to support this belief, and numerous caveats are in order to prevent simplistic conclusions. One caveat relates to observations made in the animal literature that yoked-control situations that reflect a false belief in controllability can quickly become stressful and ultimately exhausting. The belief in controllability will lead people to engage in active control behaviors, which, however, will sometimes fail to produce the desired result because the context is misunderstood. If it is not immediately obvious why such coping efforts fail, people may reattempt the same coping strategy, hoping that on the next try they will succeed. The belief system of compulsive gamblers, for example, fits this description; their repeated attempts at problem solution via more gambling actually aggravate the money loss because they misunderstand probability statistics.

A second problem with a categorical suggestion that all "personal control is good" relates to the cost of control (Folkman, 1984). Folkman argues that active control requires effort, and this effort is particularly great when the suggested control behavior is not natural for the individual. For example, individuals whose tendency is to go through a stressful medical procedure by simply trusting health professionals may suffer adverse emotional consequences by attempting to exercise control; this behavior would be dissonant with their habitual response and require considerable mental effort to resolve.

Applying findings about the outcome of coping effectiveness studies to SM is a difficult task for a variety of reasons. First, the lack of a shared taxonomy and continuing changes in the field of coping make much of the efficacy research a comparison of "apples and oranges." Also, given that coping effectiveness is at least in part determined by varying context factors, blanket prescriptions for ideal cross-situation coping recommendations are not justified. At a practical level, it makes more sense to teach problem recognition and solution process skills that can and need to be adapted to varying situations. Given the wide range of coping styles and terms that have been used by various writers, there is not even a clear consensus on how to categorize and describe coping behaviors, although I find the Skinner et al. (2003) model very appealing and progressive. In consequence, the coping literature is too complex, shifty, and fuzzy to offer useful, decisive suggestions for what to teach in SM. A suggested commonsense solution would be to teach people as many different, operationally well-defined coping behaviors as possible so as to enhance their awareness and repertoire of choices, but any attempt at declaring a particular coping behavior as universally "good" or "bad" is probably counterproductive. Ultimately the most important skill to teach and learn is a process skill, involving problem analysis and solution planning, thereby strengthening people's abilities to critically evaluate the probability of coping success in a narrowly defined situation prior to the actual initiation of coping attempts.

Cognitions and Distress

In Chapter 1, theoretical models of stress were presented that described how attributions, interpretations, and appraisals create, mediate, or maintain sustained fight-or-flight responses. In Lazarus's (2002) primary-secondary appraisal model, the fight-flight response is quickly reversed if the stressor is judged not to be relevant for the individual. Also, even if the stressor is relevant, arousal will evaporate if people can convince themselves that they possess the necessary coping skills. From an intervention point of view, it would be critical to identify thought patterns that prevent accurate appraisals and that magnify stress responses beyond what is required for the immediate response and resolution. In fact, some 2,000 years ago, the Greek philosopher Epictetus stated, "Humans are not disturbed by events, but by the view they take of them." This line of thinking has formed the basis for cognitive therapies, the underlying models of which assert that some cognitions may be maladaptive, but exactly how *maladaptive* is defined varies between writers. The earliest model of dysfunctional thinking was proposed by Ellis, who rewrites Epictetus' words by creating an A-B-C model where A stands for antecedent (stressor), B stands for belief (a cognitive response), and C stands for consequence (i.e., the resulting emotional state; Ellis, 1962). Ellis offers a list of "thinking errors" that all create problematic beliefs and consequences and result in unnecessary suffering; examples of such thinking errors and flawed assumptions are "I should be well liked by everybody" and "Everyone should agree with me." Similarly, Beck (1993) presented a model where individuals make logical errors in their thinking and interpretation of the world surrounding them that include overly negative views of the self ("I can't do anything right"), the future ("It will probably rain all summer"), and ongoing events ("My date is not at all interested in me"). Ellis and Beck share the idea that some people make thinking errors that unnecessarily increase their anxieties, their perception of lack of control, and that contribute to indecision, rumination, and depression. Such errors in logical thinking (Beck, 1993) have also been referred to as the use of imperatives (having a fixed idea of what one must do in the absence of objective anchors), all-or-nothing thinking (seeing a situation as all bad or all good), arbitrary inference (assigning a negative meaning without evidence), mind reading (believing that one knows what others think), and overgeneralization (believing that a well-defined negative event forecasts many such future events, like a student interpreting a failing grade on one test to mean he will never graduate). Intervention consists of a Socratic-style debate between therapist and client, who is also encouraged to conduct experimental tests of his categorical and maladaptive beliefs. Such a test often consists of homework to test the veracity of these beliefs. An assignment might be to look 10 strangers, encountered while shopping, in the face while smiling and saying hello. A client who believed that nobody would smile back under such circumstances might then find that his prediction of "Nobody will smile back" was simply wrong, that in fact 8 of the 10 people did smile back. A particularly anxious and distressed person might convince herself that the brief presentation she will need to give to her boss the next day will turn out to be a disaster and get her fired, and that set of beliefs will make her sleep terribly that night.

Stress management manuals that have sections on maladaptive thought patterns have typically adopted these from the depression and anxiety literature, given that there does not appear to be a distinct literature on whether subjective stress feelings are the result of faulty logic. Primary tools for changing faulty beliefs begin with instruction about existing categories and discussion of the beliefs' likely veracity. Next may be keeping records of belief systems related to stressful daily events and later reviewing this diary in the training and treatment session. An interesting connection can be drawn here between the observation of problematic delayed physiological recovery from stress and the parallel observation that delayed recovery is often due to ruminative thoughts regarding the ongoing stress situation (Schwartz et al., 2000).

The literature on depression, distress, and irrational beliefs is very convincing when applied to people who are depressed in the absence of factual problems and who have much to look forward to. Psychotherapists refer to these individuals as YAVIS clients because they posses all or most of these features: Young, Attractive, Verbal, Intelligent, and Successful. In consequence, they are also likely to have good lives ahead of them so depression makes little objective sense. The irrational belief models are much more difficult to apply to people with severe health problems that threaten at least their immediate futures or even forecast steadily declining health (examples are a heart attack or the early signs of Alzheimer's disease). When offering stress management to these individuals, one cannot sensibly argue that fear of the future is irrational and worry is unjustified, although categorical and overgeneralized thought habits may still benefit from being challenged. In consequence, some writers have argued that "pure" cognitive therapy is difficult to apply in cases of chronic, life-threatening disease and its associated distress; a spiritual-existential approach is needed for a constructive use of cognition in emotion regulation and for the embedding of cognitive restructuring efforts in a reassessment of life goals (Fox & Linden, 2002; McGregor, Davidson, Barksdale, Black, & MacLean, 2003).

Behavioral Skills

Frequently mentioned skill-learning elements of broad-based SM approaches are assertion training, time management, and problem solving. All three approaches have largely been created by practitioners who needed useful content for teaching and modeling. The theorizing behind all three approaches is mostly behavioral and social learning based, but this theorizing is often superficial and only loosely connected to the resulting intervention protocols. Review of a sample of convenience of introductory clinical psychology textbooks ($N = 4$) revealed that three of these books did not list problem-solving training, assertion training, or time management at all, and only one textbook gave at least a cursory description of these techniques, whereas books on stress management routinely include such sections.

The relative absence of useable theory for skill-learning approaches is most likely the result of the fact that what's called a skill is often subjective, and culture and situation dependent. When a senior employee with a long service history asks for a raise, then it may be readily granted; however, if a junior staff member who has not yet proven himself asks for the same, it may not only be refused but actually harm his promotion opportunities. Knowing the difference as a function of the context is clearly a skill, but it is not one that is easy to convey in a normative fashion. The area of skill learning resembles the literature on coping, which also offers "menus" of strategies to choose from but no ready, universally true rules for application. Therapists and trainers teaching any of these approaches cannot help but teach them from the vantage of what they subjectively think is appropriate for a given circumstance. On the other hand, these approaches are usually taught in group form, and appropriateness of a suggested skill or solution can be tested on the microcosm of peers represented by the group; to some degree, the decision of appropriateness of a behavior does become a matter of group consensus.

Assertion Training is best understood in the spirit of the times when it was developed. The 1960s in North America brought with them a focus on the individual right to happiness and a profound challenge of old traditions about the work ethic, expectations of being nice, and obedience to authority. Part of this movement was the recognition that people have rights and that it is OK to assert these rights (Lange & Jakubowski, 1976). Among the specific recommendations and techniques that seem shared by experts in Assertion Training are (a) the use of "I" to communicate one's feelings and intentions clearly to others; (b) the use of confident body language, volume, and tone; and (c) cognitive and speaking skills that portray sound and easy-to-understand argumentation. Assertion Training in its purest form saw its heyday in the 1970s, and has since been criticized as too narrow in its focus. The content of what used to be Assertion Training is now covered under the broader umbrella of social skills training. Assertion Training was and is considered appropriate for situations where standing up for one's right is critical (e.g., refusing an unreasonable request made by a phone solicitor for a donation to an unknown charity or being asked to complete a lengthy market survey in the middle of dinner time), but the needed skill set for asserting oneself is better integrated into the a more comprehensive approach of teaching social skills that also places emphasis on building relationships and maintaining supportive networks. Especially in the latter regard, social skills training overlaps with social support interventions (see the corresponding section in Chapter 3).

The importance of *time management* skills can be derived from extensive representative surveys on sources of stress in which people often reported feeling overwhelmed by how much they felt obliged to do in a fixed amount of time. In the absence of the proverbial need to make days 48 hours long, workplace stress experts developed a set of time management strategies that form a relatively homogeneous set of techniques and procedures to be taught (Aamodt, 2004). The proposed mechanism by which time management works centers around the clarification of short- and long-term plans, which in turn facilitates decision making about which work items are of the highest priority. An important proposed mediator in this process is the benefit arising from a perceived sense of control. Jex and Elacqua (1999), in a sample of 525 employees, showed that use of time management strategies was indeed related to lower perceptions of strain, and that these benefits were mediated by feelings of control over time.

Problem-solving training can be considered an expansion or broadening of assertion and social skills training that embeds prescriptive teaching of how-to skills in a reflective set of process skills for planning and anticipating outcomes arising from available behavioral choices; it adds some cognitive processing skills to purely behavioral ones (D'Zurillia, 1998; D'Zurillia & Goldfried, 1971). Problem-solving training (PST) has also been called "applied problem solving" and "interpersonal problem solving." The presence of psychopathology has long been associated with simultaneously observed deficits in the ability to solve problems. The earliest writers on the topic of problem-solving training (see Mahoney, 1974) clearly anticipated what the coping skills literature would conclude some two to three decades later (Coyne & Racioppo, 2000), namely that problem-solving skills were generic abilities that transferred well from one problem situation to another.

The definition of a "problem" in problem-solving training is akin to emergence of a "stressor" in the stress management literature, and a "solution" is akin to a "coping response" that is effective in bringing about a lasting resolution that maximizes positive gains and minimizes negative effects. In contrast to the more prescriptive approach of social skills training, PST is an application of Lazarus's (2000) ipsative-normative strategy for coping and offers a structure and a logical sequence of stress coping efforts that teach the following steps:

1. *Identify the problem:* People are encouraged to gather relevant information, clarify the nature of the problem, set realistic goals, and reappraise the situation for long-term personal and social well-being.

2. *Generate alternative solutions:* It is critical at this stage to withhold any judgment of options and to use "brainstorming" so as to assure that the potentially most creative solution is not a priori blocked simply because it was not obvious or appeared too unconventional at first glance.

3. *List and weigh the advantages and disadvantages of each approach:* This can be done by creating two-column lists (+ and −) for each option.

4. *Make a rational choice:* The best choice results from comparing the advantages/disadvantages of each option under Step 3 with consideration of the relative importance of each; this step needs to include the anticipation of outcomes including consideration of obstacles to be expected.

5. *Evaluate the desired outcome* (with the option of returning to Step 2 or Step 3 if the observed outcome is undesirable).

Teaching this sequence of suggested steps can be achieved quickly, but it is the application of this tool set to hypothetical and real-world, idiosyncratic problems that is both critical and time-consuming. D'Zurillia (1998) provides a brief review of the association of PST skills and overall intelligence. On the whole, there is a fairly strong correlation between intelligence test scores and problem-solving abilities such that the attainable level of problem-solving skills is limited by lacking intelligence.

Nevertheless, especially among individuals with relatively high IQs, there is marked variability in problem-solving skills, with many individuals revealing a lack of skills. Subgroups that may be particularly in need of PST are those with high impatience and low inhibition thresholds and/or low emotional intelligence (examples are people with attention-deficit disorder or hyperactivity, developmental delays, or fetal alcohol syndrome).

Buffers

Personality

In Chapter 1, a brief review was provided of evidence for personality as a predictor of negative health outcomes. Attempts to show direct links using single-factor linear models revealed relationships that were weak at best, and often nonexistent. Much stronger evidence emerged when personality interactions were tested with coping style preferences, genetic predispositions, or high environmental stress. On the whole, little about disease consequences is learned when studying modest individual differences in personality traits; otherwise interesting individual differences along dimensions of introversion-extraversion, openness to experience, conscientiousness, agreeableness, or locus of control have not revealed much of interest for health outcomes. The constructs of interest are those in which personality differences overlap with problematic affect regulation and psychopathology, namely hostility or chronic anger, depression, and anxiety (Booth-Kewley & Friedman, 1987; Rutledge & Hogan, 2002). Also of interest to health (recall the discussion above) is the construct of defensiveness.

When differences in personality take on extreme forms they overlap with psychopathology; for example, extreme tidiness becomes obsessive-compulsive disorder. Regarding the practice of SM, it should be noted that the experience of pronounced subjective distress is an integral feature of affective disorders and personality disorders and that naïve SM trainers without a background in psychopathology may easily miss an otherwise duly indicated psychiatric diagnosis; and they may wonder why a group participant is not benefiting from SM or is even disruptive to the group process, hostile, and antagonistic. When there is any reason to believe that the subjectively high stress level that brought a participant to an SM training program is due to or the by-product of a psychiatric illness, then a referral is in order. Another reason for the need to screen for psychopathology and refer out is the fact that personality is rather stable over a lifetime and difficult to change; extended psychotherapy would be required for success. This raises a question of practical importance—namely, the type of training required to conduct efficacious SM training. Does the practitioner/trainer need to be a well-trained mental health professional with knowledge of psychopathology and general psychotherapy? At a minimum, it is argued that these qualifications would be useful even if they were not absolutely mandated.

Mood

When discussing the role of mood in the stress process, it is posited that mood can play a dual role; a positive mood is of course a desirable and enjoyable outcome of effective stress reduction. Mood, however, can also play a buffering role in that a positive (or negative) mood state can exist at the emergence of a stressor and can play a moderating role in the stress process (see the stress process model earlier in this chapter). Irrespective of the type and threatening quality of a stressor, the individual response magnitude is influenced by the current mood state such that exposure to preceding negative life events sets the stage for exaggerated responses to a new stressor, and that the presence of positive life events serves as a buffer for future stress responses. Imagine a young woman who wakes up late, discovers a run in her pantyhose just before leaving the house, and then misses her bus. She will be much more upset than another woman who also missed the bus but had previously enjoyed a good breakfast and discovered a little Valentine's gift left behind by her lover. The case for the importance of efforts directed at creating positive mood states is supported via numerous studies, including two investigations where the additive effects of positive versus negative life events on blood pressure has been shown. Light and her colleagues (1999) have shown prospectively that research participants with a family history of hypertension and high current life stress were more stress reactive than were those with low life stress, and over a long prospective study period were more likely to develop high blood pressure. Similarly, the presence of negative and positive life events affected blood pressure levels in adolescents but in opposing directions (Caputo, Rudolph, & Morgan, 1998). Interestingly, the positive buffering effects of positive life events on blood pressure were stronger than the corresponding effects of negative events on worsening blood pressure levels. Research on nuns followed over six decades (Danner, Snowdon, & Friesen, 2001) revealed that those nuns who had expressed positive emotions in an autobiographical essay required at the point of entry into the order had a 2.5-fold difference between highest and lowest longevity quartiles.

Further, a positive mood is not simply the counterpoint of a negative mood state; these affective states and their effects are orthogonal. There is an extensive literature on coping and affect self-regulation (described above) indicating that the creation of a positive mood state is worthwhile and frequently under the control of individuals.

Exercise

Physical exercise has been extensively studied, and its physical benefits are well established. One pathway for the benefits of exercise is through the use of exercise as an arousal reduction technique that serves to buffer acute stress arousal. Of greatest interest for stress management is aerobic exercise, a subtype that derives its name from the repetitive movement of large muscle groups that affect oxygen consumption patterns; aerobic exercise includes walking, running, swimming, and cycling. Psychological changes can be equally brought about by exercise that uses anaerobic metabolism for energy, including activities such as weight lifting.

The stress-relevant physiological benefits of exercise derive from cardiovascular adjustments that can be achieved only by aerobic activities. In this section, evidence will be discussed that shows how physical fitness achieved by regular exercise behavior can affect health and also shows how physical fitness can affect acute physiological stress reactivity. With respect to the psychological effects, there is consistent and replicated evidence that bouts of acute exercise and a maintained level of good fitness lead to psychological improvements as shown via decreased anxiety and depression, increased feelings of vigor, greater self-esteem and self-efficacy, and better sleep (Sarafino, 2002).

The pathway for physical fitness and health includes reduced autonomically mediated cardiovascular responses to physical stress that are apparent in reduced plasma norepinephrine concentrations of physically fit individuals. Interestingly, however, study of the immediate physiological stress response indicates that physically fit individuals do not necessarily show lesser physiological stress responses; physically fit individuals do recover more quickly from stressors, and this observation is in line with research findings on the importance of physiological recovery (Linden, Earle, Gerin, & Christenfeld, 1997). Using a daily diary approach, Steptoe, Kimbell, and Basford (1998) were able to show, within the same person, that positive moods were rated as more positive on exercise days than on nonexercise days, and events that had stress potential were considered less stressful on exercise days as well. These observations clearly strengthen the case for exercise as a stress buffer, in term of both physiology and subjective experience.

Numerous reviews show the health benefits of exercise (Roth, Bachtler, & Fillingim, 1990), and these reveal that even a single bout of physical exercise can reduce anxiety, anger, tension, and confusion. In addition, there is evidence that fitness moderates the negative effects of stress for life events (Roth & Holmes, 1985, 1987). Physical activity can be a planned effort (e.g., participation in an exercise class) but is also highly variable as a function of the general lifestyle and type of work that people do. Hence, research is needed to elucidate whether all kinds of physical activity can lead to the same health and stress-reducing benefits. Rothenbacher and his collaborators (Rothenbacher, Hoffmeister, Brenner, & Koenig, 2003) studied the degree of physical activity in 312 coronary heart disease patients and 479 age- and sex-matched controls and the effect of activity on underlying inflammatory response. Physical activity was subdivided into work-related strain and leisure physical activity. Leisure-time physical activity had a clear inverse relation with coronary heart disease whereas physical work strain did not. Inflammatory response was reduced in physically active individuals and thus elucidates a pathway of how physical activity reduces heart disease risk.

When exercise is considered not only for its immediately physiological benefits but also as a long-term stress management strategy, it appears that the benefits may come about via both *direct* and *indirect* channels. In terms of direct effects, the increased cardiovascular efficiency of fit individuals accelerates recovery from stress. Indirectly, exercise leads to better sleep (itself a restorative process) and subjective reduction of tension and anxiety. Interestingly, the psychological benefits of exercise do not appear related to actual improvement of physical fitness, and Flood and Long (1996) provide microtheories to explain this lack of needed synchrony. Exercise may serve as an attention diversion activity that reduces ruminative thoughts about stress (a distraction hypothesis). Also, people may feel compelled to perceive benefits of exercise to justify the time and effort involved in engaging in exercise (a cognitive dissonance explanation), exercisers who maintain a regular exercise program may see themselves as in control of their lives in general (a self-efficacy explanation), and they may carry a set of positive expectancies regarding social norms endorsing exercise as well as opportunities for social activities related to their workouts (an expectancy theory). All four explanations can coexist and thus strengthen the motivation for continuing regular exercise habits.

Nutrition

The literature on nutrition and health outcomes is complex and a source of perpetual disagreement, even among experts (Sarafino, 2002). In consequence, the populace is confronted with contradictory popular media coverage that confuses readers. Given this confused state of the evidence on nutrition and overall health, little attention is given here to nutrition prescriptions as SM techniques.

It is posited here that the main cause for these disagreements lies in frequent overinterpretation of the available data and in the nature of badly needed but ethically problematic and logistically challenging studies on nutrition and health. In order to "prove" the benefit or danger associated with a particular food item or nutritional pattern, experiments would require people to be randomized into a lifetime study where all relevant conditions (e.g., work stress, environmental health threats, exercise patterns, availability of food) remain stable and unconfounded while one group is fed a particular diet (let's say a "no-carbohydrate Atkins diet") whereas another is fed a comparison diet of high fat/high carbohydrate nutrition (the typical North American diet), or a high complex carbohydrate/ low fat diet (which is recommended by nutritionists). In order to be of scientific use, all participants in these studies would have to adhere strictly to their assigned type of diet for many decades until unmistakable signs of disease develop. To put it bluntly, this type of research cannot be done; the inherent ethical and logistical issues are not resolvable. More limited questions about nutrition and health can be answered in the animal model, where food intake is indeed controllable and confounding can be avoided; and much of our knowledge derives from this approach. Other knowledge is derived from comparisons of ethnic cuisines and mortality/ morbidity studies of countries in which these cuisines are prevalent (e.g., the Mediterranean diet). These studies are excellent sources for the development of research questions but provide no definitive answers because of confounding problems with socioeconomic status, race, differences in exercise habits, and so forth. In a related manner, no studies could be identified that specifically investigated the long-term effects that nutrition may have on stress. Conversely, however, there is overwhelming evidence that individuals under stress have more difficulty adhering to healthy eating patterns (Vitaliano, Zhang, & Scanlan, 2003).

A second reason for limited coverage of the topic of nutrition and stress management is that excessive mental occupation with food becomes a stressor in itself, as documented by elevated cortisol levels in restrained eaters

(Laessle, Tuschl, Kotthaus, & Pirke, 1989). Further, the very preoccupation with food that characterizes restrained eaters then becomes a trigger for unrestrained eating, and a vicious, destructive cycle of guilt, more restraint eating, low self-efficacy, and more lapses in healthy eating are initiated (Polivy & Herman, 1985).

There does appear to be support in the literature that all known classes of nutrients (proteins, fats, carbohydrates, vitamins, minerals) are needed for survival, that some fats are better than others (shunning hydrogenated and saturated fat), and that complex carbohydrates are better than simple ones.

Social Support

Hold on to affection's smallish stuff; I thought. For otherwise it is all hell in a bucket.

—Resolve of a character
in Leon Rooke's *Shakespeare's Dog,* 1983
(cited in Colombo, 2000)

The concept of social support is part of everyday language and seems to need little definition and explanation. Literature on the health benefits of social support began with epidemiological approaches that targeted easy-to-quantify features of social support, in particular social network size and time spent in social interactions. Early reviews (House, Landis, & Umberson, 1988) provided strong support for social network size being positively related to longevity and other health outcomes, but other reviews contended that sheer quantity of social exchange should not be confused with quality of social relationships and that perceived support was actually more closely linked with good health outcomes than was network size.

When it comes to understanding how the quality of social exchanges can serve as a stress buffer or moderator, the support construct is subdivided into perceived support, received support, and reciprocal exchanges of support. Perceived support is quite distinct form network size because it reflects a subjective perception of available support that requires neither a factually large social network nor activation or receipt of support. Perceived support is instead considered a cognitive individual difference factor that may exert its beneficial impact via beliefs about coping self-efficacy and subsequent threat appraisals (Lazarus & Folkman, 1984). Enacted or received support, on the other hand, is more objective and taps actual supportive interchanges between a recipient and support providers (Schwarzer & Leppin, 1991); these exchanges include physical assistance with a task, receipt of positive feedback, or listening to somebody's description of a tough day at work. While perceived support and received support are meaningfully clustered together under "quality of social support," they are largely nonoverlapping and at a maximum share 21% of variance (Dunkel-Schetter & Bennett, 1990). This distinction of received versus perceived support is further important because perceived support (which is a more stable, traitlike characteristic) typically correlates positively with mental and physical health outcomes whereas received support is more likely associated with increased levels of subjective distress and physical symptom reports (Schwarzer & Leppin, 1991). Interpreting the "greater distress–more received support" linkage is difficult because (a) it may accurately reflect the fact that in times of distress more support is actively sought, (b) receiving support can also be perceived as a threat to one's self-esteem and sense of efficacy, and (c) actually needing to activate one's support network is likely to reveal that some anticipated support provision ends up being of poor quality or does not happen at all. In contrast, perceived support may never actually be tested and is therefore more likely a stable belief.

Further useful distinctions of support activities evolve from the nature of support provided, differentiating instrumental support (loaning a friend a truck to help with a move), esteem support (assuring a friend that a recent breakup is not indicative of his overall lack of attractiveness to members of the opposite sex), or informational support (referring a friend to a plumber who can be trusted for competence and fair pricing). Ultimately, the success of support systems hinges on the skills of all parties to perceive available support where it exists, to interpret support offers correctly for what they are, and to link the type of support provided to the specific needs of the situation and the recipient.

The differential health outcomes of support systems that either fail or work can be demonstrated via Baker, Szalai, Paquette, and Tobe's (2003) research on 103 married men and women. These researchers conceptualized marriage as a potential source of both stress and stress buffering, and they tested their hypotheses by studying the long-term effects of marriage on 24-hour blood pressure and left ventricular mass changes (referring to the size of the heart) over a 3-year period. Their focus was on marital quality (as in index of support quality), using indices of cohesion and marital satisfaction. High satisfaction and cohesion were associated with a desirable 8% decrease in left ventricular mass, but a 6% increase for the low marital satisfaction group. Couples with low cohesion also had less contact time with each other over the 3 years. Also, diastolic blood pressure was lower after 3 years in the high marital satisfaction group. In sum, social support can contribute to health in instrumental ways (spousal reminders for medication taking or medical appointments) or via provision of emotional and esteem support. The seemingly most effective way of benefiting from support is to live in a bidirectional support network where individuals both receive support and provide it to one another. In this respect, marriage is a critical moderator because it can be a stressor by itself (as Baker et al.'s data suggest), but it is also the single strongest source of support provision for most people (Story & Bradbury, 2003). Understanding marriage and stress is a complex issue because high and low levels of marital quality have clearly opposing effects on stress processes and outcomes (Story & Bradbury, 2003). When marriage does work, it is bi-directional—spouses receive from each other and give to each other. This bi-directionality is likely advantageous because (a) it stabilizes the mutual exchange structure and (b) gives emotional satisfaction and meaning to the provider himself or herself.

Restorative Environments

The field of environmental psychology has taken an interest in the physical qualities of the environment that may contribute to raising (or lowering) subjective well-being and physiological arousal (Hartig, in press). This line of work has included comparisons of urban versus rural landscapes and blending of various colors and textures, with people routinely preferring and benefiting most from exposure to nature rather than urban life. Explanations for the documented benefits (Hartig, Evans, Jamner, Davis, & Gaerling, 2003) include a natural inclination toward esthetic shapes and objects, opportunities for attention divestment, and avoidance of the stimulus overload that is typical of densely populated urban habitats. The ability to routinely spend at least some of one's time in a natural, low-stimulus environment may represent a buffer from stress but could also be considered a physiological recovery strategy when a stressed individual *actively seeks* a restorative environment to spend time in. Many relaxing leisure time activities (walking one's dog in the park, retreating to the den to listen to classical music, or going for a long hike on a weekend) can be embedded in this restoration mode of thinking. At this time, there is no systematic research that has assessed long-term health benefits of habitually seeking out restorative environments.

Meaning of Life, Optimistic Outlook

In Chapter 1, numerous studies were described that studied health mediating effects of positive and negative psychological states and traits. An effort was made to introduce the concept of *positive psychology* where writers have made the case that a sense of coherence, spirituality, optimism, and resilience may serve to buffer against stress. There is a growing body of studies showing the benefits of positive psychological qualities; however, the literature has not matured to the point where strategies to create spirituality or increase one's sense of coherence are included in stress management packages or come described in ready-to-use treatment manuals. Correspondingly, there is no systematic therapy outcome literature that shows how such positive states can be created, and what additional health benefits they confer. There is a clear need for such research (and an excellent opportunity for researchers to raise their profiles).

Physiological Stress Response: Recovery or Exhaustion

The typical physiological fight-or-flight response was described in Chapter 1. An argument was made that some time-limited activation and arousal is necessary, adaptive, and generally perceived as pleasant. Just as blood sugar levels must rise and decline as a function of food processing and metabolic balance, people naturally seek variation in mood; neither flat affect nor wild fluctuation is considered pleasant or adaptive.

One critical element in the maintenance of physiological self-regulation systems over which people do have control is sleep. Sleep is a critical element in maintaining a healthy balance of activation and relaxation, and people simply cannot go without sleep for long (Sarafino, 2002). Many Europeans and North Americans are believed not to get enough sleep and are therefore held to be more emotionally irritable and less alert than they could be. To some degree, sleep problems are made worse by traditions and preferences people have developed and that could therefore be changed. One of these is the creation of a society that presumes 9 A.M. to 5 P.M. are good working hours, when clearly not all people operate on the same circadian rhythm (Czeisler, Moore-Ede, & Coleman, 1982). Another artificially created problem is that of sleep disturbances arising from shift work. It may be easy to make a case for the 24-hour availability of medical emergency services, but the daily, three 8-hour–shift organization of conveyor belt work in a factory is usually created for financial exigencies arising from the advantages of continuous machine use. This profit motive forces many workers into stress-creating sleep patterns.

As surveys on coping habits have taught, people will use psychological strategies to balance mood but also use chemical helpers for this goal. The "chemical helpers" are subdividable into uppers and downers. Caffeine and nicotine serve to increase short-term alertness and thus possess tremendous reinforcing properties (Lovallo, 1997) that explain the high frequency of their consumption. The same can be said for downers such that modest ingestion of alcohol is greatly enjoyed at the subjective level (and actually associated with enhanced longevity). Flight into habitual use of strong uppers and downers, of course, turns to substance abuse, is very harmful in the long run, and is difficult to change. That notwithstanding, the beginnings of a substance abuse disorder can be conceived as attempts at mood regulation and thus a form of stress management that was meant to be adaptive but went astray. There is a high prevalence of abuse and trauma history among substance abusers that in turn supports (a) the notion of chemicals being used for affect regulation and (b) the observation that those with early trauma exposure have a greater predisposition for stress. Earlier in this book it was shown how trauma histories like abusive childhoods, lack of attachment, or war trauma in survivors create a psychobiological predisposition for pronounced stress responses, which then require extra efforts at affect regulation. These emotions may be so overwhelming that drug use becomes a routine emotional stress management tool. It therefore appears critical (barring successful avoidance of trauma altogether) that as a society we offer support and teach a wide range of coping skills for emotion regulation that reduces the likelihood of developing drug dependency or that facilitates rehabilitation.

The need for recovery (and an awareness of this need) is also apparent in the way the work world is organized, such that school children go to school 5 days a week and have long vacations, and that working people (especially when they are unionized and have good contracts) define full-time work as 35 to 40 hours a week, with evening and weekends free and annual vacations. This orderly layout of built-in recovery phases is disturbed for the case of shift workers, and many self-employed people take few vacations, if any. During such recovery phases, people may seek out restorative environments like a weekend cabin or a comfortable living room, read, listen to music, spend time with friends, or walk the dog. A schematic display of how recovery strategies can be systematically used in planning a day is shown in Figure 2.2, where a typical day with

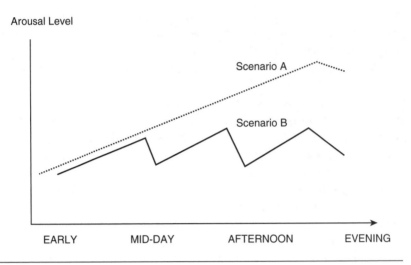

Arousal Level

Scenario A

Scenario B

EARLY   MID-DAY   AFTERNOON   EVENING

Figure 2.2   Schema of Two Days, One With Nonstop Stress, One With Effect of Recovery Breaks

continuously rising stress and arousal is displayed as the dotted line and a better planned day (the goal of good SM and time planning) is represented in the zigzag pattern of the second line.

The dotted line in Figure 2.2 represents a day with steady demands, no recovery breaks, and steadily rising stress/arousal (scenario A); the solid line represents the same amount of demand (i.e., total additive incline in arousal), but because of recovery breaks the resulting arousal level at the end of the day is much, much lower (scenario B). Although this figure is clearly a simplistic way of making a point for the importance of recovery, showing it to participants in SM programs has been very effective in convincing them of the benefits of recovery breaks.

Implications of Basic Stress Research for Intervention Protocols

This section is intended as a summary of the implications of basic stress research and its underlying theories for building a comprehensive rationale for what stress management could and should target. Extracting this information and laying it out in front of the reader in a transparent and convincing form is pivotal to the overall intention of this book, and it prepares for the discussion of various interventions and their rationales that follow in Chapter 3.

Review of stress research leads to the conclusion that a comprehensive stress management intervention should contain teaching and practice of the following tasks:

1. Identifying relevant idiosyncratic stressors in a given person's life, with emphasis on the identification of chronic and social stressors

2. Examining the changeability of this stressful environment and development of knowledge about the needed skills for stressor manipulation

3. Teaching cognitive and behavioral skills needed to manipulate stressors and maximize coping (at both an intrapersonal and a social-interactive level)

4. Acquiring knowledge, skills, and habits regarding effective creation and use of stress buffers (social support, exercise)

5. Teaching acute physiological arousal reduction skills

6. Developing structures, habits, and supportive beliefs that build "scheduled recovery" into people's daily lives

This list of tasks appears to imply a need for sequencing in the order given; however, it is posited here that at first only Tasks 1 and 2 need to be targeted for maximal efficiency and durability of effects. Tasks 1 and 2 represent a needs assessment to ensure that subsequent SM teaching and practice (especially as they are relevant to stressor manipulation in Task 3) are also ecologically relevant. The other objectives and tasks probably do not need tackling in any particular order, keeping in mind that an individual needs assessment (as represented by Tasks 1 and 2) may also reveal that not all SM learners have actual deficits in each area described as Tasks 3 to 6. The need for sequencing of intervention components is also discussed in Chapter 4, where conclusions and suggestions are provided. Examination of previously used stress management protocols (Ong, Linden, & Young, 2004) indicates that Tasks 1, 2, and 6 were often neglected in the past and that their proposed addition to an intervention protocol is novel and promising.

Another approach to understanding the sequencing rationale and necessity is by superimposing the structure of currently used models of prevention onto the step model of stress used here. Understanding and manipulating stressors (Task 1) is akin to *primary prevention* such that nonaffected individuals are protected from exposure to stressors (or the negative consequences of stress exposure). The teaching of coping skills for adaptive handling of Task 2 represents *secondary prevention* where efforts are made to identify those most affected and then treat or teach skills to minimize the risk inherent in having been exposed to the stressor. The active creation of buffers can be considered a valuable addition to secondary prevention. Finally, teaching skills for arousal reduction represents tertiary prevention where those affected by stress are "treated" to minimize the impact of the "disease" (i.e., the stress exposure), and maximize the speed of recovery and rehabilitation.

A comprehensive stress management program is enriched by knowledge of the client's unique predispositions to react to a variety of stressors in an idiosyncratic fashion, but that may require one-on-one therapy to achieve. Also, any attempt at change should be embedded in a clear understanding of what the individual's life context, priorities, and meanings are. The implied need for individualizing SM treatment targets and strategies is further supported by a literature on stress coping that sees effective coping as an interaction of behavior and unique situational demands. There is no evidence or consensus in the literature that specific coping behaviors can be categorically classified as "good" or "bad," as adaptive or maladaptive; in fact, at least for the purpose of this exposition on stress management, the research literature on coping was judged to be so fuzzy, inconclusive, and in such flux that it had little to offer in terms of normative advice for SM.

The coping literature does have the potential to help SM learners understand their usual coping patterns, organize and label their coping needs, and raise awareness of the range of available options. The critical skill that needs to be taught is how to match likely effective coping behavior to the specific situational needs. This includes the meta-skills of anticipating probable outcomes associated with each possible coping option, and with the simultaneous consideration of the facilitative (or hindering) roles that others will play. This type of training is probably best done by embedding coping behavior training in a program of problem-solving training that is meant to enhance these process skills (D'Zurillia & Goldfried, 1971). Problem-solving training does not involve fixed teaching of good versus bad coping; it is oriented toward process skill building that can be applied to an infinite number of future problem situations.

Without a doubt, these broad goals and targets for SM as listed above are lofty; if such a broad mandate were required of all stress management programs, they would effectively embrace the equivalent of long-term psychotherapy and a demanding program of skill acquisition that would likely take many months or even years to acquire and master. Given this broad, idealistic, and likely unreachable array of expectations for a "perfect" stress management program, translation into manageable clinical practice models raises many questions:

- Has anybody developed, described, and evaluated such a broad program?
- If a massive, long-term intervention is neither economically feasible nor desired by the populace, can there be a scaled-down version that still captures at least some critical features of the aforementioned six core tasks? Does such a bottom-line program exist, and does it show clinically meaningful benefits?
- Is there a minimal set of techniques that is required to attain benefits of clinical significance?
- If so, which techniques are most promising and least redundant with each other?
- Is there a minimal threshold for length of SM before benefits are apparent, and if SM program length is extended, is there a point of diminishing returns?

Reviews of different techniques and their applications and outcomes as provided in the next chapter are meant to answer these questions. Global conclusions and recommendations are crystallized and discussed in the final chapter.

3

Descriptions, Rationales, and Outcomes of Stress Management Interventions

Descriptions

Chapter 2 ended with a list of "desirable ingredients" for SM that made it look like a cooking recipe: Take two pinches of relaxation, a cup of wisdom, and three teaspoons of insight; mix well and bake at medium heat for 45 minutes. This list of ingredients was derived from a model of the stress process that suggests natural sequencing of steps and the existence of moderating and mediating factors, and it was supported by a review of empirical evidence that justified the importance and the potential of each component of the model. Chapter 3 begins with a comparison of the desired or ideal model with what clinicians and researchers actually do. Thereafter it moves on to descriptions of techniques and associated outcomes.

This section is titled "Descriptions" rather than "Definitions," because a search of the literature does not reveal an agreed-on, "classic" definition of stress management (Carlson, 1999). Nevertheless, the available attempts at definition do share many features: "Strategies to reduce stress" (Feuerstein, Labbe, & Kuczmierczyk, 1986, p. 186); "Stress management is the ability to reduce stress arousal or to cope in a competent manner with stressors" (Girdano, Everly, & Dusek, 1993, p. 7); and "The goals of stress management are to increase your understanding of yourself and your own stress cycle and to help you exercise what control you do have over this cycle" (Brehm, 1998, p. 8). Brehm also acknowledges that stress management may contain changes to the stressors themselves so that the likelihood of subsequent stress responses is reduced.

The current text largely adopts Feuerstein et al.'s (1986) perspective because these writers define good stress management by its theoretical main ingredients:

> Conceptually, the reduction of stress is comprised of three basic elements: (1) physical alteration of environmental stressors, for example, relocating a factory to an industrial zone; opting out of the "rat race" in the case of an executive promoted beyond the level of his or competence; (2) modification of a person's cognitive attributions, for example, focusing thought or reinterpreting situations as less emotionally threatening, and (3) alteration of behavioral and physiological responsivity, for example, the use of various relaxation techniques or pharmacological methods. (p. 186)

That being said, the model developed and presented throughout this text (see the preceding chapter) considerably broadens Feuerstein et al.'s description by also considering the possibility that rigid personality styles may be maladaptive, that coping can be cognitive *and* behavioral, and that arousal reduction strategies may seek to alter acute physiological responsivity as well as abnormally elevated resting states.

Another approach to seeking a definition of SM is via a systematic analysis of what stress management researchers actually do in their clinical protocols. This type of review has been undertaken by Ong, Linden, and Young (2004), who culled 153 studies using Internet science search engines with the key words "stress management," "stress reduction," "stress management program," "stress reduction program," "outcome," and "effectiveness." The search resulted in the largest pool of studies described in the literature so far, and all identified references are included in this book as a reference section titled "Therapy Outcome Studies Reviewed by Ong, Linden, and Young (2004)." Ong and her collaborators reported that most often studied were SM applications for health problems (40% of the sample of studies), workplace interventions (22%), studies with students (16% of studies [note, however, that one could also consider these to be workplace studies]), sports applications (3%), psychiatric problems (3%), and "Other" (16%). The Other category included studies of spouses of the elderly, patients undergoing acute medical procedures, and individuals with low social support or poor problem-solving skills. Although there was wide variability in the protocols, the authors noted that a modal type of stress management program exists, and that it is characterized by the following:

1. A preferred group treatment format (59% of studies were group only; 18% paired group and individual sessions)

2. The teaching of a modal number of six to eight different techniques

3. A typical treatment length of six sessions and a mean session duration of 1.5 hours

Attempts to classify stress management studies by their theoretical orientation indicated that 77% used an approach that broadly qualifies as a "cognitive-behavioral approach," 85% taught some form of relaxation, 15% used at least one form of biofeedback, 10% were classified as based on a systems model, and 6% could not be readily classified. Note that these percentages do add up to more than 100%, because almost all studies used multiple techniques and these were often classifiable as derived from varying theoretical orientations. These similarities notwithstanding, Ong et al. (2004) reported large variability in treatment length and choices of techniques, with the great majority focusing only on relaxation and cognitive and behavioral coping skills. As is typical for reviews of the therapy outcome literature, many studies were seriously flawed in design quality and measurement. Intervention descriptions were frequently cryptic and would be difficult to replicate by another researcher. Especially confusing was the use of certain technique descriptions and labels such that (a) techniques might appear to vary across studies although they were actually comparable upon close inspection, (b) some technique descriptors were so vague as to be meaningless, and (c) levels of categorization were often mixed up. These observations are further elaborated on below.

When scrutinizing every second paper (for the sake of parsimony, not all studies were selected), a total of 225 different terms for techniques were used, although most researchers would probably agree that only a fraction of that figure could actually represent truly different techniques (see also the remainder of this chapter). It was often easy to see that two different terms undoubtedly meant the same thing (e.g., Jacobson's relaxation vs. Progressive Muscular Relaxation) or were likely the same (diaphragmatic respiration vs. deep breathing). Difficult to comprehend was the fact that reviewers and editors had accepted vague descriptors like "creativity techniques were used" or "various methods were taught." Particularly confusing was the indiscriminate use of broad versus narrow, superordinate versus subordinate categories. Researchers occasionally claimed to use such things as "diaphragmatic breathing, time management, and stress management techniques," obviously not recognizing that these terms represent highly different levels of categorization, with one subsuming the others.

Key conclusions from Ong et al.'s (2004) review were the following:

1. A modal type of a stress management protocol exists, suggesting some consensus in practitioners' minds.

2. The reporting of intervention protocols was generally poor, barring successful attempts at replication.

3. The SM protocols were sufficiently different so that a review of the outcome literature on SM would not be meaningful if reviewers uncritically accepted the notion that the term SM also possessed truly comparable meaning across different studies.

Ong and her collaborators urged journal editors to set a much higher standard for the reporting of SM treatment protocols and challenged SM researchers to develop a consensual theoretical model for SM that is based on sound knowledge of stress physiology, that leads to a clinically sensible, at least partially standardizable, and also a socially responsible SM treatment approach. This entire book is, of course, an attempt to respond to these challenges put forth by Ong and her collaborators.

When relating these observations of what stress management researchers actually do to the "desired ingredients" list at the end of Chapter 2, it becomes abundantly clear that systemic, preventive efforts and the building of social support buffers, as well as the deliberate creation of positive emotional states, are not part of typical SM protocols.

Rationales and Outcomes

Organization of This Section

Ideally, evidence for the effectiveness of SM would draw from the entire literature of controlled trials that includes SM as a descriptor (provided that every writer actually had the same idea of what stress management is). Analyses of outcomes could then be organized around (a) populations studied (e.g., SM for schoolteachers or garbage collectors), or (b) disease categories that might be caused or worsened by stress (bruxism, hypertension, etc.), or (c) specific endpoints that had been measured (e.g., SM effects on self-reported distress, blood pressure, natural killer cell activity, or absenteeism at work). Each of these three organizing principles can be further subdivided according to other organizing principles; that is, SM effects in schoolteachers can be studied separately for healthy schoolteachers and for teachers with asthma versus hypertension versus headaches, and so forth. In addition, each of these could again be broken down for type of measure.

One can readily see that a review with this complex, three-dimensional categorization strategy would be enormous in scope, and this is powerfully demonstrated by some quick calculations. With an exclusive focus on occupational stress management, Van der Hek and Plomp (1997) reviewed 24 studies (far fewer than the 153 SM outcome studies identified for all applications by Ong et al., 2004). These 24 studies targeted 14 different workplace populations (e.g., teachers, nurses, managers, hospital janitorial staff) and used 33 different measures, with the latter consisting of 6 different physiological indices (e.g., blood pressure, skin response), 12 work-related outcomes that were either self-report (e.g., job satisfaction) or objective indices (e.g., medical malpractice claims, sick days), as well as 15 different psychological constructs (e.g., self-esteem, depression, and burnout). Using these data on the effects of SM just for workplace studies, there would have to be at least 14 (different workplaces) × 4 (classes of measurable endpoints) = 56 resulting cells to be considered in a meta-analysis. Breaking this down into each type of construct that was measured (instead of clustering them as families of similar outcome indices) results in 462 cells of outcome studies that needed filling. Of course, including the third dimension, namely diseases, increases that figure to many thousands. Any attempt at a comprehensive meta-analysis is further complicated by the fact that a minimum number of studies would have to be available in *each* cell to allow determination of the stability of results and calculation of a fail-safe statistic for all cells. Add to that that none of these hypothetical "numbers games" addresses the fact that different researchers also have highly variable operationalizations of what stress management actually is (Murphy, 1996; Ong et al., 2004; Van der Hek & Plomp, 1997), and that a review might crudely aggregate highly different interventions under a single broad label of "SM." Hence, it cannot come as a surprise that searches of the published literature revealed no such broad, quantitative (meta- analytic) or narrative reviews of the overall effect of SM. There are, however, reviews of the outcome of SM for narrowly defined applications, and there are numerous reviews of the effectiveness of a variety of individual techniques that fall under the global descriptor "SM."

Reviews of SM when defined as a package of interventions and its effects on particular populations or endpoints are not tackled first because that might imply to the reader that these studies can be easily and meaningfully aggregated. In my view, however, they should be read with a very critical eye and a sense of reluctant belief. Although a section on the outcome of broadly defined SM interventions will follow later in this chapter, readers are strongly encouraged to interpret all results with caution because any reporting of such outcomes in an aggregated form belies the previous observation that one researcher's SM is not equal to another's, and that to some degree "apples and oranges" are being compared in these reviews. Note also that conclusions about outcomes for SM packages are derived from a relatively small number of pertinent publications.

Reviews of specific technique applications of narrowly defined SM techniques and their results are dramatically more prevalent in the literature and form the great majority of this section. In fact, there are so many narrow-focus reviews that this section is effectively only a summary of summaries, or a review of reviews. Consistent with Ong et al.'s (2004) recommendations, these reviews will be organized around names of techniques or interventions that appear truly distinct from one another, begin with a description of the technique, and then proceed to documented outcomes.

General Principles and Strategies for Reviewing Therapy Outcome Studies

A summary of possible review strategies for outcome research may help to understand some of the positions taken when interpreting results and conclusions from various review articles. Reviews generally fall into one of three categories: narrative, box score, or meta-analysis. In terms of the history of any growing literature on outcomes, narrative reviews are likely the first ones to be conducted in any given area of outcome studies because they do not require an absolute, minimum number of studies with similar protocols for a review to make sense. Narrative reviews also have the distinct advantage of being the most inclusive; they are, by their very nature, qualitative research in that broad sampling, searches for patterns, and derivation of future testable hypotheses are more important than deriving hard numbers, effect sizes, and categorical conclusions. Narrative reviews often form the first step in the formulation of specific hypotheses to be tested in subsequent clinical trials and then for later aggregation in quantitative reviews. Their drawback is that different reviewers, even when analyzing the exact same pool of studies, may focus on different measurement, population, or treatment protocol features, and may also draw variable conclusions. To be trustworthy, narrative reviews should spell out a priori exactly how studies were retrieved from the literature, what search criteria were used, and what features the reviewer was most interested in.

Box-score reviews are wedded to the rigid use of a probability criterion (typically $p < .05$) as a cutoff that determines whether treatment was a success or not. The advantage is that results can be tabulated quantitatively (in "box" form as the name indicates), and researchers can be objective in claiming that therapy x is superior to therapy y because, for example, in 8 out of 10 comparisons, therapy x had produced significantly stronger outcomes than y for the treatment of cancer, for example. Although box-score reviews can be considered an improvement over narrative reviews insofar as they require less inference and interpretation, they are flawed because they often ignore questions of statistical power and invite unreasonable acceptance of statistical significance as clinically meaningful differences. Unfortunately, psychologists have a long history of conducting seriously underpowered research that in turn leads to volatile conclusions on therapy outcomes that are often difficult to replicate (Linden & Wen, 1990).

Meta-analysis, on the other hand, culls a shared statistic from each study that integrates means and an index of variability into the calculation of an effect size that is then readily comparable across studies and does not suffer from distortion due to uneven sample sizes (provided, of course, that the researcher follows standard procedure and differentially weighs effect sizes for underlying sample size; Rosenthal, 1984). The most frequently reported effect sizes are Cohen's d and the coefficient r, and in the reviews below it will be spelled out each time which effect size statistic was used.

Meaningful meta-analyses can be laborious because the researcher is expected to sample comprehensively, describe study identification with sufficient detail to permit replication, and ensure that only truly comparable studies are contrasted with each other. Further, measures need to be clustered into meaningful families. Ultimately, the strength of meta-analysis is to provide few but sufficiently meaningful "hard" numbers to permit a conclusion; this paring-down process is also its greatest weakness—meta-analysis by its very nature often fails to account for seemingly small but potentially critical differences in treatment protocols, choice of measures, and so forth. In sum, all modes of review have inherent flaws and strengths that can, however, be minimized (although not eliminated) with diligence and objectivity. Some of the weaknesses of box-score analysis have been overcome with meta- analytic approaches, and there appears little value to continue with box-score outcome reporting; however, the relative strengths and weaknesses of narrative relative to meta-analytic review balance each other out, implying that we had best continue using both, in a complementary fashion, in order to advance science. These principal issues notwithstanding, not every research question of interest for stress management has been investigated with all possible review modalities, and conclusions drawn here often suffer from the absence of adequate reviews.

In order to facilitate interpreting the review on outcomes presented below, the reader should take note of my approach to review and interpretation. Search strategies were primarily directed at locating high-quality meta-analytic reviews because of the resulting high transparency and comparability of results. Narrative reviews were especially sought out when they were comprehensive in nature. Literature searches used Internet search engines (ISI Web of Science, MedLine, and PsychLit, as well as searches of secondary sources). Of great interest were systematic reviews that applied consensual criteria for judging evidence. Sometimes no systematic reviews were available; the material presented here is therefore an attempt at a first systematic review of topics not previously subjected to this level of analysis (examples are the sections on time management interventions and forgiveness therapy).

Each following section in this chapter will comment on the generalizability and trustworthiness of findings, given the extremely wide diversity in existing versus absent evidence for outcome. Note also that a distinction is made between clear evidence of negative findings (i.e., demonstrations of SM's *in*effectiveness in strong trial protocols) and the absence of published attempts to show clinical outcomes. The latter is sometimes attributable to the novelty and uniqueness of an approach (e.g., forgiveness therapy), but it is more often a reflection of popular beliefs and myths about the value of an approach when there is precious little evidence in support of these beliefs. As is shown below, humor therapy and time management are prime examples of positive beliefs about effectiveness that run far ahead of existing data that justify such beliefs.

Review of the Effects of Specific Techniques, Rationales, and Outcomes

Given the large number of techniques that can be subsumed under SM, some categorization of interventions may be needed to enhance the clarity of this section. For consistency with the SM model proposed in this book, the discussion of techniques and their outcomes is clustered into interventions that fit into the proposed sequence model: (1) stimulus or environmental manipulations, (2) teaching of coping skills, (3) creation of buffers, and (4) arousal reduction interventions.

Techniques for Stimulus or Environment Manipulation

To really save one man you must transform the community in which he lives.

—Social reformer J. S. Woodworth, 1977
(cited in Colombo, 2000)

The concept of stressor, or stimulus, manipulation interventions as distinct parts of SM has received minimal previous attention and no distinct literature review can therefore be found that reports outcomes of interventions labeled as stressor manipulations. Nevertheless, a number of interventions could be found that fit under the conceptual umbrella of stressor (or stress environment) manipulation, and the variety inherent in these methodologies demonstrates the many creative ways in which this goal can be achieved. Most of the research stems from organizational behavior research and relies typically on case studies where changes within one work unit (factory, office, etc.) are measured preintervention and postintervention (Karasek, 1992). In this area of research, the controlled trials with random assignment that are typical in health research are largely unknown.

A critical indicator of the possibility of stress affecting job satisfaction and productivity is a high rate of absenteeism. Only about 30% to 35% of absenteeism is due to documented illness; an average of about 10% of absenteeism is attributed by employees themselves reporting stress overload and another 10% is attributed to "personal needs," a vague term that may well hide another subgroup also being overwhelmed by work demands. A good example of detective work regarding absenteeism and an attempt at stimulus control (with a true spirit of primary prevention) is the extensive work that has been done on repetitive stress injury. Repetitive hand and wrist physical stress is clearly not the same as psychological stress, and the reader may wonder why this is discussed here at all. The reason will become clear soon. Many of the discomforting symptoms resulting from extended work on computers are nonspecific (like sore eyes, neck stiffness, lower back pain) and may be prematurely classified as symptoms of psychological stress, and the responsibility for stress coping is then likely placed on the individual worker. A thorough investigation, however, revealed that repetitive stress injury is very real and expensive to employers and employees (Grossman, 2000). Use of ergonomic knowledge that is translated into workplace redesign can produce tremendous gains in productivity, decreases in compensation claims, and greater job satisfaction. Industrial/organizational psychology textbooks can provide the reader with numerous creative examples of how employers have dealt with this problem (e.g., Aamodt, 2004).

The way stressor manipulation is defined in this book is sufficiently novel that no literature exists that readily answers the question of the comparative efficacy of such interventions. That notwithstanding, the literature on workplace stress offers many examples of how employers and unions may cooperate by offering stress-reducing practices. In a 2002 survey (cited in Aamodt, 2004), 64% of employers offered flextime, 30% allowed employees to bring a child to work in case of emergency, and 68% offered an employee assistance program. These figures represent a much welcomed employee-centered approach to workplace stress reduction; it is unfortunately likely that less employee-centered companies did not participate in the survey, thus leading to a positively skewed impression.

A Swedish group of researchers reported two studies about workplace stress and the handling of layoffs (Arnetz, 2003). In study 1, the staff of a hospital were followed for 7 years. Twenty percent of staff had been laid off at the beginning of the study and beds were reduced by a corresponding 20%. Departments that increased their efficiency had also reduced subjective stress reports. Study 2 was an intervention where the staff in a bank was taught stress management techniques individually and the bank intervened at the system level to increase efficiency. As bank productivity went up, perceived stress went down, which was paralleled by reductions in prolactin and thyroid-stimulating hormone levels. Unfortunately, the description of this project did not clearly discriminate between benefits achieved at the individual level via "stress management" teaching versus organizational change.

Johnson (1990) calculated effect sizes (pre/post intervention) for a variety of systematic strategies that companies have used to reduce absenteeism. Unfortunately, these interventions allow only pre/post effect size computations because no control groups were studied. The number of studies contributing to each effect size was relatively small (ranging from $N = 4$ to $N = 12$), but the resulting effect sizes drew a clear picture of what seemed to work and what did not. The effect sizes for distress reduction were: Good pay $d = -0.86$, Flextime $d = -0.59$, Compressed work schedules $d = -0.44$, Discipline $d = -0.36$, Recognition $d = -0.30$, Wellness programs $d = -0.18$, Financial incentives $d = -0.17$, and Games $d = -0.08$. These strategies reflect a rather mixed bag of types of interventions with many simply being contingency contracting strategies that do not fit a preventive objective. Nevertheless, recognition and wellness programs do represent strategies to change the nature of the workplace, and these were at least moderately positive in their impact.

Given that stress management approaches in the workplace vary greatly in the degree to which they are systemic versus person-based (Giga, Noblet, Faragher, & Cooper, 2003), Karasek and Theorell (1990) have developed a useful taxonomy for different strategies and presented a crude, quantitative analysis based on review of 19 case studies conducted worldwide. Karasek (1992) differentiates four levels of intervention, beginning with the individual and moving up to the system:

1. Person-based interventions (relaxation, cognitive reappraisal)

2. Communication pattern interventions (building interpersonal trust, elimination of conflict-inducing communication)

3. Task structure interventions (job enrichment, formation of autonomous teams)

4. Work organization and production process interventions (change in management styles, labor-management dialogue, participatory interaction, sociotechnical design alternatives)

Interventions at levels 3 and 4 can be differentiated again as a function of whether the restructuring is expert-guided or based on a worker participation process. Applying this taxonomy to the 19 case studies and comparing outcomes, Karasek (1992) concluded that the person-centered coping enhancement approach (i.e., what typical SM programs do) was the least effective. Level 3 and 4 interventions (task and large-scale work reorganization) were judged to be moderately effective, with the greater effects appearing as the result of task and workplace reorganization that was guided by experts *with active worker participation.* Clearly, only level 3 and 4 interventions as classified by Karasek qualify as "stressor manipulations" and primary prevention efforts. Karasek's results and the findings of Munz, Kohler, and Greenberg (2001) clearly support the value of first targeting the stressor environment instead of focusing mostly on boosting workers' coping skills.

Skill Learning/Coping Techniques

Social Skills Training

Social skills training has been applied broadly to children and adults with social anxiety disorder, antisocial aggressive behavior, anorexia,m depression, alcohol abuse, personality disorders, schizophrenia, as well as some medical problems (diabetes, cancer). Many of these applications are irrelevant or of tangential value for evaluating the outcome of SM. There have been numerous published reviews (narrative and meta-analytical) that reveal a rather mixed bag as far as the effectiveness of social skills training is concerned, although results in adults look more promising than they do in children. Note that no studies could be found that specifically applied social skills training as a method for stress reduction; some readers may therefore consider the discussion of findings from social skills training outcome research to be of marginal importance to stress management.

In child populations, aggregation of social skills training outcomes across different areas of application reveal consistently small to moderate-sized effects (overall effect size $d = 0.40$ [Schneider, 1992]; $d = 0.47$ [Beelmann, Pfingsten, & Losel, 1994]). On a more detailed level, effects tended to be positive and consistent in the short term, but the limited follow-up research available suggests that gains weaken over time and do not generalize well to new environments. Also, shy children showed more relative improvement toward an adaptive level than did aggressive children, and neither child age, length of training, nor quality of research design correlated with outcomes (Magee-Quinn, Kavale, Mathur, Rutherford, & Forness, 1999).

Results are stronger and more indicative of skill maintenance in adults. Taylor (1996) published a meta-analysis of social skills training effects specifically applied to social phobia and reported moderate effect sizes for skill improvement ($d = 0.65$ for pre/post treatment compared to $d = 0.13$ for untreated controls). Social skills training effects were significantly greater than those of drug treatment or attention placebo ($d = 0.48$). Meta-analysis of 73 studies reported results separately for groups of developmentally delayed, psychotic, nonpsychotic, and offender populations (Corrigan, 1992). Social skills training was reported as effective for acquisition of skills ($d = 1.43$ pre/post), overall adjustment ($d = 0.99$), generalization of learned skills to other settings ($d = 0.92$), and maintenance of gains in adjustment ($d = 1.2$). The greatest benefits were seen for developmentally delayed adults ($d = 2.07$) and the least for offenders, who did learn the skills but showed poor generalization ($d = 1.06$). Psychotic and nonpsychotic populations fell in between with $d = 1.31$ and $d = 1.33$, respectively.

In sum, social skills training appears to be quite effective for adults, both short term as well as generalized, but noticeably less so for children. Most of the applications for social skills training are of limited use for understanding effects of SM. In terms of use as a stress reduction tool, there is a stronger rationale for the more narrowly defined assertion training than there is for broadly defined social skills training; unfortunately, however, the literature, especially meta-analysis, does not provide results specifically for assertion outcomes.

Time Management

Using the search term "time management," a quick search of Web sites identifies a large number of sites, reflecting almost exclusively commercial enterprises offering time management in industrial settings and some additional sites that describe time management courses offered through business schools and colleges. After perusing these more-commercial Web sites, the reader comes away believing that time management has been demonstrated to be effective in reducing subjective stress and enhancing organizational effectiveness. The following section on controlled evaluations of time management provides a test of these implied claims of effectiveness of time management training programs.

Review of publications and course outlines on time management (as found in SM manuals and on Internet sites) suggests a high degree of homogeneity and similarity in the rationales offered for the use of time management, and also in the steps and techniques that are routinely taught under this umbrella term. Such high level of agreement is, of course, welcome and compares favorably with other, much more varied SM technique operationalizations described in this book. As such, it facilitates the task of reviewers who can largely treat time management programs as actually comparable with each other.

The rationale for time management training is fairly straightforward. Feeling overwhelmed and not in control, chasing after deadlines, and feeling that the demands outstrip the time available to deal with them is a routine sentiment expressed by workers. Industrial psychologists also have conducted observational studies of how workers use time and noted that a tremendous amount of time at the workplace was not used productively. Identified problems that contribute to the sense of lack of control and permanent strain are role confusion, lack of clear priorities, and having to deal with frequent disruptions. Although there is no doubt that an objectively high workload contributes greatly to work stress, there also is evidence that people's work habits and lack of organizational skills worsen the problem. In response to these observations, time management strategies are geared toward directing workers' attention to the most important, need-to-get-done-today items, to institute realistic plans and expectations, and to embed these activities in a review of personal (or organizational) values and long-term plans. Core components of time management are set out below:

1.   Step 1 is a structured reflection on priorities derived from long-, medium-, and short-term plans of the person or organization. Essential to this priority setting is the resulting knowledge that a well-developed short-term activity list is part of systematic long-term planning, and this makes it easier to focus on the most urgent tasks at hand while reducing the need to worry about long-term outcomes.

2.   A pivotal tool in time management is a list for daily activity organization that arises from the prior clarification of priorities; work is categorized into high, medium, and low priority on the basis of the known consequences of not completing a given task on that day. High-priority items are to be done first because that reduces perceived pressure and prevents procrastination.

3.   An often elaborate set of tips for everyday applications of time management techniques is frequently offered, and such tips are to some degree specific to the workplace or particular occupation of time management participants. Such tips include

- constructive use of breaks,
- learning about one's unique, most productive time of day (to be reserved for challenging tasks),
- allowing for brief relaxation and effective peer support,
- reasonable expectations regarding the probability of disruptions,
- recognizing the inefficiency of perfectionist attitudes,
- a "touch everything only once" rule (to make a decision on what to do with an item right away),
- strategies for effective communication (via memo, telephone, e-mail, and direct contact),
- sufficient detail to engage in a self-help time management program (or use of Internet-based resources to create such a program) is easily extracted from the Internet. An example of a particularly detailed and helpful Web site can be found at http://www.mindtools.com.

The programs are usually offered in group form and at the workplace; the descriptions given on commercial Web sites leave an unclear picture of how much time is typically spent in completing a time management workshop. Time management studies can be coarsely subdivided into two types: first, those offering generalist techniques to a wide variety of employees with the hope and expectation that these skills are transportable to other workplaces, and that they may also help employees to organize their private lives or achieve an adaptive balance of work and home life. A second type of intervention is workplace-specific, can be reactive in nature (i.e., triggered by a critical incident), and/or may be preceded by a systematic analysis of the unique needs of a well-circumscribed workplace like a hospital ward, a medical practice, or a school. In this case, the observed benefits may not generalize well to other sites but are meant to be of acute value for the target organization.

An empirical test of the underlying components of a modal type of time management was conducted by Hoff Macan (1994) via two large workplace surveys ($N = 176$ and $N = 177$), using causal modeling procedures. Hoff Macan found that time management training was perceived as having rather small effects on its intended targets (i.e., setting goals/ priorities, making lists, and developing a preference for organization), but when change in establishing priorities and preference for organization had been brought about, these changes were found to be strongly associated with greater perceived control over time, which, in turn, led to reduced job-induced tension and greater job satisfaction. Interestingly, job performance itself was not affected by perceived control of time.

An intensive search of the literature using multiple scientific Internet search engines with the key words "time management" paired with "outcome" or "effectiveness" or "intervention" or "results" revealed not a single published, controlled trial of the effect of time management on any hard, stress-related index. This absence of findings applied to control group designs as much as it applied to simple pre/post comparisons. Therefore, reported claims about the effectiveness of time management strategies are mostly based on anecdotes. This conclusion, in turn, is in striking contrast to the considerable enthusiasm with which commercial time management program providers pitch their wares to potential customers. Given that time management programs have a clearly described set of steps, concrete learnable skills, and a convincing rationale, one would expect positive outcomes, which makes the lack of research all the more striking.

Problem-Solving Training

The basic steps involved in problem-solving training have already been described in Chapter 2 under behavioral coping skills. Problem-solving training typically has a brief, largely standardized component that consists of educating people about the structure and sequence of effective problem solving, whereas the larger, more time-consuming portion involves practice and home assignments that are designed to help learners sharpen and fine-tune these skills, to make them a habit. This practice phase is usually specific to the problem type that is to be solved; examples are anticipation of consequences in children with poor impulse control, or development of habits to protect oneself from cancer risks. The observation of a two-step learning process logically leads to the empirically testable question of how much time is needed for "technical" problem-solving knowledge to turn into an effective problem-solving habit.

Problem-solving training has been used for a wide variety of target problems: suicidal tendencies, depression, attention deficit, impulse control problems, coping with cancer or minimizing cancer risk, chronic psychiatric problems, stress and anxiety, academic underachievement, alcoholism, cigarette smoking, vocational indecision, and marital and family problems (D'Zurillia, 1998). While D'Zurillia provides an excellent overview of the theory, history, practice, and outcomes of problem-solving training, a Web-based literature search failed to reveal the presence of any systematic review of the effectiveness of problem-solving training (neither narrative nor meta-analytic reviews were found). This was surprising because a number of writers (D'Zurillia, 1998, in particular) reported favorably on the outcomes of problem-solving training for the many varied applications listed above.

In the absence of systematic reviews, at least a few illustrative summaries of recent controlled trials can be provided here. A sample of young incarcerated offenders was randomized to either problem-solving training or a treatment control condition (Biggam & Power, 2002); reductions in anxiety, depression, and hopelessness were reported posttraining, as was an improvement in self-perceived problem-solving ability. Gains were reported as maintained at 3-month follow-up. Two studies targeted cancer (Allen, Shah et al., 2002; Schwartz et al., 1998). In Allen, Shah, and colleagues' study, all participants were recently diagnosed breast cancer patients and had just begun chemotherapy. The intervention consisted of two in-person and four telephone-session interactions with an oncology nurse over a 12-week period. Among the 149 study completers (91% completion rate), better mental health was reported at 4 months; the outcome was mediated by initial level of problem-solving skills such that participants with initially low skills also showed fewer benefits. In the second study (Schwartz et al., 1998), participants were relatives of women recently diagnosed with breast cancer; random selection assigned 144 to problem-solving training and 197 to an educational information control group. The goal was to help participants devise strategies to reduce their own risk and to find ways they could help their family member. Both interventions consisted of a single 2-hour session, and all participants received extensive handouts with cancer information. Both groups showed decreases in cancer-specific and general distress; additional benefits of problem-solving training for cancer-specific distress were apparent in those who practiced more.

With a sample of schizophrenic patients, problem-solving training led to improvements in social skills, and the gains were maintained at 4-month follow-up (Medalia, Revheim, & Casey, 2002). A wide range of improvements was seen in 99 children with early-onset conduct problems (Webster-Stratton, Reid, & Hammond, 2001) who had been randomized to problem-solving training or the wait-list control condition. At post-treatment, externalizing problem behaviors at home were reduced in the treated children, more prosocial behavior was seen with peers, and more positive conflict management strategies were demonstrated. At 1-year follow-up, most gains were shown to be maintained.

A brief, 1-hour problem-solving intervention was developed for family caregivers of individuals with advanced cancer; in addition to the 1-hour intervention, participants received a detailed home care guide and completed a follow-up survey (Cameron, Shin, Williams, & Stewart, 2004). The 34 caregivers who completed the study reported reduced emotional tension, greater caregiving confidence, and a more positive problem-solving orientation.

In sum, there have been many applications of problem-solving training to a remarkable range of problem areas that are typically stress related, and it appears that outcomes are predominantly positive. However, this optimistic conclusion is tempered by the absence of a systematic review of problem-solving training outcome, especially in regard to its comparative effects relative to other active treatments.

Cognitive Restructuring

There is no systematic review that narrowly determines the effect of cognitive restructuring as a single treatment specifically designed for stress reduction. This is not surprising for at least two reasons. First, all recent forms of cognitive therapy contain at least behavioral elements and are generally best described as cognitive-behavioral therapies (CBT). It is critical to cognitive therapy that testing of presumed flawed attributions and overgeneralizations involves behavioral experimentation to test the veracity or erroneousness of various thought patterns. This introduces a necessary behavioral element into CBT. Indeed, there are pervasive and convincing arguments that a distinction between behavioral therapy and cognitive therapy makes little sense because the testing of faulty cognitions usually involves a form of behavioral experimentation. An exception to this claim would be the application of behavioral contingency programs with clients of very low verbal intelligence (i.e., very young infants, autistic or developmentally disabled individuals).

One controlled trial could be located that directly targeted irrational thinking in 39 health practitioners in training (Kushnir, Malkinson, & Ribak, 1998). Irrationality (defined along the lines of Ellis's [1962] rational-emotive therapy model) was significantly reduced in the treated group, and psychosocial professional efficacy improved correspondingly.

These observations notwithstanding, the prevailing emotions associated with stress are anxiety, anger, and depression, each of which has been subjected to extensive clinical trials of psychotherapy with high-quality meta-analyses available to judge their merits.

Reviews of the outcome literature are quite consistent in their conclusions about the success and limitations of CBT for generalized anxiety (Persons, Mennin, & Tucker, 2001). Generalized anxiety disorder is very distressing for the affected individuals, there appears no need to uncover early trauma, and psychological treatment benefits brought about by CBT are comparable in size to drug treatments but tend to endure whereas the drug benefits quickly disappear when the drug is discontinued. Barlow and his colleagues (Barlow, Raffa, & Cohen, 2002) further argue that the best outcomes may be achieved with a combination of relaxation training and cognitive interventions. In one small meta-analysis (Chambless & Gillis, 1993) describing results from seven studies, large effects were observed: The pre/post effect size for reduction of self-reported anxiety was $d = -1.69$; and the pretest to follow-up effect size was $d = -1.95$. Westen and Morrison (2001) reported aggregated effect sizes (pre/post treatment) of $d = -2.23$ for depression, $d = -1.55$ for panic, and $d = -2.09$ for generalized anxiety disorder. Note that these large effects should not be compared directly with effect sizes resulting from comparisons of CBT with a wait-list control or attention placebo group, which are usually quite a bit smaller. Meta-analyses based on larger samples tend to show smaller benefits ($N = 61$ comparisons for anxiety disorders, $d = -0.70$ for CBT, and $d = -0.60$ for pharmacotherapy; Gould, Otto, Pollack, & Yap, 1997). Unfortunately, positive results from well-controlled clinical trials with volunteer participants do not always translate well into similar benefits for broad-based clinical practice (Westen & Morrison, 2001) where initial treatment benefits may weaken over time and be of limited clinical significance.

This discussion of the efficacy of cognitive restructuring for generalized anxiety can easily be considered tangential to the evaluation of SM outcomes; cognitive restructuring of anxiety-producing and -maintaining irrational thoughts possesses a strong and convincing rationale, but it is questionable to what degree individuals with high self-reported stress can attribute their high stress levels to irrational thinking patterns. If their stress levels can be tied to specific events like pending tests or fears of eviction due to inability to pay the rent, then it makes little sense to call such fears irrational.

The most recent and most comprehensive meta-analysis of anger treatments is based on a review of 57 publications that embraced 92 treatments and described outcomes for 1,841 participants (DiGiuseppe & Tafrate, 2003). Determinations of effect sizes d revealed an overall between-groups difference of $d = -0.71$ for anger reduction at posttest, suggesting typically large effects that approached the typically observed effects for CBT. Self-reported aggression, attitudes, and more frequent use of positive behaviors showed the relatively largest improvements ($d = -1.16$, -0.81, and -0.83, respectively), whereas physiological arousal reductions were smaller overall ($d = -0.52$). Although effects weakened with extended follow-up, benefits were largely retained. DiGiuseppe and Tafrate (2003) reported generally comparable effect sizes for different treatment forms but assigned little importance to this observation because the majority of all interventions were of a CBT-type to begin with and not sufficiently different in rationale or protocol to promise substantive differences. A number of critical moderator variables were identified. Studies that used a manual and integrity checks (only $n = 3$) showed much larger benefits than those with a manual but no integrity checks ($n = 25$), with corresponding d's of -3.15 versus -0.91. Individual treatment ($n = 11$) produced noticeably larger effect than group treatments ($n = 25$), with $d = 1.16$ versus d $= 0.68$, respectively.

Forgiveness Therapy

Chronic interpersonal stress plays a particularly important role among distinguishable stressors because recovery has been demonstrated to be slower than recovery from other stressors (see Chapter 1). This type of situation is particularly demanding if the individual with whom one has problems is a part of day-to-day life (e.g., spouse or coworker). In this case, every day serves as a reminder of an unresolved conflict or past wrongdoing. Interpersonal stress is typically maintained for a long time, and it is of a pernicious quality when one or both parties believe that the other has behaved wrongly whereas they themselves have not contributed to the problem. If this one-sided perception is held equally by both parties, there is gridlock. In extreme, well-defined cases, people can resort to the court system to sort out right and wrong, but that is at best a very slow and usually still unsatisfactory solution. An alternative is that at least one party decides that maintenance of the relationship as a whole is more important than being right or wrong about guilt attributions of the past. Note that such an ability at perspective taking is, of course, a major defining characteristic of a lasting marriage.

Long-term emotional distress is predictable when somebody has been factually victimized (e.g., rape or child abuse). However, no matter how much empathy the victim receives, lack of emotional resolution by the victim is held to have extensive negative health consequences.

A critical role in resolving such conflicts, or in reducing the understandable anger of a victim toward an offender, is given to the concept of forgiveness. This term has gathered much interest recently. A major advantage of forgiveness as a conflict resolution tool is the fact that each individual has full control over it. The other party in such a conflict needs not be involved at all. Forgiveness is seen as having two major components (Thoresen, Luskin, & Harris, 1998): letting go of negative thoughts, feelings, and behaviors, and seeking a more compassionate understanding of the offender. Chapman and colleagues (2001) presented a 20-step learning program and applied it in a pilot outcome study to 17 male forensic patients who had been abused. The treatment program was described as proceeding in four distinct phases: (1) uncovering phase (dealing with feelings of hurt, working through shame, etc.), (2) commitment phase (realizing that past strategies have failed, considering forgiveness as an option), (3) work phase (attempting to see the wrongdoer with new eyes, developing empathy), and (4) deepening phase (finding meaning in surrender, realization of not being alone, shifting away negative feelings to greater dominance of positive feelings). The results drew a clear picture of possible change in that in the treated group of $N = 9$, forgiveness and hope increased significantly as did self-esteem (relative to controls). Despite these promising initial data, the literature on forgiveness and especially the outcome of forgiveness therapy is too recent to have permitted accumulation of forgiveness therapy outcome studies that could place effects in the context of other intervention effects.

Buffer Creation

Humor Therapy

No complicated psychological theorizing is required to make a positive (albeit subjective) case for the use of humor in daily life. Laughter and the use of humor in general are universally held to be positive behaviors and experiences that may lead to reduction of stress, promotion of good health, and enhanced quality of life. Also, it is rather difficult to think of negative side effects for the use of humor (or the application of humor therapy), except those occasional muscle spasms that might follow hearty laughing (and even those are harmless and transient). A sense of humor can make a person appear particularly likable and thus facilitate the building of friendships and support networks, and a good joke can serve as a welcome distraction in otherwise grim circumstances. Having watched almost all episodes of the TV series *M.A.S.H.*, the author recalls vividly how the—often rather black—humor of the M.A.S.H. staff made many otherwise horrifying moments more bearable. Numerous experimental studies on analogue samples back up these global and anecdotal claims, but very, very few clinical trials with patient populations are available.

Given that having a sense of humor is typically considered a stable individual quality, how does humor therapy achieve its end? Does it mean that humor therapy can transform a dull, unimaginative introvert into the life of the party? Probably not! However, humorous activities can be divided into *passive humor* (like reading jokes in magazines or on the Internet or renting funny videos) and *active humor production* (like writing a funny story, telling a good joke with the right emphasis, or playing a trick on a colleague). Obviously, it is easier to engage people in passive exposure to fun than it is to "make them all-round funny people."

The expression "laughter is the best medicine" has been around for centuries, but until recently there was no evidence to support this popular claim. When Norman Cousins (1976) incorporated humor therapy into his treatment of ankylosing spondilytis, however, the medical world began to take notice of the healing power of humor and of the positive emotions associated with it. Cousins's premise was this: "If stress and disease can have negative physiological repercussions, can positive thoughts and actions produce positive affects throughout the day?" The answer to this question comes in Cousins's report that 10 minutes of laughter from watching TV provided him with 2 hours of pain-free sleep that was badly needed for recovery.

Prior to engaging in a review of the outcomes of humor manipulations, it is wise to identify the specific nature of a humor intervention that could be meaningfully subsumed under stress management. In the section below, the application of humor in a psychotherapy process is not being considered because this application is considered too tangential to the SM theme. Therapists sometimes make jokes in therapy; these can be unrelated to a client's presenting problems and are meant to strengthen the building of an alliance with a patient (Franzini, 2000, 2001). Also possible is to seek humor in patients' responses or make interpretations more interesting by pointing out ironic twists, but this latter application can backfire because of differences in definitions of what is funny and also because a patient may lack the ability to be self-critical and open (in fact, an inability to be constructively self-critical is usually a part of the presenting psychopathology, and a patient who is able to see himself or herself in a funny light is probably close to therapy completion). Alas, these applications are seen as quite different from the kind of humor therapy that may be relevant to SM, and evaluating their usefulness is not helped by the lack of controlled research.

Outcome: Clinical Analogue Studies. In this section, a review is provided of studies that have evaluated subjective, behavioral, and physiological responses to acute exposure to humorous stimuli. This literature reveals a plethora of creative humor inductions, and many endpoints have been studied in a variety of participant populations. Numerous questions about the characteristics of respondents who did derive benefit from humor and critical features of the stimuli themselves have been revealed.

A small series of studies employed similar protocols in that college students and other healthy volunteers were exposed to various humorous stimuli and the effect of this exposure on mood was studied under controlled conditions (Cann, Calhoun, & Nance, 2000; Cann, Holt, & Calhoun, 1999; Mueller & Donnerstein, 1977; Ribordy, Holes, & Buchsbaum, 1980; Singer, 1968; Trice, 1985). Possessing a sense of humor (understood as a trait-type quality) sometimes enhanced the humor benefits (Cann et al., 1999), but this did not apply to all studies evaluating this effect (Cann et al., 2000). Evidence also suggests that aggression reduction effects following humor exposure applied to women but not to men (Mueller & Donnerstein, 1977).

Valuable additions to the studies that relied exclusively on self-report are those that also tap relevant behavior and biological activity. Weisenberg, Tepper, and Schwarzwald (1995) tested a time-limited experimental analogue of a clinical intervention, during which cold pressor (a test of physiological reactions to immersion of a hand into ice water), neutral, repulsive, and humorous films were offered. Pain tolerance increased in repulsive and humorous conditions; this was attributed to the distraction propensity of the humor stimuli.

Physiological pathways were tested in two studies by Berk et al. (1989; Berk et al., 2001). Their first study tested 10 healthy volunteers whose neuroendocrine changes were monitored during the watching of 60 minutes of a humorous video (5 participants were neutral controls, 5 were actively exposed to humor). Despite the rather small sample, many significant effects were apparent in the form of reduced cortisol, dopac (the major serum catabolite of dopamine), epinephrine, and growth hormone. This result suggests powerful physiological effects for a relatively small dose of humor with effects showing throughout the task period and typically lasting well into the 30-minute recovery. Interestingly, results were attributed to laughter (an active behavior), although the article failed to mention whether participants' laughter had been objectively recorded or not. Berk et al. (2001) expanded their earlier work by repeating the $N =$ 10 study with a similar humor induction but a much larger sample ($N =$ 52 healthy men), longer follow-up testing, and by including a wide range of immune function indices. Humor boosted natural killer cell activity, immunoglobulin level, T-cell activity, and cytokine interferon, and the effects lasted well beyond the length of exposure to the humor stimuli; many indices showed continued boosting effects at 12 hours postexposure.

Martin and Dobbin (1988) studied the effect of hassles (a form of accumulating minor stressors) on immune function as indexed by immunoglobulin A in 40 participants. Mood levels tracked over a 6-week period revealed that participants scoring high on measures of sense of humor as an inherent trait did not show the correlation of stressor exposure and immune change, whereas those low on humor trait showed a negative link ($r = -.32$), which suggests that the trait absence of a humorous outlook was paired with greater negative affect. The same pattern of a stress buffering effect of humor use was apparent for all three types of humor measures. The findings represent a direct and successful test of the stress buffering hypothesis of exposure to humor.

Another study's results bear on the stress buffering rationale. Newman and Stone (1996) showed participants a stressful video with images of a gory industrial accident. The task was to describe the events seen in either objective-neutral terms or ways that could be construed as humorous. Measures were galvanic skin response, heart rate, and skin temperature. When asked to enact humor in even this contrived environment, arousal was reduced relative to a neutral control condition.

In a shock anticipation experiment (Yovetich, Dale, & Hudak, 1990), participants benefited from humor induction (relative to controls) in that subjective anxiety ratings as well as physiological reactivity were attenuated, but this main effect was also moderated by a trait-type predisposition for humor. Similarly, induced depressive mood was reversed by humor exposure (Danzer, Dale, & Klions, 1990), as was apparent on self-report and zygomatic muscle activity (which reflects actual smiling behavior). Finally, a series of three studies tapped the immunoglobulin and subjective responses to humor induction in student volunteers (Lefcourt, Davidson-Katz, & Kueneman, 1990). Findings confirmed that possession of a trait-type sense of humor was a critical moderator of the mood benefits of humor induction.

Outcome: Field and Clinical Studies. A total of only four studies could be located for the critical applied testing of long-term benefits of humor induction (McGuire, Boyd, & James, 1992; Vance, 1987; Ventis, Higbee, & Murdock, 2001; Witztum, Briskin, & Lerner, 1999). Vance's work is in the area of instructional design, and humor applications were tested in three classes of first-grade school children ($N = 58$). Participants were not in any way preselected, and the humor manipulation was tested with respect to its effect on learning and retention (mood or distress were not tapped). Vance (1987) tested immediate and delayed humor contingency models and found that humor presentation prior to learning accelerated retention but that humor interspersed within a learning unit did not facilitate learning. In the strict sense, this study (while an applied study in nature) is not relevant to stress reduction, although one could claim that the humor benefits upon learning may have been mediated by a relaxed attitude and openness to learning that can result from humor exposure.

A truly clinical application with a controlled design was used by McGuire and colleagues (1992), who used long-term exposure to humor via watching funny movies to the improve quality of life for elderly residents of a long-term care facility. The researchers carefully evaluated the humor potential of a long list of commercially available movies, and randomized participants into either humorous, neutral, or a control condition. All subjects had experienced pain for at least 6 months. The humor and the neutral condition subjects watched movies for 3 hours per week for a 12-week period in total. Endpoints were self-reported health and affect, and pain medication requests. Watching funny movies resulted in broad-based improvement in mood state, weak and mixed results regarding self-perceived health, and no apparent benefits for pain medication requests. In another trial, 40 spider phobics were randomly assigned to systematic desensitization, humor desensitization, or untreated control. Both active treatments showed improvement and were superior to the no-treatment control, but were not different in effect from each other. The humor desensitization consisted of instructions to engage in humorous depictions of the feared spiders via imagery or the use of jokes or cartoons. Lastly, an uncontrolled intervention of humor for treating schizophrenia patients also showed some benefits (Witztum et al., 1999). Twelve schizophrenics were studied before and after a 3-month humor therapy; the intervention led to reduction in behavioral symptoms.

Conclusion. Use of humor as a therapeutic tool has been enthusiastically accepted by laypeople and mental health professionals and is being applied in a wide variety of contexts: schools, offices, and hospitals. Humorous material is made available to healthy people as a simple distractor and mood enhancer as well as to patient populations to facilitate emotional coping.

In sum, review of the experimental literature reveals a fairly consistent picture that humor induction in the laboratory can enhance positive moods and minimize distressed affect under a variety of experimentally induced distressing conditions (pain induction, performance stress, viewing of unpleasant films). The evidence is predominantly based on self-report, but a few well-controlled studies also reveal parallel effects on physiological indices of arousal. The shown benefits for immune function enhancement are particularly impressive (Berk et al., 1989; Berk et al., 2001) because they were apparent even in a small sample, they were replicated, and they lasted well beyond the humor exposure episode itself. There is suggestive evidence that at least for transient humor induction experiences, people do not need to possess a trait-type sense of humor to benefit from exposure to humorous materials, although a trait-type sense of humor appears consistently to accentuate the derived mood benefits. There is no clear evidence that actual laughter is required for benefit. The stimuli most often used were movies, a form of passive humor exposure. There is a critical absence of data about whether research participants can effectively be taught or encouraged to become active producers of humor (Martin, 2001). It is posited here that the ability to create humor actively (finding and retelling of jokes, using witty one-liners, or playing a prank) may actually have greater potential to be sustainable and to lead to reciprocity by encouraging others in the immediate social field to participate. Although men and women have been subjected to humor inductions, gender differences were rarely tested, and when they were tested, both genders appeared to benefit equally. There is no evidence so far that researchers have captured the cultural specificity underlying humor, and the most often used humor stimuli were North American–made comedies.

In light of the relatively good analogue research support on the acute benefits of humor, there is a stunning absence of controlled research into the longer-term effects of systematic, stress-reducing, and mood-enhancing humor use for healthy or clinical populations. The available studies are small in terms of sampling and have at best modest-quality protocols. Clinical practice (e.g., in the form of humor-material libraries in cancer wards) is way ahead of a literature base that actually supports its benefits. Analogue studies are supportive of positive outcomes, but evidence from controlled clinical trials is sorely missing to support claims for routine clinical applications. In consequence, there are exciting opportunities for researchers to close this gap.

Social Support Interventions

Presence of support has repeatedly been linked to good long-term health outcomes based on demonstrations of better immune function, lower blood pressure, and reduced mortality (see Chapter 2). Acute provision and general availability of support are meant to buffer individuals from the negative effects of stress exposure, and there is strong experimental research to support this claim. As Hogan, Linden, and Najarian (2002) have shown, however, there is a no ready translation from time-limited, acute support protocols in experimental studies to enduring support creation in the real world. That notwithstanding, researchers have created many unique approaches to support creation. Examples of particularly promising protocols are given in the next section. The reader interested in more detail on such interventions is referred to Hogan et al.'s (2002) review and tabular descriptions.

Social support interventions have taken many forms and have targeted highly varied populations. It is difficult to see a natural order in the several types of support interventions that have been used unless a brief description of the concept's many critical features is provided first. Commonly held critical features are structural aspects of social networks (e.g., the size of a person's social circle or the number of resources provided), functional aspects of social support (e.g., emotional support or a sense of acceptance), and enacted support (e.g., provision of specific supportive behaviors, such as reassurance or advice, in times of distress), as well as the subjective perception of support by the recipients (Lakey & Lutz, 1996). When support is defined interpersonally, as an exchange between providers and recipients, three main types of supportive social interactions emerge: emotional, informational, and instrumental (Antonucci, 1985; House & Kahn, 1985; Kahn & Antonucci, 1980). Emotional support involves verbal and nonverbal communication of caring and concern, and is believed to reduce distress by restoring self-esteem and permitting the expression of feelings. Informational support, which involves the provision of information used to guide or advise, is believed to enhance perceptions of control by reducing confusion and providing patients with strategies to cope with their difficulties. Instrumental support involves the provision of material goods (e.g., transportation, money, or physical assistance), and may also help decrease feelings of loss of control. It can be readily seen from this description that support can play an acute and lasting buffering function in the stress response process.

Understanding the nature of social support is at times impeded by the fact that support can emerge from both natural and more formal support systems. Natural support systems include both family and friendship networks. More formal support is provided by professionals (such as mental health and medical professionals), through interventions with groups of individuals with similar problems, and through social or community ties (such as clubs or religious groups). Presumably, natural support networks are a more enduring source of support, while other forms of support may be more transient. Whether one or the other is a superior source of support is not clear, however. How support is conceptualized and operationalized within an intervention may be critical in determining the ultimate success of that intervention.

Outcome of Support Interventions. Despite a massive literature on the benefits of support, there is equivocal evidence about how, and how well, social support interventions work. Only a single, systematic review of social support intervention outcomes could be located (Hogan et al., 2002). Using a computerized search strategy, 100 studies had been identified that evaluated the efficacy of such interventions. For the purpose of review and evaluation, Hogan et al. (2002) subdivided studies into three large clusters: (1) group versus individual interventions, (2) professionally led versus peer-provided treatment, (3) interventions where an increase of network size or perceived support was the primary target, versus those where building social skills (to facilitate support creation) was the focus. Since the search was not limited to a particular patient population, the interventions targeted a wide range of populations, including the elderly, those suffering from medical illnesses or from psychological disorders, women during labor, smokers, substance abusers, caregivers, and breast cancer and cardiac patients, to name a few. The review was primarily narrative in nature because the wide range of different social support interventions and targeted populations prohibited evaluation of treatment outcome using meta-analysis (i.e., there were not enough studies in all the resulting cells to permit meaningful comparison).

Close attention was paid to how support had been conceptualized by identifying whether a given intervention was targeted at directly providing support (e.g., providing emotional, informational, or instrumental support, or increasing enacted support), or whether it attempted to produce enduring changes in naturally occurring support (e.g., developing or improving social skills so that support is increased in the natural environment, strategies to improve perceived social support, or making changes in social networks). These two different approaches have very different conceptual underpinnings. Support provided by others is believed to strengthen coping resources, render a sense of being supported, and ultimately lead to a reduction in psychological or general health symptoms (Lakey & Lutz, 1996). On the other hand, interventions targeted at training social skills or improving the naturally occurring social environment are based on the belief that people can create and maintain support systems (or their perception of the support received from these systems) if they acquire the necessary skills. The resulting improvements in support are assumed to improve health and well-being.

Finally, it is important to determine the source of the support within a given intervention. This is most applicable to interventions focused on providing support. Support provided by a family member or friend and by other persons with similar difficulties (hereafter "peers") was discriminated from support provided by a professional caretaker (e.g., medical professional, psychologist, nurse, social worker). Other interventions may not specifically provide support from a certain source, but may work to increase the support received or perceived in the participant's natural environment.

Group Interventions That Provide Support Through Family and/or Friends. Support interventions that include family members or friends in treatment have the benefit of using the patient's natural support system; eight such studies were identified. Benefits from the core treatment were observed in all eight studies; three studies reported additional gains attributable to the inclusion of significant others in the interventions, while two others failed to do so. Effects tended not to last when evaluated at follow-up. Seven out of the eight studies did not include a measure of support. One particularly creative study is described here to demonstrate the potential richness of variations in protocol. Wing and Jeffrey (1999) tested a comprehensive support intervention that included intragroup activities, alternating providing and receiving support, group problem solving, and an intergroup competition. The support intervention was evaluated with friends recruited by the participants, as well as with teams of three other people the participants had not previously met. The support manipulation improved the maintenance of weight loss for those recruited with friends and those who were not, and showed that alternating between receiving and giving support may be most beneficial.

Group Interventions That Provide Support Through Peers (Self-Help Groups). Peer support, or "self-help," groups constitute a large portion of the health services system. In the United States alone, between 3% and 4% of the population is involved in self-help groups over a 1-year period (Kessler, Mickelson, & Zhao, 1997). Self-help groups provide an arena within which participants can both provide and receive support (most often emotional support), and this reciprocity is hypothesized to foster more favorable well-being (Maton, 1987). Furthermore, peer support groups provide members an opportunity to develop friendships and to rebuild lasting social networks after a crisis. Despite their widespread use and popularity, there are relatively few outcome studies; only 6 of 100 fit into this category. Five out of six studies reported improvements in general well-being or specific symptomatology, although it is important to note that none of the six studies reviewed employed a randomized control group design, and the generalizability of results are seriously threatened by concerns about self-selection into self-help groups.

In addition, this group of studies allowed conclusions to be drawn about the type of support protocol that may be most effective. Maton (1988) examined the relationship of social support to well-being and group appraisal among members of three different self-help groups: Compassionate Friends (time-delimited stress), Multiple Sclerosis (chronic stress), and Overeaters Anonymous (behavioral control). The social support measure included three subscales, namely Support Provided, Support Received, and Friendship. A fourth subscale, Bidirectional Support, was defined as persons high on both Support Provided and Support Received subscales (note that Support Received is equivalent to perceived support.). Receiving social support increased perceived group benefits and group satisfaction, while providing support and friendship were positively related to well-being and group appraisal. Bidirectional supporters reported more favorable well-being and group appraisal than Receivers or Providers. These results provide insight into the process of peer support groups, as providing *and* receiving support had beneficial effects on well-being and group satisfaction; those who did both fared better than participants who engaged in only one or the other.

Self-help groups may be of particular appeal to individuals with stigmatized concerns (e.g., AIDS, alcoholism, breast or prostate cancer), and lowest for equally damaging but less "embarrassing" diseases (e.g., heart disease). The differences are not trivial; for example, AIDS patients were *250 times* more likely to participate in a self-help group than hypertension patients.

Support Groups as a Means for Providing Social Support. Sixteen studies were identified in which organized support groups were led by a professional (e.g., psychologist, psychiatrist, nurse, or social worker). While typically nondirective, the leader facilitates discussion of the emotional issues and personal experiences of the group members. Similar to peer support groups, these support groups provide members with an opportunity to both receive and provide support. Formal skill training is not a component of these groups.

Eight of the 16 studies reported favorable outcomes of support group interventions on psychological and medical outcome measures. A further 4 studies reported moderate improvements on only psychological outcome measures; however, in one of these studies the support group did not outperform a stress management condition (Shearn & Fireman, 1985) and in 2 others the support group was inferior to a cognitive-behavioral treatment (CBT) condition at posttreatment (Bottomley, Hunton, Roberts, Jones, & Bradley, 1996; Edelman, Bell, & Kidman, 1999). Given that the support treatments failed to produce results similar to those found in SM or CBT controls, it can be concluded that they must also be inherently different in rationale and process (i.e., there must be more than nonspecific factors at work here).

Social Support Skills Training Group Interventions. Interventions that target social skills attempt to improve naturally occurring support systems by teaching relationship skills; the professional group leaders are directive and follow a defined curriculum. Although group members may be encouraged to be supportive of each other, the primary focus is the teaching and practicing of specific social support skills.

Nine of the 13 studies in this category reported benefits of social support skills training, and were mediated by increases in personal support networks. Much of this appeared to stem from increased contacts with professional caretakers, however, and does not hold much promise for generalization beyond the acute contact phase with professionals.

Five studies targeted psychiatric populations, and the skills training approach consistently improved assertion and social functioning. Again, one particular study deserves detailed mention. Brand, Lakey, and Berman (1995) investigated the efficacy of a treatment designed to increase perceived support that combined psychoeducation, social skills training, and cognitive behavioral techniques. This treatment is quite different from others described in this section because its primary objective was to increase perceived support. Perceived social support (measured by a well-validated measure) was found to increase when from family members, but not from friends, in the intervention group. Brand et al. suggest that observed changes in self-esteem and frequency of self-reinforcement might have mediated the increase in perceived support. Interestingly, changes in self-cognition were larger than changes in perceived support.

Group Interventions That Combine Provision of Support With Social Skills Training. One randomized controlled trial study was located that combined provision of support with social skills training; it aimed to improve support and decrease distress and grief in HIV-seropositive and HIV-seronegative homosexual men who had recently lost a friend or partner (Goodkin et al., 1999). The supportive component of treatment involved group discussion and the provision of mutual support, while the skills component focused on social support skills and coping styles. Treatment groups were homogeneous in terms of HIV-serostatus. At posttreatment, overall distress was reduced and grief recovery accelerated in men who received the intervention, but there was no change in depression or anxiety.

Individual Interventions That Provide Support Through Family and/or Friends. Although there is a variety of studies on support provision by close family members or friends, discussion here is limited to interventions in which improving social support was one of the explicit goals of treatment; four such studies were located. Three of the four studies reported beneficial effects from including significant others in individual treatment.

Individual Interventions That Provide Support Through Peers. Peer interventions at the individual level have taken many different forms. The results are encouraging because there is a critical mass of studies and the clear majority show favorable outcomes (9 out of 14). Peer support has proven efficacious with many patient populations, including coronary bypass patients awaiting surgery, nursing home residents, women with chronic depression, and mothers of children with juvenile rheumatoid arthritis. Interestingly, Scharlach (1988) observed beneficial effects of the support condition on the peer supporters as well as on the support recipients, providing evidence for the advantages of providing support.

Worth mentioning separately is a very well-designed study in which advocacy services were provided to women with abusive partners. Advocates focused on helping the women access needed community resources (i.e., instrumental support) while providing emotional support (Sullivan, Campbell, Angelique, Eby, & Davidson, 1994). At posttreatment, women who received the advocacy intervention reported increased effectiveness in obtaining desired resources, increased perceived social support, and improved quality of life. At 6-month follow-up, improved quality of life was maintained, but differences in perceived social support subsided. This may be due to the transient nature of the provided support, which could be corrected by providing as-needed services.

Individual Interventions That Provide Support Through Professionals. In most cases, these support interventions involved a combination of emotional support, informational support, and/or instrumental support, making it difficult to assess the unique contribution of support provided by a professional. Nine of the 18 studies reported generally positive effects of professionally led individual support interventions.

Social Support Skills Training: Individual Interventions. Teaching social skills to unassertive persons through use of rehearsal, modeling, instruction, and behavioral feedback has proven effective in the laboratory, and seven studies evaluated individually based interventions focusing on teaching social skills rather than direct provision of social support. Overall, the results of these investigations are promising in generally unassertive populations and in samples with specific diagnoses, and treatment effects were often reported to generalize.

Comparison of Different Types of Individual Support Treatment Structures. Only one study compared different forms of individual support. Pistrang and Barker (1998) examined the effects of emotional support provided by a partner versus a fellow patient on women with breast cancer. The participants engaged in a semi-structured communication task that required the discussion of the personal problems of the women. Trained observers rated the conversations with a fellow patient to be more helpful, empathetic, and supportive, less critical, and involving more self-disclosure than the conversations with partners.

Social Support Interventions That Combine Group and Individual Therapy. In this section, interventions that combine group settings with one-on-one support are described. In many cases, these interventions involve both professional leadership and support provided by family members, friends, or volunteers. A clinically sensitive and ecologically promising approach was evaluated by Hawkins, Catalano, and Wells (1986), who found that a social support skills training group followed by a "buddy" program was effective at reducing drug use; coping with relapse; and improving social interactions, interpersonal problem solving, and stress coping in a sample of drug users residing in therapeutic communities.

Group Versus Individual Interventions. Group and individual interventions were compared in three different studies, but the results were uneven, possibly due to lack of power and low-design-quality threats. One approach worth describing in more detail was a skills group that was compared to peer telephone support for multiple sclerosis (MS) patients (Schwartz, 1999). Participants randomly assigned to the skills intervention were taught approaches to goal setting, strategies to deal with cognitive deficits, and ways of improving communication with caregivers, and also participated in discussions about their emotional difficulties. Thus, these participants received emotional support as well as structured skills training aimed at improving coping and naturally occurring social networks. Participants randomly assigned to the peer telephone support condition received nondirective emotional support from volunteers who also had MS and who were trained in active listening. Results indicated that the skills training intervention produced gains in psychosocial role performance, coping behavior, and well-being, while the peer support intervention increased external locus of control but did not influence other variables. The peer support intervention was most helpful among participants with affective symptoms. Possible mechanisms behind the success of the skills training group are proposed by Schwartz, including modeling, reframing, increased commitment, and the directive nature of the group. Improved communication with caregivers may have led to increased support, which may have played a role in treatment outcome. Interestingly, compared to the supported patients, the peer telephone supporters reported more change in both positive and negative outcomes and showed improvements on psychological variables (e.g., self-esteem, depression). These findings, in combination with those reported by Scharlach (1988), suggest that systems of *mutual* support that encourage reciprocity may be especially helpful.

Discussion. A coarse summary of the results in a box-score format indicated that support interventions were reasonably successful given that of the 100 studies reviewed, 39 reported that supportive interventions were superior to no-treatment or standard care controls, 12 reported that interventions were superior or equivalent to alternate (also successful) treatments, 22 suggested partial benefits of support interventions, 17 suggested no benefit, and in 2 studies treated participants got worse. Eight of the studies had no controls to allow comparison. In sum, 73 of 92 studies (or 83%) reported at least some benefits from support interventions relative to either no-treatment or active controls. Unfortunately, this crude summarization was considered of limited use because many different types of interventions, delivery formats, and populations were lumped together. Support provided by friends and/or family members and by peers appears beneficial, and social support skills training may be especially useful. These findings held across both individual and group interventions, and for peer- and professionally directed protocols. Further, it was noted that interventions that emphasized reciprocal support (e.g., both giving and receiving support) demonstrated more encouraging results, suggesting that merely receiving support may not be as potent as mutual exchanges of support. Conceptual and methodological problems prevented much confidence in simplistic reporting of results. While reviews of therapy outcome routinely criticize studies for their methodological flaws, the support intervention literature was judged by Hogan et al. (2002) to reflect particularly serious problems. Far and away the most salient problem was that *most* of the studies examining the efficacy of support interventions failed to include a measure of social support. This was particularly striking because investigators usually posited that improved support was the reason for otherwise observed benefits. Attempts to improve the quality of social intervention studies may also need to carefully consider the need for matching the type of support to the type of recipient and the type of situation, because some support attempts have been shown to backfire. Positive ties with others were significantly related to well-being only when they involved positive affect and sociability rather than specific provision of support. A related concern is support attempts that fail because of minimization (i.e., challenging the seriousness or existence of a problem) and maximization (i.e., catastrophizing the problem or being overly protective; Dakof & Taylor, 1990; Hemphill, 1997; Lehman & Hemphill, 1990). Interestingly, Hemphill noted that some kinds of support, such as tangible and informational assistance, were perceived as especially helpful or unhelpful, depending on the characteristics of the stressor (i.e., physical incapacitation, controllability, or trajectory). Further, at least two well-designed studies show that support can worsen outcomes (Helgeson, Cohen, Schulz, & Yasko, 1999, with breast cancer support groups; and Frasure-Smith et al., 1997, with female cardiac patients). Women with breast cancer in peer discussion groups who initiated treatment with high support levels experienced decreases in physical functioning over the course of the group, and female cardiac patients who received nursing support also fared worse than their untreated counterparts. It appears that social support interventions should not be considered innocuous, and that women may be particularly open to negative outcomes.

There is discussion in the literature about matching interventions to patient characteristics. Hogan et al. (2002) provided a lengthy discussion of patient characteristics that may maximize the usefulness of support interventions and situations, as well as other patient characteristics that may not necessitate support interventions or that promise failure. On the one hand, there are psychiatric diagnoses (psychosis, personality disorders) for which support interventions are unlikely to lead to the creation of a patient-maintained network, and there also are people who neither have nor seek support. Support may be particularly beneficial in cases of transient stress phases, or acute disruptions in previous support.

A timely question is that of the usefulness of online support but no research was located that evaluated the efficacy of "computer" support. The Internet, however, by providing access to online support groups and chat rooms, may provide a potentially very useful form of social support (Davison, Pennebaker, & Dickerson, 2000). Interestingly, in their investigation of who pursued online support, Davison and her colleagues found that sufferers of debilitating diseases that present physical barriers to attending support groups (e.g., multiple sclerosis and chronic fatigue syndrome) showed the highest rate of online support group participation. Such groups provide an opportunity for persons whose disability impairs mobility, for rural and other isolated populations, and for those who desire anonymity.

Pet Ownership

Over the past decade or so a remarkably consistent body of literature has emerged that shows the stress-reducing benefits of owning a pet, although this body of research derives its strengths from time-limited lab stress manipulations rather than from an accumulation of controlled clinical trials. Acquiring a pet can be considered a special form of social support intervention in that pets provide esteem or emotional support (Allen, Blascovich, & Mendes, 2002), and this rationale is easy to accept. The benefits of pet ownership even derive anecdotal support in TV shows and Hollywood movies where a well-trained dog brings the owner's slippers when arriving home or fetches a cold beer from the refrigerator! Unfortunately that portrayal is a little too Hollywood-ish; if it were true, however, it could be seen as the dog providing instrumental support.

A key feature of the pet's supportive qualities is that the pet is loyal, nonjudgmental, and nondemanding, and this aggregate of qualities can lead people to sport bumper stickers saying, "I love my dog" or "The more I learn about people, the more I love my dog" (or cat, or fill in the blank with a pet of your choice). These little stabs notwithstanding, the presence of pets has consistently been shown to reduce acute arousal in demanding laboratory situations. Most often studied are blood pressure responses. In the great majority of studies where owners could bring their pets to the laboratory, the pet's presence was associated with smaller physiological stress responses than were seen in the presence of friends or a spouse or under a variety of control conditions where participants were alone while performing a comparably demanding task (Allen, Blascovich, & Mendes, 2002). It is less clear whether people who own pets have a priori different personality dispositions than those without pets, or whether "prescribing" acquisition of a pet to those who have never considered owning one would have the same beneficial effects.

Allen and Blascovich (1996) assessed the value of service dogs for people with ambulatory disabilities. Forty-eight individuals with severe and chronic ambulatory disabilities requiring the use of wheelchairs were recruited from advocacy and support groups for persons with muscular dystrophy, multiple sclerosis, traumatic brain injury, and spinal cord injury. Participants were matched on age, sex, marital status, race, and the nature and severity of the disability in order to create 24 pairs. Within each pair, participants were randomly assigned to either the experimental group or a wait-list control group. Experimental group members received trained service dogs 1 month after the study began, and subjects in the wait-list control group received dogs in month 13 of the study. Data collection occurred every 6 months over a 2-year period, resulting in five data collection points for all subjects. Participants showed substantial improvements in self-esteem, internal locus of control, and psychological well-being within 6 months after receiving their service dog. Socially, all participants showed similar improvements in community integration, and behavioral indices of change also improved (school attendance, part-time employment, needed paid and unpaid assistance hours). The authors concluded that trained service dogs could be highly beneficial and potentially cost-effective components of independent living for people with physical disabilities. In some ways, this study does not readily fit in the category of SM; on the other hand, the physical mobility limitations of these patients can be seen as a stressor and the dog's assistance was instrumental in increasing mobility. It is also likely (although not directly assessable in this type of protocol) that the pet's presence surreptitiously provided emotional and esteem support. Alternatively, the patients' improvement in affect may have been a reaction to the increased mobility that the trained dog facilitated. Either way, the intervention's benefit was apparent across a number of different indices and of surprising strength given the relatively small sample of the study.

Additional benefits of pet ownership and its inherent stress reduction potential are the fact that (a) some pets (dogs in particular) need to be walked daily, thus creating an opportunity for sustained exercise; and (b) pet care requires routines that create stability and a sense of responsibility that is of benefit to some.

Similar to the domains of time management and humor therapy, the popularity of pet ownership and its claimed benefits for health are based on good short-term, experimental evidence of benefits, but the ultimately critical, controlled, randomized trials are lacking. Although this appears to represent an exciting opportunity for researchers to distinguish themselves, such studies will not be easy to conduct because people self-select in whether or not they want pets in the first place. It is possible, or even likely, that those who decide to acquire a pet are metaphysically different from people who do not. Lack of perceived social support may be one strong motive for pet acquisition, whereas those high in support may elect not to have a pet; conversely, if people high in support were randomly assigned to have a pet (provided that they agreed in the first place), they might not benefit because the vacuum that the pet fills elsewhere does not exist here. Correspondingly, it may not even be possible to representatively sample petless individuals who then agree and follow through with a random assignment to pet ownership or a no-pet control group.

Psychological Effects of Exercise

The known acute physiological effects of exercise and their long-term implications are widely documented and provide strong reasons for inclusion in a lifestyle habit (Rostad & Long, 1996). Narrative and meta-analytic reviews have been published to help assess the usefulness of exercise components in SM programs.

A meta-analysis of the associated psychological benefits of exercise treatment in cardiac patients identified 15 studies of exercise rehabilitation that also monitored psychological changes in patients undergoing an exercise program (Kugler, Seelbach, & Krueskemper, 1994). These researchers reported that exercise alone without any specific attempt at psychological intervention produced significant reductions in anxiety (effect size $d = -0.31$) and depression ($d = -0.46$).

Long and her coworkers (Flood & Long, 1996; Long & Van Stavel, 1995; Rostad & Long, 1996) have diligently reviewed the literature and concluded that there is consistent evidence supporting aerobic exercise for coping with stress. In a meta-analysis, 40 studies were used to extract 76 effect sizes expressed as d. Exercise implementation was associated with an average within-group effect of $d = -0.45$ and a between-group effect of $d = -0.36$ in stress reduction. The outcomes indexed by these effect sizes were self-reported anxiety and tension. Predictably, participants with higher initial anxiety also derived greater benefits ($d = -0.48$ vs. $d = -0.32$), whereas the much greater benefit observed for men was surprising (men showed a between-group effect of $d = -0.49$ but women benefited only marginally with $d = -0.14$). It is comforting to see the replicability of effects when comparing the remarkably similar effect sizes for anxiety reduction in the Kugler et al. (1994) meta-analysis of cardiac patients with the data from Rostad and Long's (1996) more mixed samples.

Whereas people readily acknowledge the demonstrated benefits of an exercise habit, a major concern for all health practitioners is to assist in creating a stable, lasting exercise habit. Unfortunately, even among those convinced of the benefits, only a small portion actually engage in routine exercise, and researchers have placed considerable research emphasis on learning about methods to help people initiate and maintain exercise. The outcome of such efforts has been reviewed in a meta-analysis (Conn, Valentine, & Cooper, 2002), and researchers concluded that behavioral interventions are helpful in increasing physical activity but the resulting average effects sizes were small ($d = 0.26$). When linking protocol differences to outcomes, a number of clear recommendations emerged. Conn et al. (2002) concluded that patient populations were more likely to respond to a prescribed exercise regime than were nonpatients and were more successful if they focused on behavior (rather than broad health education), incorporated self-monitoring, used group formats, and were based on intensive contact between participants and interventionists.

Arousal Reduction Techniques

This section on the rationales and benefits of different arousal reduction strategies is kept relatively short because differences and similarities between various methods have been extensively discussed elsewhere (Lehrer & Woolfolk, 1990; Linden, 1990; Vaitl & Petermann, 2000). Further, as the reader will see below, the outcomes are much more similar than they are different (Benson, 1975) although protagonists of specific techniques tend to stress uniqueness and differences. The primary purpose of arousal reduction methods is to help people recognize sympathetic hyperarousal and to provide them with techniques to reduce such arousal. More recently, applied psychophysiology researchers have come to see relaxation methods as tools for achieving a balance between sympathetic and parasympathetic activation. In addition to just being expected to learn a technique, most proponents of relaxation methods (in particular those of meditation and Autogenic Training) also stress that experienced relaxation practitioners experience a shift in their overall arousability pattern and adopt a more distanced, reflective view of potentially stressful situations (Linden, 1990).

When researchers came to see the many similarities and shared features of arousal reduction strategies (e.g., a vehicle for focus, removal of external stimuli, a comfortable body position, perceived permission to focus on oneself; Benson, 1975), they started to challenge the idea that relaxation techniques had more to offer than would other inactivity like sitting quietly and resting or listening to classical music. Alexander and colleagues (Alexander, Robinson, Orme-Johnson, Schneider, & Walton, 1994), however, showed that a comparison of meditation with simple "eyes closed, rest" activity showed three to four times greater effects on skin resistance response, respiration, and plasma lactate changes for the mediation practitioners, thus supporting the notion of arousal reduction techniques as possessing unique and valuable properties.

Even though arousal reduction strategies achieve more than mere physical inactivity does, it is considerably more challenging to show differential benefits and/or "ideal matches" of particular strategies to specific applications. Benson's (1975) position is that all arousal reduction interventions share critical features that, at least for the most part, account for the benefits. These include provision of a rationale, permission to focus on oneself, spending time in a stimulus-reduced environment, and the use of a vehicle to facilitate attentional focus. Where methods differ most is in the use of the type of vehicle for attention focusing. In meditation it is the mantra, in Progressive Muscular Relaxation it is the clearly structured and sequenced following of tensing-relaxing steps for various muscle groups, in biofeedback it is the availability of a physiological monitor and displays of one's functions, and in Autogenic Training it is the structured sequence of attending to formulas that suggest particular physiological changes. Their shared target is to produce a relaxation response that shifts the pattern of the electroencephalogram (i.e., increases dominance of alpha activity), reduces muscle tone and blood pressure, and reduces breathing rate with simultaneously greater inspiration and expiration depths. Aside from physiological arousal reduction, these techniques are also likely to lead to accompanying changes in subjective arousal, and it is worthwhile for researchers to measure and report biological and psychological changes separately, given that they may not always occur in synchrony. One arousal reduction technique that is somewhat distinct and growing in popularity is that of mindfulness stress reduction (Davidson & Kabat-Zinn, 2004; Grossmann, Niemann, Schmidt, & Walach, in press; Kabat-Zinn, 2003). Although mindfulness stress reduction has some of its origins in meditation as practiced on the South Asian subcontinent, it is not be confused with traditional meditation like transcendental meditation because mindfulness meditation is not passive acceptance, but focuses on achieving an astute awareness and the ability to see and accept without judgment one's own behavior and interactions with the environment (Kabat-Zinn, 2003). A potential problem with discussing mindfulness meditation in a comparative sense with other arousal reduction methods is that mindfulness meditation is considered more of a multicomponent approach, more of an intervention program rather than just a unitary, single-technique intervention (Davidson & Kabat-Zinn, 2004; Smith, 2004).

Although the choice of arousal reduction method can occasionally be tied to specific outcomes (Lehrer, Carr, Sargunaraj, & Woolfolk, 1994), it is more often a function of the therapist's and client's preference, and of less importance for generic stress reduction. This claim to equivalence does not apply to certain demonstratedly "ideal" matches of technique to target, as in the case of electromyographic pelvic floor feedback for urinary incontinence.

One of the most extensively reviewed areas of arousal reduction is Autogenic Training (AT). This technique and its outcome are described in more detail to illustrate some specific technique-outcome matching effects. In AT the patient learns a set of six formulas that are subvocally repeated and that suggest specific autonomic sensations (see Linden, 1990, for a detailed description of the clinical procedures). These six formulas and their intended target areas are (1) "My arm is very heavy" (muscular relaxation), (2) "My arm is very warm" (vascular dilatation), (3) "My heartbeat is very regular" (stabilization of heart function), (4) "It breathes me" (regulation of breathing), (5) "Warmth is radiating over my stomach" (regulation of visceral organs), and (6) "There is a cool breeze across my forehead" (regulation of blood flow in the head). Supporting research has shown that measurable physiological changes accompany the practice of these imagery exercises (for reviews of the underlying conceptual issues, see Lichstein, 1988; Linden, 1990; or Luthe, 1970).

Two recent, detailed reviews are available to evaluate the efficacy of Autogenic Training and other comparison treatments (Linden, 1994; Stetter & Kupper, 2002). Both of these reviews have the unique advantage of drawing on English- and German-language studies. Quantitative findings suggested that Autogenic Training was associated with medium-sized pretreatment to posttreatment effects ranging from $d = -0.43$ for biological indices of change to $d = -0.58$ for psychological indices in the Linden (1994) review, and $d = -0.68$ (biological indices) and $d = -0.75$ (psychological outcomes) in the Stetter and Kupper review (2002). The pooled effect size estimates hide considerable variability in behavioral/psychological effects for individual target problems. Moderately sized improvements were reported for tension headache and migraine, hypertension, coronary heart disease rehabilitation, asthma, somatoform pain disorder, Raynaud's disease, and anxiety and sleep disorders.

The proponents of various arousal reduction strategies are often as wedded to their underlying theories and philosophies as are other psychotherapists to their alignments and particular theoretical orientations. Arousal reduction methods can be organized around Western versus Eastern origins (biofeedback, muscular relaxation vs. meditation, yoga), and around the degree to which they require imagination (e.g., there is a high need for imagery capability for meditation, and a low need for imagery in the learning of muscular relaxation). Along these lines, there is empirical support for the stress-reducing propensities of tai chi chuan (Sandlund & Norlander, 2000), but it is unclear whether tai chi chuan is more appropriately placed under the physical exercise or under the arousal reduction "umbrella" given that it combines some physical effort with an attentional distraction and focusing element.

Ultimately, however, it is an empirical question whether any one method is more effective than another, and this answer is, at least in good part, already available. Data from seven meta-analyses permit aggregation and comparison of results (Eppley, Abrams, & Shear, 1989; Godfrey, Bonds, Kraus, Wiener, & Toth, 1990; Grossmann et al., in press; Hyman, Feldman, Harris, Levin, & Malloy, 1989; Linden, 1994; Luebbert, Dahme, & Hasenbring, 2001; Stetter & Kupper, 2002), as well as observed effect sizes *d*, are displayed in Table 3.1.

Table 3.1   Average Effect Sizes for Arousal Reduction Strategies

Review	Pre/Post	Arousal Reduction vs. No Treatment	Arousal Reduction vs. Placebo	Arousal Reduction vs. Other Active Treatment
Hyman et al. (1989)	−0.51	−0.58	−0.66	N/A
Eppley et al. (1989)	N/A	−0.63	N/A	N/A
Godfrey et al. (1990)	−0.40	N/A	N/A	N/A
Linden (1994)	−0.53	−0.52	−0.37	−0.03
Stetter & Kupper (2002)	−0.75	−0.61	N/A	−0.28
Luebbert et al. (2001)	−0.49	N/A	N/A	N/A
Grossmann et al. (in press)	N/A	−0.56	−0.54	−0.43

One case of a very focused application of relaxation training is that documented by Luebbert and her collaborators (2001) in a meta-analysis of relaxation for cancer patients. Fifteen studies could be identified, and they revealed significant effects on affective distress for patients undergoing chemotherapy, radiotherapy, bone marrow transplantation, and hyperthermia. Outcomes could be clustered into biological indices (blood pressure, heart rate, nausea, pain), and the corresponding aggregate effect size was $d = -0.49$ (weighted for sample size) for the pre/post comparison. Outcome for subjective distress (depression, tension, anxiety, mood) also was $d = -0.49$.

Hyman et al.'s (1989) conclusions are based on 48 studies covering various relaxation techniques for a variety of applications. Linden (1994) focuses on evaluations of Autogenic Training ($N = 24$ studies), as do

Stetter and Kupper (2002). Eppley et al. (1989; $N = 146$ studies) evaluated the effects of various relaxation strategies for anxiety reduction. Unique to Linden's review is the separate reporting of effect sizes for biological indices of stress versus self-reported arousal reduction; for the pre/post comparison the effect sizes were $d = -0.47$ and $d = -0.58$, respectively; for the active treatment versus control comparison they were $d = -0.36$ and $d = -0.67$, respectively; and for comparison with placebo the scores were $d = -0.51$ and $d = -0.24$, respectively. Interestingly, while effect sizes for self-reported distress weakened with increasing levels of nonspecific effects inherent in different controls, the effect sizes for biological indices of stress remained at the same level. Note that the effect sizes in Table 3.1 reflect the *average* of effect sizes for self-report and biological indices.

Eppley and his colleagues (1989) subdivided their studies into relaxation, meditation, and other relaxation (i.e., neither mediation nor muscular relaxation) and found effect sizes of $d = -0.61$, $d = -0.69$, and $d = -0.58$, respectively (the effect size reported in Table 3.1 is the average of these three individual effect sizes). Grossmann et al. (in press) culled 64 empirical studies on mindfulness-based stress reduction from the literature and computed effect size for a variety of pre/post effects and control conditions. Unfortunately, only 20 of the 64 studies met reasonable standards for methodological quality and permitted inclusion in the effect size comparisons. The authors concluded that the average effect size for mindfulness stress reduction was around $d = 0.5$. As Table 3.1 indicates, it may have potential to be superior to other arousal reduction approaches because of all tested approaches it showed the largest effect superiority when pitched against active treatment comparisons (average $d = 0.43$). Such claims need to be interpreted with caution, however, because they are based on only a small number of studies with varying target populations.

In sum, Table 3.1 reveals a consistent picture of comparable, moderate effect sizes across all seven meta-analyses; subgrouping for techniques produced no meaningful differences (Eppley et al., 1989), and effect sizes for pre/post changes are essentially the same as for active treatment versus no-treatment controls. Notably, those reviews that subdivided results into outcomes on self-report versus biological indices consistently reported that biological indices of change were as large as self-report indices. This is in striking contrast to effect size computations for various cognitive-behavioral therapies where self-reported change in distress is typically twice as large as the effects associated with biological indices of distress.

Given that the aggregation principle of meta-analysis means sometimes indiscriminate "lumping," there still remains the question of which technique is the best match for which problem. Note, however, that the literature on arousal reduction methods is much broader than is needed for a discussion of stress management and arousal reduction techniques. Applications that are not considered to be greatly affected by psychological stress (e.g., bladder control problems following surgery, neuromuscular rehabilitation, or attention deficit disorder) are ignored here although they do often show strikingly positive results, especially for some biofeedback applications. Lehrer and his collaborators (1994) have presented a detailed review of effective technique to area of application matches for arousal reduction strategies. These researchers classify techniques on the basis of their cognitive versus behavioral/autonomic emphasis, with meditation and mindfulness forming the more cognitive end of the spectrum, Autogenic Training possessing both a cognitive and an autonomic rationale, and muscular relaxation and biofeedback being the most physiological, autonomically based techniques. Stress, anxiety, and phobias (applications most relevant to this book) were considered most responsive to interventions with strong cognitive *and* behavioral elements.

Stress Management Effects for Specific Populations

How should *population* be defined for this type of review? In principle, an infinite number of population subgroupings is possible, and one could divide healthy and ill individuals, women and men, people in varying occupations, older and younger participants, and study different cultural groups separately. For the current purpose, this section considers only different populations that are healthy; research on target populations that are defined by an existing illness (like asthma or hypertension) is described in the following section, which organizes studies by their targets.

Targeting population subgroups by characteristics other than ill mental or physical health requires a reason; some a priori theory or observation should justify why somebody wants to study population subgroups. As is shown here, these reasons and rationales are generally not hard to come by, and different rationales tend to lead to correspondingly different protocols. Teaching SM to healthy individuals is by definition primary prevention, and this makes it very difficult to show the clinical benefits of an intervention due to floor effects: Self-reported stress or muscle tension would appear to be an excellent outcome measure in many instances, but if it is already low, how could one show "improvement"? The alternative is to think of SM as a primary prevention strategy where participants' health changes are tracked over many decades and compared to a group that lived similarly challenging lives but had no exposure to stress management. This type of prospective approach has not been applied to date and may never succeed because the creation of an unconfounded control group is not feasible. More likely successful, of course, is the teaching of SM to people at high risk for stress-related disease, or to those who clearly show the disease. Alternatively, SM can be provided as part of a course of rehabilitation; that is, SM serves as a secondary and tertiary prevention effort.

Similarly good arguments can be raised for differentiating genders in outcome research because of growing evidence that women have different treatment needs and preferences than men (Cossette, Frasure-Smith, & Lesperance, 2001). Also, treatment results in one group may not readily generalize to other population groups that differ in SES or racial/ethnic background, given preexisting variations in resources and challenges.

Lastly, members of a particular community or those sharing a workplace may be selected and treatment targets can be tailored to (or respond to) an a priori environmental needs assessment. Examples might be communities that had to cope with natural disasters like an earthquake, or a firm that has seen drastic changes in personnel structure through cutbacks or mergers. A useful schema for classifying such studies is provided by Van der Hek and Plomp (1997), who lay out a 3 (level of interventions) × 3 (level of outcome measures) grid. Each axis organizes studies on a continuum of focus on the individual, on the individual-organizational interface, and on the organization itself. These researchers also supplied a table where the 24 outcome studies they reviewed were categorized according to these nine resulting cells; the results are rather revealing. Only 2 of the 24 studies targeted the organization, and only 2 more focused on the person-organization interface. The great predominance of studies exclusively targeted individuals. About half of the studies, however, included measures of outcome that affected the organization (burnout, absenteeism, etc.). Similarly, a review of 16 studies of stress management effects conducted by Giga et al. (2003) revealed that 81% of all interventions were directed at the individual, and only 19% addressed systemic change. The emerging picture is that of a workplace culture that clearly places the "stress problem" within individuals who are presumed to require better SM skills so as to make the company more efficient.

Review of the published literature on SM outcomes for healthy population subgroups revealed six reviews of workplace interventions, one of which is a meta-analysis of outcome (Godfrey et al., 1990). Van der Hek and Plomp (1997) reviewed the outcomes of 24 workplace studies published between 1987 and 1994 (narrative review) and concluded that the results were so variable that no overall conclusions of SM effectiveness was justified. Sixty-four workplace studies were identified by Murphy (1996); he concluded with a more positive view on SM's benefits than did Van der Hek and Plomp in that benefits were typically apparent, and that larger benefits were reported with studies that used a combination of techniques. Nevertheless, Murphy also cautions the reader to tread lightly because of the large variety in protocols, measures, and study design quality. He further suggests that interventions that target the stressors themselves (i.e., the workplace environment) may hold more promise than those targeting individuals and their coping skills, yet this type of work is particularly underdeveloped. Similarly, Jones and Johnston (2000) aggregated results from 36 SM trials with nurses in practice or in training; their sample of studies also included preexperimental interventions and those with quasi-control conditions. They concluded that SM tends to decrease subjective distress but questioned whether the observed statistical improvements were of a clinically relevant magnitude. Not surprisingly, they roundly criticized the available studies as frequently flawed in design, highly variable in content, and largely ignoring the person-organization interface, being predominantly focused on the individual.

A review of SM interventions for medical trainees identified 600 seemingly relevant articles, 24 of which actually reported intervention programs and of which, in turn, only 6 met rigorous scientific standards for trustworthy protocols (Shapiro, Shapiro, & Schwartz, 2000). Demonstrated benefits included improved immune function, decreases in anxiety and depression scores, increased spirituality and empathy, improved knowledge of stress, and better conflict resolution skills. Similarly, a systematic review of stress management interventions for mental health professionals identified a total of three studies that were actual interventions (Edwards, Hannigan, Fothergill, & Burnard, 2002). All three studies reported positive results but the type of measure varied from one study to another, revealing increasing job satisfaction in one study and decreased exhaustion in two others.

On the whole, the results from the narrative reviews are mirrored in the effect size computations of Godfrey and her collaborators' (1990) meta-analysis. These researchers culled 46 published studies of workplace stress reduction efforts and found that only 19 actually reported statistical results, and another 2 reported results in such an incomplete fashion that they could not be used for the analysis. Godfrey et al. reported results for studies that were subgrouped into either primary prevention (coping skills teaching and or stressor manipulation) versus secondary prevention (i.e., consisting only of teaching an arousal reduction strategy). Given that few studies had control group designs, the reported effect sizes reflect within-condition pre/post changes. The cluster of primary prevention interventions was reported to have been more effective (reductions of $d = -0.80$) than the secondary prevention approach ($d = -0.49$); and these results imply that multitechnique protocols produced better outcomes than single-technique efforts, although this finding may have been confounded by differential treatment length. Additional subanalyses were undertaken but the resulting cell sizes were so small that they were not very trustworthy; note that no fail-safe n statistic had been provided. Worth mentioning, however, is that subgrouping of secondary intervention efforts ($n = 7$ studies) revealed an effect size of $d = -0.40$ for relaxation training.

These reviews of SM effects on largely healthy populations tended to report significant changes despite the fact that floor effects were likely reducing the probability of demonstrable change. This suggests that so-called healthy populations still have room for improvement in self-reported stress levels or related biological and behavioral stress indices, and that SM is sufficiently powerful to lead to changes even if baseline scores on outcome variables are not particularly elevated.

A subtype of stress management is stress inoculation, which prepares individuals for stressful encounters and is thus truly preventive in its rationale. In a review of eight stress inoculation intervention protocols applied to children and adolescents, Maag and Kotlash (1994) identified protocol features that might aid or interfere with obtaining positive outcomes and reported that none of the eight studies identified the nature of the trainees' specific deficits, applied individually tailored interventions, or employed any generalization programming. It is disappointing that an appealing and well-reasoned approach such as stress inoculation training has received so little quality evaluation in the literature.

Stress Management Effects on Specific Endpoints

Consistent with the previous section on the physiology of stress and behavioral and subjective responses to excessive stimulation, this section can be organized into physiological measures (again subdividable into endocrine, immune function, and cardiovascular measures), self-report tools, peer or clinician observation, and behavioral indices (like alcohol consumption or absenteeism at work). It is sensible to evaluate different classes of endpoints in one study, and it is highly recommended to avoid simplistic or overly narrow definitions of stress. There are a few reviews that bear directly on SM effects on specific endpoints.

Immune Functions. Miller and Cohen (2001) reviewed psychological interventions and their effects on the immune system; this meta-analysis does not specifically focus on stress management, but it does provide outcome comparisons for five presumably different types of interventions, one of which is referred to as "stress management." Discussing this review needs to start off with the caveat that these authors subdivided psychological interventions into the following categories: conditioning, relaxation, stress management, disclosure interventions, and hypnosis with immune function suggestions. They do not provide documentation that these five types of interventions are nonoverlapping and that study categorizations can be reliably replicated. Problematic is Miller and Cohen's claim that relaxation is distinct from stress management. In contrast, throughout this book (and many other texts on SM) relaxation is subsumed under stress management and is not held to be distinct. Similarly, one can argue that a disclosure intervention is a form of emotional coping skill training and also broadly subsumable under stress management.

A total of 59 studies that included 2,135 individuals were identified; these had to be randomized controlled trials and meet at least minimal design quality criteria; up to 15 immune function indices were extracted. For understanding the review's results it may be necessary to point out that depending on the specific disease to be treated, the desired goal of immune function interventions may be suppression *or* activation. The results of comparative effect size computations revealed that (a) relaxation techniques and stress management had essentially no impact on immune function indices, (b) disclosure interventions led to mixed results with considerable heterogeneity suggesting both small improvements and worsening of immune function depending on the index used, and (c) conditioning studies and hypnosis with immune function imagery indicated moderate benefit; that is, immune function changed in desired directions. Note, however, that hypnotic imagery designed to *enhance* immune efficiency failed to produce effects ($r = .00$) whereas those studies that suggested *imageries of suppression* had the intended benefit ($r = .27$). The effect of conditioning interventions was comparatively large ($r = .57$) but only natural killer cell activity had been studied as an endpoint.

Cardiovascular Outcomes. A number of reviews (narrative and quantitative) can be found for psychological treatments applied to hypertension and those offered as part of cardiac rehabilitation (Jacob, Chesney, Williams, Ding, & Shapiro, 1991; Linden, 2000, 2003; Linden & Chambers, 1994; Linden, Stossel, & Maurice, 1996; Oldridge, Guyatt, Fischer, & Rimm, 1988; Spence, Barnett, Linden, Ramsden, & Taenzer, 1999). Not all interventions described in these reviews were specifically labeled as stress management, but inspection of these studies' rationales suggest that reduction of distress is a primary psychological target of psychological interventions for these patient groups, so subsuming these studies under SM appears justifiable. Note that the disease itself can be interpreted as a stressor requiring adaptation, and that the presence of the disease as a stressor is potentially orthogonal and independent of stress levels in existence prior to the illness.

Outcomes of Distress Reduction in Cardiac Rehabilitation. Many outcome evaluations for psychological treatments in cardiac rehabilitation have not been specifically labeled SM interventions, yet they have rationales and technique descriptions that fit well under the umbrella of SM. Researchers routinely see the diagnosis and treatment process of cardiac patients as a major stressor that requires coping, and there is a growing belief and supportive data that affective distress may contribute to the development of coronary artery disease and may impede rehabilitation (Rozanski, Blumenthal, & Kaplan, 1999).

Treatment outcomes have been carefully evaluated via narrative and meta-analytic comparisons. Efficacy reviews of psychological cardiac rehabilitation can be subdivided into those that are preventive in nature (i.e., targeting those at risk for heart disease) versus those in which patients clearly have diagnosed heart disease. The one available meta-analysis on psychosocial interventions for the primary and secondary prevention of coronary artery disease (CAD) focused exclusively on the modifiability of Type A behavior and its associated health benefits (Nunes, Frank, & Kornfeld, 1987). Seven of the 18 studies reviewed by Nunes et al. represented samples with documented CAD, whereas the others were samples of healthy individuals. Effect sizes were noted to increase with more intensive intervention. The effect of psychosocial treatment relative to controls (typically on medication) was evaluated for mortality and morbidity at 1-year and 3-year follow-up. At the 1-year follow-up, the effect size was $d = 0.34$ for mortality reduction (ns), $d = 0.45$ for recurrent myocardial infarction (MI) reduction (significant at $p < .05$), and $d = 0.57$ for combined MI recurrence and mortality (significant at $p < .05$). At the 3-year follow-up only the combined mortality and morbidity figures suggested further enhancement of the clinical benefit with $d = 0.97$ (significant at $p < .001$).

While providing empirical support for the inclusion of stress reduction in cardiac care, there remained a gap in knowledge about the unique effect that psychological interventions might have relative to nutrition and exercise interventions. Our own research group attempted to fill this gap in knowledge (Linden et al., 1996) by performing a statistical meta-analysis of 23 randomized controlled trials that evaluated the *additional* impact of psychosocial treatment for rehabilitation from documented coronary artery disease. Mortality data were available from 12 and recurrence data from 10 of the 23 studies. Follow-up data were clustered into short (less than 2 years) follow-up and long (more than 2 years) follow-up to allow testing of long-term benefits of interventions. The longest follow-ups included in this analysis were 8 and 5 years. The average length of follow-up in the less-than-2-years category was 12 months; the average length of follow-up in the more-than-2-years category was 63 months (5.2 years). The results were quite consistent with those of previous reviews, both narrative and meta-analytic. The observed odds-ratio reflected a 46% reduction in recurrence for the less-than-2-year follow-up and a 39% reduction for the longer follow-up. The analyses of the tests of psychosocial treatment on mortality (using fully randomized trial data only) revealed treatment-related mortality reductions of 41%. For follow-up greater than 2 years there was a continuing trend for mortality benefits (26%), but this was not statistically significant. The benefits of psychological treatment for reduced reoccurrence of cardiac events were very similar in magnitude, and mapped onto the reductions in mortality.

With respect to psychological distress and biological risk factors, patients in the control conditions changed very little (compared to pretest); if anything, they got worse. Psychological intervention, on the other hand, was associated with reductions in psychological distress ($d = -0.34$), heart rate ($d = -0.38$), cholesterol ($d = -1.54$), and systolic blood pressure ($d = -0.24$).

The previously described reviews presented a rather positive set of conclusions about the impact of psychosocial treatments for cardiac patients and underline claims made previously that stress reduction is likely to benefit multiple health indicators, both psychological and biological in nature. Since publication of the review by Linden et al. (1996), another meta-analysis (Dusseldorp, Van Elderen, Maes, Meulman, & Kraail, 1999) and four large-scale clinical trials have been published that appear to undermine claims that psychological treatments are beneficial, and that represent somewhat of a "roller coaster" of ambiguous conclusions about usefulness of psychological interventions.

Jones and West (1996) reported the results from a very large trial where additional psychological intervention was contrasted with standard care in a sample of 2,328 post-MI patients. A multicomponent stress management rehabilitation program had no apparent additional benefit for mortality, clinical complications, anxiety, or depression. Treated patients reported less angina and less medication usage. Note that apparently all cardiac patients were randomized into one of the two treatment conditions, irrespective of whether or not elevated stress, anxiety, or depression was present. Of importance is the fact that the mortality rate for both groups was only 6% over the following 12 months, thus making it difficult to distinguish experimental from control treatment results due to low base rates. Another very large recent trial with disappointing results was the one conducted by Frasure-Smith et al. (1997) that found no significant benefit of psychological treatment overall but a trend toward greater mortality in treated women. Finally, the largest psychological trial conducted on cardiac rehabilitation patients to date deserves mention as well (The Writing Committee for the ENRICHD Investigators, 2003), although it is not really appropriate to consider this study a trial of stress management given that the target of the intervention was depression and, to a lesser degree, improvement of social support. In a randomized clinical trial methodology, 2,481 post-MI patients (1,084 women, 1,397 men) were enrolled in eight participating centers and were assigned to a usual-care control group or to the experimental treatment. ENRICHD failed to show benefits for psychological treatment on mortality outcomes but was successful in reducing depression and improving support despite the fact that the usual-care condition was not actually inert but represented a minimal intervention control.

These confusing results benefit greatly from the clarification provided by a meta-analysis (Dusseldorp et al., 1999) in which standard care was compared with additional psychological treatment (as was done by Linden et al., 1996). The researchers noted reductions in mortality odds for psychological treatment that ranged from 6% to 52%, depending on the length of studied outcomes. Aggregated across all studies, psychological treatment had no significant positive impact on short-term MI recurrence (−16%) but still showed 41% reductions in medium- and long-term follow-ups. Most striking was a comparison of outcomes for those studies where psychological treatment failed to produce psychological changes with those where it succeeded. When psychological distress was not reduced by the treatment (as was true in Jones & West's study, 1996), patient mortality was higher than that of the controls (odds-ratio 0.88:1) and MI recurrence was not affected (odds-ratio 1.03:1); when, however, psychological distress was reduced, then the odds-ratios for mortality were 1.52:1

and for MI recurrence were 1.69:1. The importance of demonstrating this mediational effect was also underlined by Cossette et al. (2001), who reanalyzed the disappointing M-HART results and concluded that cardiac benefits did occur when psychological distress was also effectively reduced. More specifically, they found that short-term anxiety and depression reduction predicted 1-year status (i.e., treatment response stability) and that distress reduction was associated with reduced mortality from cardiac causes and with reduced number of readmissions. Such findings direct attention to the yet-to-be resolved question of which patients are most likely to benefit from which treatment approach. Along these lines, it needs highlighting that the earlier rehabilitation studies tended to offer treatment almost exclusively to men, who in turn tended to be younger than the female cardiac patients. Older patients (who most often were women) benefit less from standard treatment approaches, and treatment needs vary for women and men. At this time, it cannot be ruled out that older female patients may actually be better off without therapy.

Cardiac patients are the fortunate beneficiaries of improved cardiologic care and its associated lower post-event mortality rates, and researchers, as a consequence, need to consider trial protocols with other endpoints, which are likely to change over time and which are important prognostic indicators. Such endpoints can be psychological in nature (e.g., distress) or be intermediary, hard cardiac endpoints like ischemia, premature ventricular contractions, or heart period variability. This latter approach is reflected in a stress management intervention trial (Blumenthal et al., 2002; Blumenthal et al., 1997) where outcomes were contrasted with those from an exercise control condition. The treatment was a small-group, cognitive-behavioral intervention lasting 16 weeks with one 1.5-hour session per week; patients were not preselected for high psychological distress. During the 5-year follow-up (Blumenthal et al., 2002) the stress management group had only a relative risk of 0.6 of event recurrence in comparison to the usual care controls (1.3 events), and in addition the researchers were able to show significant cost reductions for stress management (relative to the other conditions) in the long-term care of ischemia patients. Ischemia was also more positively affected by stress management than by exercise. Stress management was uniquely associated with significant reductions in hostility and self-reported stress but not with any unique advantages for reducing depression or trait anxiety.

Although results in the area of psychological stress reduction in cardiac rehabilitation may appear confusing, some fairly clear conclusions are possible given the many patients who have completed randomized controlled trials of stress reduction programs and the diligent reviews that have scrutinized the aggregated knowledge base. Hoped-for stress reduction in cardiac patients is of no use if distress was not present to begin with (a floor effect problem), if not all patients benefited equally (especially, older women derived few if any benefits), or if treatment length positively correlates with better outcomes. Where stress reduction was indeed achieved, event recurrence and mortality were also reduced, with follow-ups reaching 5-year observation periods.

Hypertension. Although psychological stress is widely considered to contribute to the development of essential hypertension, and the epidemiological evidence for the stress–high blood pressure (BP) linkage is very convincing, the biopsychological pathway that would explain how stress can lead to disease is less clear (Schwartz et al., 2003). Consistent with research findings that link stress to hypertension, psychological treatments are designed to reduce stress in one of two possible ways. One approach is to emphasize arousal reduction through relaxation training, meditation, and/or biofeedback, all of which are designed to improve a person's self-regulatory skills. A second approach is to conceive of stress as a multistep process involving triggers, coping behaviors, cognitions, and—finally—physiological stress responses. Research using this second model to conceive of stress–BP linkages targets deficient cognitive and behavioral stress coping skills.

Therapy outcome reports and resulting consensus opinions tend to reveal small effects if aggregated uncritically into reviews. The U.S. report (Joint National Committee on Detection, Evaluation, and Treatment, 1988) and the earlier Canadian Consensus Conference (Canadian Consensus Conference on Non-Pharmacological Approaches, 1990) have been complemented by a more recent Canadian Consensus Conference (Spence et al., 1999) and by meta-analyses on the effectiveness of nondrug approaches to the treatment of hypertension (Andrews, McMahon, Austin, Byrne, 1984; Linden & Chambers, 1994; Ward, Swan, & Chesney, 1987). Together, these reviews clarify agreements and differences between various research studies, although their positive recommendations vary considerably in strength. Andrews et al. (1984) sampled 14 drug studies and compared resulting effect sizes with the outcomes from 37 nondrug studies. The drugs were noted to be very effective, with effect sizes about twice as large as the magnitude of the most effective nondrug approaches—for example, weight loss ($d = 1.6$), yoga ($d = 1.4$), and muscle relaxation ($d = 1.3$). Other nondrug approaches were associated with effect sizes that did not differ from placebo-associated outcomes ($d = 0.6$–0.7). Note that the relaxation training studies in the Andrews review referred to standardized, single-technique interventions.

Ward et al. (1987) included only studies that met criteria for high design quality, leaving a total of 12 studies. Therapies designed to produce arousal reduction (predominantly relaxation) were associated with effect sizes of $d = 0.54–0.65$ for systolic blood pressure and $d = 0.40–0.58$ for diastolic blood pressure, based on pretreatment to posttreatment within-group changes or comparisons of active treatments with wait-list controls.

Jacob and his collaborators (1991) also reviewed the outcome on relaxation therapy for hypertension (although not using a full meta-analytic approach) and identified 75 controlled clinical trials. Jacob et al. highlighted how design features and entry criteria had significant impact on the observed clinical effects; patients who had high pretreatment BP values also showed much greater improvements with treatment ($r = .75$ for systolic and $r = .64$ for diastolic blood pressure). The issue of differential pretreatment levels had not been considered in the recommendations of the two earlier North American consensus groups or previous reviews and may have led to an underestimation of the effects possible with psychological treatments.

The narrative review approach of Jacob et al. (1991) was subsequently complemented with a meta-analysis and sampled even more psychologically based treatment comparisons (Linden & Chambers, 1994). Although drug treatment is the accepted gold standard for efficacious hypertension treatment, neither of the Consensus Conference papers (Canadian Consensus Conference, 1988; The Joint National Committee on Detection, Evaluation, and Treatment of High Blood Pressure, 1988) directly compared drug effects with nondrug effects. Therefore, Linden and Chambers (1994) investigated whether or not the findings of the narrative reviews could be corroborated by quantitative, meta-analytic findings, including comparisons with pharmacological agents. Specifically, they wanted to know how the total amount of blood pressure change achieved with nondrug approaches compared to drug treatment results. The objective of this review was to explicitly answer the question a patient might ask his or her practitioner: "How much blood pressure reduction can I achieve with the available treatment options?"

The Linden and Chambers (1994) meta-analysis included a total of 166 studies that evaluated the effects of three types of medications, weight reduction, sodium and alcohol restriction, physical exercise, calcium and potassium supplements, single-component and multicomponent relaxation therapy, and individualized, cognitive-behavioral therapies. Of the nondrug approaches, weight reduction/physical exercise, and individualized, cognitive-behavioral psychological therapy were particularly effective and did not differ from drug treatments in observed raw effect sizes for systolic blood pressure reductions.

Linden and Chambers (1994) confirmed Jacob et al.'s (1991) observation that initial blood pressure levels strongly influenced the magnitude of observed treatment effects irrespective of what the treatment actually was. After adjustment for differences in initial blood pressure levels, the effect sizes for nondrug therapies increased, and the effect size of individualized psychological therapy matched the effect sizes of drug treatments for systolic and diastolic pressure reduction. These findings suggest that some nondrug therapies may be quite effective, especially when differences in pretreatment blood pressure levels are taken into account. In terms of technique-specific outcome, the adoption of a standardized treatment, relative to an individualized approach, is associated with smaller reductions in blood pressure (Linden & Chambers, 1994).

The above considerations formed the basis for a different kind of clinical trial, namely a study using conservative measurement strategies (ambulatory blood pressure as an endpoint), high initial blood pressure, and individualized, one-on-one treatments (Linden, Lenz, & Con, 2001). Treatment led to a significant reduction in ambulatory blood pressure, and total change at 6-month follow-up was −10.8 and −8.5 mmHg, respectively. The level of blood pressure at the beginning treatment was correlated with pressure change ($r = .45$ and 0.51, respectively). The amount of systolic blood pressure change was positively correlated with reduction in psychological stress ($r = .34$) and change in anger coping styles (r ranges from .35 to .41). This study suggested that psychological interventions offered by professional therapists in an individualized manner can be an efficacious treatment for primary hypertension. Significant and clinically meaningful reductions in both systolic and diastolic 24-hour mean blood pressure were observed.

Applications of SM to Other Health Outcomes. Stress is presumed either to contribute to or play a role in the rehabilitation and treatment of numerous medical disorders. Distress is a frequent and predictable response to a disease diagnosis, and the knowledge of having a disease, often aggravated by salient symptoms, leads to affective distress, typically in the form of anxiety and depression. Ong et al. (2004) had identified 40% of 153 studies as applications of SM to various health concerns. Aside from frequently studied SM applications to hypertension, cardiac rehabilitation, and immune system improvements, there are many other areas of application with typically positive results that, however, have not been investigated with systematic outcome reviews. Such positive results are encouraging but not definitive, and reviews are badly needed.

The fact that cancer patients have to cope with the stress and fear of the unknown has led numerous researchers to offer distress reduction efforts to cancer patients; these studies consistently support the value of stress management for affect and quality-of-life improvements (Fawzy et al., 1993; Jacobsen et al., 2002; Schwartz et al., 1998; Speca, Carlson, Goodey, & Angen, 2000). A promising new direction in the psychological treatment of cancer patients goes beyond attempts to just reduce distress, and also seeks to add a dimension of "meaning-making," encouraging patients to find ways to identify potential benefits from the disease experience (Bower & Segerstrom, 2004). This promise became apparent in one intervention where cognitive-behavioral treatment for early-stage breast cancer with the target of meaning-making not only reduced distress but also showed improved immune function. The immune function improvements were in turn correlated with relative success in meaning-making, thus indicating a potential mediating pathway for psychotherapy and disease outcomes.

Applications to rheumatoid arthritis have been described in a review by Savelkoul, de Witte, and Post (2003) that identified 13 studies on psychological treatment for arthritis. Only 3 of these described coping interventions, and only 1 was supportive of positive outcomes. Further supporting evidence from individual studies is available for diabetes (Henry, Wilson, Bruce, Chisholm, & Rawling, 1997; McGrady, Nadsady, & Schumann-Brzezinski, 1991), fibromyalgia (Kaplan, Goldberg, & Galvin-Nadeau, 1993; Wigers, Stiles, & Vogel, 1996), multiple sclerosis (Schwartz, 1999), dermatitis (Habib & Morrissey, 1999), injury and illness prevention in athletes (Perna, Antoni, Baum, Gordon, & Schneiderman, 2003), and HIV-positive patients (Antoni, 2003; Antoni et al., 1991; Lutgendorf et al., 1997; Lutgendorf et al., 1998).

Summary of the Effects of Stress Management

The literature revealed a massive body of outcome studies that are relevant for investigating benefits of stress management. They were organized into categories, summarized, and evaluated here. Throughout this chapter on outcome and a preceding review paper (Ong et al., 2004), the lack of a consensual definition of SM was considered a handicap for making meaningful comparisons of interventions that were described as "stress management" and that had bundled multiple techniques into one package. Nevertheless, for the sake of at least attempting comparisons, the term *stress management* was accepted as somewhat meaningful when SM intervention results for either population subgroups or areas of application were reported above. The first and largest section of this review is free of this constraint because it organized interventions by more specific technique descriptors rather than by the global term SM.

A number of core conclusions emerge from this review:

• There is no population subgroup or area of application where SM was found to be ineffective; SM appears to have little or no potential for harm, and generally produces at least moderately positive outcomes.

• SM is rarely pitched against other active psychological treatments in treatment comparisons, and reported positive effects are predominantly derived from pre/post, within-participant changes, or from SM effects compared with no-treatment controls.

• Most of the stimulus manipulation (or environmental change) approaches were tested in the workplace, and the results favor these approaches over arousal reduction strategies in individuals. No significant body of literature could be identified that evaluated social policy changes as systemic interventions, and no comprehensive meta-analyses could be found on these types of interventions.

• SM may be useful for suppression of overly active immune function but showed no potential for increasing weak immune function.

• SM has been found useful for cardiovascular problems, with the most promising findings for blood pressure reduction. In the area of cardiac rehabilitation, men appeared to benefit more than women.

• The literature on coping interventions was very difficult to interpret. This is due in part to the fact that the underlying taxonomies of coping keep changing. The limited usefulness of the coping literature for facilitating stress management is also attributable to the fact that adaptive coping is best explained with a trait-by-situation interaction model that is difficult to teach and test in standardized, random assignment treatment protocols.

• Similarly, the literature on problem-solving training provided some empirical support for its effectiveness but comprehensive reviews are lacking. This absence of a unified database may have resulted from the fact that the basic principles of problem-solving training are shared by researchers, but that the application of these principles to different populations and problem areas results in greatly different protocols that are not open to ready comparison. Problem-solving training in newly diagnosed cancer patients is by necessity very different from problem-solving training for children with impulse control problems, for example.

- Social skills training was reported as consistently effective for adults (less so for children), although not all studies showed transfer of skill acquisition to everyday life.

- Some popular and frequently practiced techniques may have strong, empirically based rationales but lack a substantive body of research on outcome evaluations; this was found true for the use of humor, pets, stress inoculation, and time management.

- Many known predispositional factors for stress are simply not open for change, at least not in the psychologist's office; these include genetics and low socioeconomic status.

- The field of buffers represents a rather mixed bag of conceptual sophistication and includes well-known and accepted concepts (physical fitness, social support) as well as promising new ones (sense of coherence, spirituality). On the whole there is some evidence that creation of social support is beneficial, and there is very consistent and strong evidence that exercise is a valuable buffer for stress, producing replicable, moderate effect sizes. Outcome research on concepts that can be subsumed under positive psychology is still in its infancy, largely untested but promising.

- In terms of arousal reduction strategies, there is a large body of research, the main conclusions of which are that many effective techniques are available, that effects are generally in the moderate range, and that techniques are largely interchangeable as effective stress reduction tools. In contrast to psychotherapy, and cognitive-behavioral treatments in particular, however, arousal reduction strategies produce similar-sized effects on self-report of affect and on biological indices of stress, whereas psychotherapy shows large effects on self-reported distress reduction that are not matched by correspondingly large biological changes.

- There is growing support that single-technique SM approaches do not fare as well as multicomponent interventions, but that observation is open to the confounding explanation that longer interventions also produce better outcomes and the fact that definitional problems interfere with the reliability of results from clustered reviews of multicomponent stress management interventions.

4

Now What?

A Summary, Reflections, and Recommendations

Small enzymes of consciousness can have large catalytic effects for a whole culture. Anyone who has made yogurt knows that.

—Former Canadian Ambassador
James George, 1995 (cited in Colombo, 2000)

Major Conclusions

An extensive body of literature, ranging from basic biology to epidemiology to social policy and to clinical practice, has been reviewed to extract critical information for a discourse on the stress management construct and the application of this knowledge for the design of useful, replicable, and transparent intervention programs. Conclusions from core questions raised throughout this book are first listed in a compressed form representing what could be called an "executive summary." A more detailed discussion and suggestions for clinical practice and research that arises from these summary observations follow in the same order.

Definition and Operationalization of Stress Management

SM as typically practiced is a hodgepodge of techniques, most of which are taught in only a minimalist, superficial fashion, and researchers often disagree on operational definitions (see also Ong, Linden, & Young, 2004).

The techniques themselves can be meaningfully organized into four categories: (1) system or environment interventions (i.e., stressor manipulations), (2) coping skills training, (3) creation of stress buffers (like social support), and (4) arousal reduction techniques. Most of the typically used specific techniques have a sound rationale and are grounded in basic research; there is generally supportive evidence for clinical utility from numerous controlled, clinical trials. Stimulus recognition and manipulation are logical first activities in an SM program, and they represent a primary prevention objective that is germane to SM. To facilitate communication, researchers and practitioners should distinguish these four classes of SM components and clearly describe which ones are built into an intervention protocol.

On the whole, controlled stressor manipulations and systemic change research have been the "orphans" in this literature, the neglected children who have received minimal and not-well-structured attention. It is noteworthy that European stress researchers see the topic (and the opportunities for change) much more as a larger societal issue whereas North Americans tend to construct the need to manage stress as an individual responsibility. Best developed is the area of workplace stress that is more likely to deal with organizational issues (i.e., the stressor environment) than are other applications; yet even here, systemic changes are often asked for and rarely researched and practiced (Giga, Noblet, Faraghe, & Cooper, 2003). Also underdeveloped is the area of social skill building meant to understand and minimize interpersonal strain, and this vacuum is particularly noteworthy because the research described in this book has identified interpersonal stress as particularly insidious, persistent, and difficult to recover from.

As a result of this discourse on stress management and its theoretical and practical roots, the following definition is offered:

> Stress management is both a set of relatively concrete techniques for distress reduction and skill building, as well as an attempt to view, organize, and shape our world to maximize quality of life even at times of adversity. These two core features do not readily form a coherent, simple definition of stress management; instead, to be meaningful, the definition embraces a broad view of stress that reflects how people interact with one another and how they construct their environment, and that accepts that stress management is both preventive and reactive in nature.

Rationales for Stress Management

On the whole, the rationales for various SM techniques map well onto the physiological, behavioral, and cognitive processes that delineate how stress can lead to disease. The simplest designs and most closely matched rationales of technique to known pathophysiology are found in the category of arousal reduction strategies. This area of coping, although recognized as very important for SM, is both vast and inconclusive. Adaptive coping is recognized as requiring a behavior-by-situation match, which does not readily lend itself to the group format of standard SM approaches. Recognition of emotional distress and socially appropriate expression of these feelings appears to be of greater benefit for women than for men. Although rationales for systemic interventions are sometimes well developed, especially in the organizational behavior literature, the intended systemic interventions still tend to place too much emphasis on individual responsibility rather than needed social policy or system change.

Emerging Trends

A promising trend in psychotherapy in general and SM in particular is the attention being paid not only to the reduction of distress but also to the creation of supportive environments and positive mood states that can serve as buffers against the negative effects of strain. There is strong basic research evidence to suggest that this emergence of a positive psychology is worthwhile in its own right and not just the opposite of distress. Absence of distress is not equivalent to the simultaneous presence of joy, a sense of meaning, and contentment, and an exclusive focus on stress reduction misses out on the golden opportunities for "antistress vaccinations" that are inherent in the creation of good humor, fitness, joy, a sense of coherence, and social support. A further distinct advantage of creating buffers is that these efforts are largely controllable by individuals and are readily available, often at no or minimal cost, and rarely need professional intervention. In this regard, there is a consistent body of research evidence backing social support creation, but very little research shows the long-term health consequences of other positive psychology constructs. Evaluations of social support intervention outcomes exist and suggest predominantly positive benefits, but they also represent a complex, and at times confusing, body of research (Hogan, Linden, & Najarian, 2002). There are no readily usable protocols to endow stressed individuals with a meaning of life or a sense of coherence.

Outcome of Stress Management Interventions

No single review of the literature exists that comprehensively reviews all SM outcomes for different applications and different populations. Chapter 3 represents the most comprehensive such effort to date. The relatively largest number of available reviews is in the area of workplace stress reduction, and the findings suggest that SM outcomes are similar in effect size to psychotherapy in general. The workplace literature also provides evidence that interventions that function as primary prevention and use environment change strategies (or stimulus manipulations) produce greater benefits than do interventions that target only arousal reduction in individuals.

The absence of a single, all-encompassing review of outcomes is attributable, at least in good part, to the sheer size of the field. There are, however, numerous reviews on more narrowly defined intervention strategies that indicate overall similar-sized effects of SM approaches to those of psychotherapy at large. No SM technique or area of application could be identified in which systematic research has shown that SM was *in*effective, and there is ample evidence for its consistent benefits. Interestingly, outcome research on some of the most popular and promising techniques is at times scant or even nonexistent; particularly striking examples are humor therapy and time management interventions.

Meaningful comparisons of SM with other classes of interventions, or contrasts of different classes of conceptualizations of SM with each other, are severely handicapped by the lack of a consensual definition of SM. Undoubtedly, it makes sense to compare SM effects with those of a no-intervention, wait-list control group, but no clear picture emerges from this literature of what an appropriate active treatment control or attention control condition might be. Frequently, SM content and outcome overlap with the contents and outcomes of cognitive-behavioral therapy, which implies that cognitive-behavioral therapy is not different enough to represent a suitable active treatment comparison. True placebo comparisons also make little sense because even minimal therapy is not inert, and blinding of participants or therapists cannot logically and credibly be achieved.

Unique to measuring outcomes of stress management is that many intervention recipients are healthy at the outset, and their scores on dependent variables often reflect floor effects, leaving little room for improvement. It is therefore likely that SM, when applied to relatively healthy samples within a primary prevention context, underestimates effect sizes that may be achievable with more distressed samples. When SM is used as primary prevention, then any judgment of its effectiveness requires prospective designs with very long follow-ups, extending over many decades, and of sufficient duration so that illness is likely to develop in at least a sizeable group of participants.

Which Protocol Features
Account for the Best Outcomes?

While a fairly typical, or modal, type of SM program can be identified (Ong et al., 2004), there is no reliable knowledge or consensus on *necessary* or *sufficient* features for high-quality SM protocols. Also, the modal programs teach an average of six to eight techniques, thus not permitting technique-specific claims for effectiveness. In addition, knowledge is lacking about required minimal length of treatment, needed qualifications for therapists/ trainers, suitability of technique for a particular population, superiority (or lack thereof) of multicomponent interventions, most sensitive outcome measures, or most suitable applications. It is likely that multitechnique packages are superior to single-technique interventions (Godfrey, Bonds, Kraus, Wiener, & Toth, 1990; Linden & Chambers, 1994; Murphy, 1996), but supporting evidence for this claim remains scant.

Identified Gaps

Building the necessary solid evidence base for the outcomes of SM requires (1) a theoretical foundation that is shared by clinicians and researchers, (2) a rationale that maps onto the known pathophysiology of the stress process, (3) a consensus on what an appropriate intervention package consists of, and (4) treatment protocols that are sufficiently well described in publications so as to be replicable in a variety of settings by other practitioners.

Chapter 2 represents an outline of a comprehensive theoretical model (and justifies its components) that may be agreeable to many readers; it was explicitly based on a review of the known interactive pathways of emotion-behavior-biology and their linkages to disease (Chapter 1). At the end of Chapter 2, a list of basic goals for intervention was offered, as were suggestions for sequencing of technique presentations. A corresponding, structured, and manualized intervention protocol has been constructed and is currently being evaluated in a randomized, controlled clinical trial (Linden, 2002, 2003). More details on the content of this protocol follow below.

Defining Stress Management
and Questioning Rationales

The previous section was meant to serve as the "executive summary"; the following sections discuss in more detail the implications of these core conclusions, and recommendations for future research and clinical practice are offered.

In many ways, arousal reduction techniques or strategies represent the "home turf" and the originating point of SM. Arousal reduction approaches map well onto Selye's concepts of activation and exhaustion, are consistent with McEwen's concept of allostasis, and they were the first techniques considered to be useful SM tools (Lehrer & Woolfolk, 1990; Vaitl & Petermann, 2000). It is almost impossible to find an existing SM protocol that does not contain some arousal reduction attempt (Ong et al., 2004). In other words, researchers and practitioners agree that arousal reduction skills are desired and needed targets for intervention; however, we still need to remind ourselves that there is no evidence that a battery of SM techniques without the inclusion of arousal reduction techniques will be less efficacious than a battery that does include them.

Arousal reduction techniques are meant to facilitate recovery and prevent exhaustion, and (albeit to a lesser degree) may reduce the excessive vigilance and alarm response readiness that characterizes individuals under stress. Hundreds of controlled clinical trials attest to the efficacy of arousal reduction interventions on their own, and these outcomes are documented in numerous meta-analyses that were described in Chapter 3. On the whole, the effect sizes associated with singular applications of arousal reduction techniques are smaller than those observed for multicomponent cognitive-behavioral therapies, but it is also noteworthy that psychotherapy effects are usually stronger on self-report indices than they are on biological measures, whereas the arousal reduction interventions used in SM tend to produce biological effects that are similar in magnitude to more subjective, self-reported arousal reduction. The therapy outcome literature does not support categorical claims that any particular arousal reduction strategy is overall superior to another one. This conclusion, however, does not preclude "ideal matches" between specific techniques and applications.

The rationales for coping skills training (whether behavioral or cognitive) are noticeably more detached from underlying physiological rationales than are the arousal reduction strategies. Moreover, the presumed pathways for how coping behaviors affect physiology are less direct. They are mediated by numerous intrapersonal and interpersonal factors. As an author, I found that writing the section on coping was the most taxing task of all; it required intense reading of written works that were complex and often contentious with each other, and described a field in continuous flux. In the end, these works provided little help for the task of extracting useful information for the teaching of adaptive coping skills to a large number of people. Maybe the most important conclusion is that no coping style is inherently and categorically adaptive or maladaptive across different contexts.

Adaptive coping is at least difficult, if not impossible, to define without consideration of such unique situational contexts and knowledge of available personal resources, and this is made difficult to evaluate because the dominant taxonomies of coping styles continue to change (Skinner, Edge, Altman, & Sherwood, 2003). The particular strength of a taxonomy like Skinner et al. lies in its use for communication, because it reduces a vast catalogue of terms into a more manageable three-dimensional model. On the other hand, even Skinner et al.'s impressive reorganization of the coping literature mostly helps to organize future research efforts at clarifying what is adaptive, for whom, and when; it does not yet help stress management practitioners answer the question of what categorically "adaptive coping" is. Correspondingly, it is most difficult to extract coping advice from this vast literature that can then be taught in a time-limited fashion as part of an SM treatment package.

While recognizing the importance of effective coping for stress management, the identified need to develop coping skills in individually tailored, situation-dependent approaches impedes their ready integration into a manualized, group-based SM intervention. I posit here that problem-solving training and coping training are largely overlapping; both provide elementary training of meta- or process skills (cognitive and behavioral) that can be offered in an educational, standardized format. To make coping and problem-solving training most effective, however, context variables need to be considered, and these methods are therefore best taught in one of four flexible formats or environments:

1. In a one-on-one setup with a professional therapist who has the needed training and experience to assess individual histories and possible rigid personality structures or personality disorders that may contribute to excessive stress levels.

2. Via a differently framed but otherwise similar approach adopted for relatively well-adjusted individuals who do not seek formal therapy but seek "coaching." Coaching is a new approach for psychologists who typically consult with executives on a one-on-one basis to maximize their efficiency and create a healthy effort-reward balance at work.

3. Via group interventions for homogeneous groups that are explicitly recruited to work within a disease- or problem-specific model of stress

management. Examples are (a) diabetic adolescents seeking to build assertion skills that allow them to adhere to a dietary regime without being made outcasts by their nondiabetic peers, (b) police officers who learn stress inoculation skills to prepare them for crowd control assignments, or (c) cancer patients who want to build or nurture emotional coping skills needed to tolerate the looming, long-term threat to their sense of safety that is typical of this disease and its complex treatment protocols.

4. Via a small-group format (with less than 10 participants) that is fairly lengthy, employs systematic homework assignments, and possesses a cohesive, trusting group dynamic so that individualizing can still be achieved. This approach would be more like group psychotherapy in its spirit and methods than just educational.

Considerable evidence was presented about which stressors and stressor qualities trigger or aggravate stress responses. The successful manipulation of stressful environments themselves represents the least coherent area of controlled stress outcome research, and little is known about the degree to which stressors themselves are modifiable to minimize frequency or magnitude of future stress responses. To a large degree, this is inevitable because the stimulus environment varies from one person to the next. In this vein, a group of junior employees fearing layoffs in their company because sales are down are far removed from the power needed to eliminate this threat effectively. On the other hand, a family that is under stress because of unruly teenagers may be able to change the family environment with the help of a family therapist.

Even if difficult to set into operation, it is logical that modifying stressors (the first step or element in the stress process) may potentially be of the greatest benefit because (1) it may prevent unnecessary triggering of stress responses, (2) multiple individuals or whole population groups could benefit from one intervention, and (3) a modified or eliminated stressor no longer requires coping and activation, thus reducing the possibility of total exhaustion. At the risk of sounding trite, even simple maneuvers like organizing an office or a kitchen, keeping updated address and phone lists, or regularly backing up important computer documents can be meaningfully conceived of as stress prevention efforts.

Especially the early research on stressors and stress responses is dominated by the use of animal models, and this approach has greatly increased knowledge of the pathophysiology of stress. It has highlighted critical stimulus features like control and predictability, and numerous findings from animal models can be readily applied to humans. Animal models have also revealed numerous potential pathways from stressor exposure to disease outcomes. On the other hand, as was shown earlier, the research emphasis on animal models of stress may be a prime reason that modification of environmental stressors has received little attention; only in George Orwell's fictional *Animal Farm* do the animals actually assemble and plot to overthrow their ruler.

A second posited reason for the relative neglect of environmental change is that it falls outside of the typical practice patterns of health professionals, who work with distressed individuals rather than consult with policy- and lawmakers. To illustrate the limitations arising from this point, one can consider poverty as a stressor. There is ample evidence that financial concerns are among the top three or four concerns listed by people in survey research as sources of stress. The other dominant concerns are relationship issues, work overload, and childcare concerns. Certain money worries are indeed the result of poor money management by individuals who do have a reasonable cash flow and, in this case, money management skills can be taught and practiced with hope of some success. Our local newspaper, for example, occasionally recruits a family to reveal their finances and offers them free time with a financial consultant. This consultant then assesses the family's earnings, expenses, habits, expectations, and current concerns, and outlines a financial plan that is designed to return a sense of subjective control as well as sound planning. Aside from this being good journalism with a human interest bent, it also is designed to be educational for readers in a similar situation and can be seen as a form of stress prevention through the use of media. Given that most people in this world are objectively poor, however, the much larger issue is how poverty can be eliminated, and that is a huge, global, societal, and political issue that far exceeds what health professionals can do on a day-to-day basis.

The purpose of elaborating on the topic of poverty was to show how stress researchers have largely ignored many stressors as global problems that also require (at least serious and aggressive attempts at) global solutions (Gardell, 1980). Achieving peace in war-torn countries, reducing crime in a neighborhood, encouraging civility on the road, or eradicating poverty requires systemic change and a strong political will.

Taking such a broad view of stress and its occasional modifiability at the source, however, may still invite a reflexive falling back onto the continuing desire to "fix" stress at the level of the individual, as has been done for many decades. Unfortunately, such a knee-jerk response ignores the very real possibilities of intervening at an intermediary level, such as the family or the workplace, where one can have more direct influence on individuals' day-to-day stress levels without blaming individuals or assigning all responsibility for coping to individuals themselves. When a psychologist who provides employee assistance to the staff of a hospital emergency room learns from a string of clients that they hate their job because their common supervisor is hostile, crude, and offensive, then it is inefficient, and maybe even morally wrong, to teach hostility coping skills to the employees. The problem is that it is the supervisor who needs "fixing"! Such "intermediate-level" interventions are still within reach of mental health professionals or human resource experts in their daily activities, although it may require innovative thinking, creative solutions, and sharpening of previously unused skills. I recall the case of a young woman with little formal education who reported severe anxiety and sleep problems to me; she was the single parent of three preschoolers and was supposed to live on a blend of welfare support and regular alimony payments by the children's father. The welfare rate available to her was reduced because the ex-husband's alimony was to make up the difference. Unfortunately, his alimony payments were highly infrequent, often represented only a fraction of the agreed-on amount, and arrived in unpredictable intervals; every first-of-the-month and the need for rent payment became a perpetual, major stress trigger. Instead of trying to treat her symptoms of insomnia and anxiety, which appeared to be understandable reactions to a perpetual threat, I decided to think more "systemic" and formed an alliance with her social worker and a lawyer to improve communication between all "players" and assure more reliable alimony payments from her "ex."

In the section on workplace interventions in Chapter 3, a string of examples illustrated how worker-centered workplace changes can affect the perceived stress load. These interventions represent intermediate-level interventions, and affect performance, absenteeism, and job satisfaction. Specific strategies included the establishment of daycare centers at work, introduction of flextime, empowerment strategies, and shifts from conveyor belt work to teamwork, to name just a few.

What About the Needed, Shared Definition for Stress Management?

Review of the literature revealed that there is both disagreement and considerable overlap in what components make up SM as it is described in the literature. A number of options for resolution are advanced here, and their respective advantages and disadvantages are outlined.

A rather radical idea that is nevertheless worth discussing is to give up the term SM for good. Every SM intervention could instead be called cognitive-behavioral therapy (CBT) for distress, and this could be done by conceptualizing all SM approaches as CBT that is being applied to people without a psychiatric diagnosis. It is not difficult to make up arguments in support of such a suggestion. Many techniques of SM are also frequently used psychotherapy techniques: cognitive restructuring, relaxation training, and assertion training. Arousal reduction is a core treatment approach to anxiety disorders (and some personality disorders). Cognitive restructuring is well documented as a useful treatment for depression, generalized anxiety, panic, and Obsessive Compulsive Disorder; and problem-solving training is offered to children and adolescents who lack behavioral inhibition. In support of this argument is Blagys and Hilsenroth's (2002) review and conclusion that CBT is characterized by a set of distinct process features that differentiate it from other forms of psychotherapy. These distinct features were listed as (a) use of homework and outside-of-session activities; (b) direction of session activity; (c) teaching of skills used by patients to cope with symptoms; (d) emphasis on patients' future experiences; (e) providing patients with information about their treatment, disorder, or symptoms; and (f) and an intrapersonal/cognitive focus. Comparing these process features of CBT with the various descriptions of SM techniques in Chapter 3 shows a great deal of overlap and supports the provocative "test case" that SM is CBT and vice versa. Hence, the argument is not just to equate SM with all psychotherapy, but to consider equating it with CBT because of CBT's heavy emphasis on skill learning and behavioral change rather than a focus on creating insight into individual behavior patterns; the latter is more characteristic of psychodynamically and interpersonally oriented therapies.

Another argument for equivalence can be derived from a hypothetical substitution experiment. If the term *stress management* did not exist and no distinctly labeled compilation of SM techniques had ever been provided, would a skilled and well-trained cognitive-behavioral therapist have enough tools in his or her arsenal to provide an individual with significant help in the reduction of distress, feelings of burnout, and in teaching better coping skills? The answer would likely be yes, and that insight puts the onus on stress management researchers to make a case for SM's "right to life."

The above hypothetical substitution scenario appears to justify supporting the radical proposition that SM is not needed at all. In support of a more balanced view, however, the commonalities and differences of psychotherapy and SM can be readily displayed in a three-column table (Table 4.1) that describes shared and varying features and the distinct emphases of the two approaches.

Table 4.1   Comparison of Psychotherapy and Stress Management,
Core Features

Characteristic	Psychotherapy	Stress Management
Assumptions about psychopathology	Typically applied to individuals with a *DSM* or *ICD* diagnostic code, seeking to remedy primary presenting pathology. Goal is insight and lasting behavior change.	Typically applied to people without a psychiatric diagnosis, some may have physical health/psychosomatic problems with affective distress consequences. Goal is to teach skills, be educational; benefits may take time to show.
Intent: reactive vs. preventive	Mostly reactive, responding to a professionally or self-made psychiatric diagnosis	Often preventive, otherwise reactive to a physical disease diagnosis or to identified problems within an organization
Delivery format	Mostly one-on-one, occasionally manual-based, most often individually tailored	Predominantly in group form, typically standardized
Theoretical orientation	Highly varied and eclectic, depending on therapist training/preference and client needs, often insight-oriented	Predominantly cognitive-behavioral in nature, most likely skill-oriented, sometimes with a systems perspective
Outcome measures	Overwhelmingly behavioral and self-report, rarely biological	Overwhelmingly self-report, frequently biological, rarely behavioral
Length of intervention	Mostly brief (5–20 one-hour sessions), occasionally long-term if needed, frequently terminated when distress is clearly reduced	Almost always brief, 6–12 hours of training, spread over 6–8 meeting times; will typically terminate at fixed time irrespective of participant progress
Homework use	Frequent, especially when the therapy is strongly cognitive-behavioral in orientation	Standard, considered critical for success
Therapist/trainer qualification	Variable, but mostly provided by professionals who possess a graduate degree in mental health	Highly variable; at times taught by people without knowledge of psychopathology. If applied to medical problems, typically provided by therapist with mental health training.

This three-column display of shared versus unique features of stress management and psychotherapy gives rise to the argument that something valuable may be lost if SM as a label were given up altogether. The two terms represent two very different places on a continuum of psychopathology, and the stigma associated with being a patient in therapy may prevent some individuals from benefiting from the learning and preventive qualities that SM can provide. SM's potential as a true primary prevention tool would be seriously weakened or lost altogether if the labels "patient" and "therapy" were to be used in the intervention. Psychotherapy "reacts"; patients ask for help with distress, the therapist assesses symptoms and then responds with a negotiated therapy plan. SM may also be reactive, especially in the case of medical patients (like diabetics or postinfarction patients) where stress may play a contributory role in symptom maintenance and an impediment to rehabilitation, but at the same time it is much more preventive and proactive in its intent. If psychotherapy is cognitive-behavioral in its orientation, then it presumes that existing distress is due to poor learning and/or poor coping on the part of the patient. It does not seriously attempt to see an individual's problem in a larger societal context and does not attempt to change the patient's environment. SM (at least the way it is defined here) begins with learning about environmental stimuli and then considers opportunities for lasting changes to the stressor environment. SM may include elements of empowerment such that systemic changes triggered by one individual on his or own behalf may later benefit other individuals in the same environment (via implementation of a functional sexual harassment policy in a workplace, for example).

While popularity is not a scientific argument per se, the SM field is very popular, and there is a journal devoted solely to the topic. A Google.com Web search on "stress management" identified 2,500,000 pertinent responses; SM books are selling well in academic and popular bookstores and many are now in third or fourth editions. In sum, complete elimination of the term SM is drastic, would be a "throwing the baby out with the bathwater" approach, would not be readily accepted, and—last but not least—is not compatible with other suggestions toward a more reconstructive approach as presented next.

On careful consideration of these arguments for and against retaining the term *stress management,* I propose that the term not be abandoned but that—instead of attempting to uphold or propagate a single global, catch-all label—one might classify different stress management approaches into three reasonably distinct categories. This newly proposed taxonomy results from considering reactive versus proactive intentions of different stress management rationales and protocols, the degree of individualizing versus standardizing of the content of the interventions, and, lastly, whether a given SM intervention is a systemic intervention or a professionally led intervention where a clinically trained stress expert works with individuals or small groups. The resulting categories and their inherent qualities (and flaws) are primary, systematic stress prevention; preventive, skill-learning stress management; and reactive, problem-solving stress management.

Primary, Systemic Stress Prevention. This label is applied to a truly primary-prevention type of SM that achieves its goals via system and policy changes. These changes are possibly triggered by empowered private individuals, but are generally implemented by politicians, administrators, or managers, and they affect workplaces and society at large (Newton, 1995). Examples would be government programs or policies to reduce poverty; to increase public safety; to minimize harassment due to gender, race, religion, or sexual preference; or to support job stability. While this approach is not the type of work that psychologists typically undertake on a daily basis, the aspirational aspect of such systemic, preventive activities is actually mandated in the Ethics Code of Psychologists in many jurisdictions, with the intent of raising the social conscience and level of emancipation of health professionals.

Preventive, Skill-Learning Stress Management. This term refers to a preventive, skill-learning–based approach to stress reduction that is not necessarily reactive to a preceding diagnosis of acute distress; it can be fairly standardized because it needs to prepare individuals for a variety of future demands with stress potential that are only partly predictable. It provides individuals with a flexible toolkit and is meant to be the psychological analogy to a "beginner's home repair toolkit" that one can buy in a hardware store. Some narrowing of objectives can be achieved by recruiting intervention participants who share a similar environment; examples would be all employees of a company or all 12th-grade students in a school. Again, analogies would be basic toolkits for plumbing jobs versus basic tool kits for woodwork. On the other hand, if participants come from all walks of life and represent varying age groups, then a broad, multitechnique approach to stress reduction may be best.

Intervention protocols that embrace multiple techniques have earned such loaded and pejorative descriptors as "shotgun" or "garden hose" approaches, but the intended use of a preventive purpose justifies the teaching of multiple techniques. If learners do not present themselves with a specific problem to solve, that is, a trigger to react to, then the acquisition of a wide arsenal of tools for undetermined future use is highly desirable. An analogy to this approach is the vaccination against multiple strains of flu when public health experts cannot foretell which of six possible strains may become the most dominant in an upcoming flu season.

Still, caveats are in order. Exclusive use of shotgun programming and global outcome assessments categorically prevent determination of the most and least effective program components in SM. Determining the potentially different effects of various components is of great theoretical and, ultimately, also of clinical interest. A research strategy is proposed here that allows specificity evaluations without raising ethical issues surrounding offers of second-rate treatments. Using a multimethod, multitool approach (and a large sample), researchers can measure skill acquisition and goal attainments for each treatment component. Next they can determine with multivariate statistics which pattern of success with various tools was associated with best overall outcomes. Similarly, the best match of patient characteristic to problem characteristic can be determined. An example of this type of approach in cardiac rehabilitation is the work by Cossette, Frasure-Smith, and Lesperance (2001), who showed distinct benefits for men who received solution-oriented, educational interventions, whereas women did not benefit from the same types of interventions.

Reactive, Problem-Solving Stress Management. The third type of SM is the most reactive; it is applied to situations that are predictably and commonly stressful, like massive layoffs in a company, dealing with a positive diagnosis of breast cancer and its pending lengthy and frightening treatment protocol, surviving in a hostile workplace, or handling the challenges faced by caregivers of Alzheimer's patients. This approach requires tailoring interventions to the situational triggers that brought the need for SM to light, and it is probably most efficacious when matched to participant preferences and individual context. A heart or cancer patient with a supportive spouse may not need or even benefit from additional support but may seek to quell her disease-specific fears with accurate information about symptoms and warning signals, as well as tips for risk reduction. Nevertheless, clinical experience and qualitative and quantitative research can be drawn on to identify frequent and typical stressors and stressor qualities, and this knowledge can be built into treatment rationales and technique selections. Using another home repair analogy, it is much more efficient for an appliance repair person to know the type and model of a broken appliance in advance of a home visit than to come without specific parts and tools.

Reflections on Communication

When it comes to describing SM protocols in manuals and research studies, use of the three category descriptors provided in the previous section is expected to facilitate a better understanding and enhanced replicability of the approaches used. In addition, I urge authors to clearly spell out which specific, preventive, system change manipulations are used, what coping skills are practiced, what buffers are created, and which arousal reduction strategies are taught. Both Ong et al. (2004) and previous sections of this book provide numerous examples of fuzzy and confusing use of terminology regarding intervention content. To create further meaningful labeling, no intervention that is meant only to reduce arousal or that teaches only time management should be called "stress management" or "stress reduction." Narrowly defined interventions should be called by a name that most closely resembles what they are actually trying to achieve: reduce arousal or teach relaxation, or teach problem-solving skills for diabetes management.

Enhancement of the comparability of SM across different practitioners and samples can be facilitated by the creation and use of manuals, and by generous sharing of manuals among researchers and practitioners. All authors, reviewers, and journal editors are urged to use (and require of authors) clear, meaningful labels, detailed descriptions, and, where possible, sharable manuals to facilitate replication.

Effective Ingredients and Delivery Modes for Stress Management

While its additional value is unproven at this time, the ideal program should include buffer creation and help participants develop an overall lifestyle that has built-in recovery habits and schedules. There is a definite vacuum in the research literature about how features of a positive psychology can be created via structured interventions and how much benefit such interventions may bring about. There has also been minimal attention paid to social skill building, although interpersonal stressors have been shown to be particularly pervasive and long-lasting.

Considerably more researcher attention needs to be directed at the question of standardizing versus individually tailoring interventions and the resulting outcomes. There is evidence that individual tailoring enhances outcomes (e.g., Linden, Lenz, & Con, 2001). The advantages and disadvantages of standardizing versus individualizing are well established.

Individual tailoring (a) is what therapy practitioners actually do every day, (b) likely enhances therapy outcome and makes it more durable, (c) makes comparisons across therapists and therapies (or SM programs) difficult, and (d) often loses the economic advantage of group interventions. A fully standardized program (especially when embedded in a randomized, controlled trial) treats therapist and client variables as mere noise that needs to be "randomized away." It is, however, ideal for comparing the differential effectiveness of *techniques* by holding therapy and client variables constant. It also underestimates the magnitude of positive outcomes that will result if a motivated client is matched to a competent therapist of his or her choice and they together seek the best solution free of theory-limited preconceptions or manual-defined procedures.

Even if one accepts that cognitive behavioral therapy and stress management are different, it makes little sense to draw a rigid boundary between them. A thorough assessment of individual stress triggers via extended diary keeping and in-session review of individual histories may reveal that emotional exhaustion may result from longstanding, maladaptive patterns. Chronic low self-esteem may feed the habit of picking abusive spouses; an anxious need for control creates pervasive tension and drives friends away; perfectionism may create intense strain because of the unattainability of "perfect" goals. In these circumstances, cognitive therapy and a change in thought patterns reflect a combination of coping skill training and stressor manipulation; in some cases, the intervention needs to take on a psychodynamic perspective.

The literature on therapy outcome research supplies some useful data for judging what a cost-efficient, recommendable length of SM training should be. Nevertheless, this available information needs to be interpreted cautiously because there is an unresolved gap between well-studied effect sizes in the controlled-trials literature and more crude estimations of what is achieved in clinical practice in natural clinical environments. Treatment lengths vary greatly in clinical practice, but the most studied type of clinical activity outcomes is for clinicians working under the umbrella of third-party payers; here the average number of sessions is five, after which only about 20% of studied patients show notable improvement (Hansen, Lambert, & Forman, 2002). In the controlled research environment, one large-scale review indicates that with a mean observed length of 12.7 sessions (roughly translating into an equivalent number of hours of exposure), between 58% and 67% of patients showed clinically meaningful improvements (Hansen et al., 2002). Therefore, it is suggested that the overly short exposure to treatment typical in third-party–paid treatment environments be avoided, and instead intervention lengths that provide about 10 to 20 hours of exposure should be targeted. There should be some variation in length depending on whether SM is taught in group or individual format, with the latter possibly requiring less therapy exposure time. Using such specific numbers for suggested intervention length needs to be paired with the qualifier that patients with comorbid conditions and longstanding personality problems are not likely to benefit from short-term interventions, and are best treated in individual therapy. The systematic use of homework assignments (as is typical in SM) may further help boost outcomes, given that a meta-analysis of additional homework benefits revealed a moderately large effect size (Kazantzis, Deane, & Ronan, 2002) that, not surprisingly, was moderated by differential homework adherence.

The reader may want to recall that the observed modal number of SM intervention length is 9 hours, typically provided in six sessions (Ong et al., 2004). Hence, the potentially achievable benefit may not be fully reached in the current, modal delivery format, and somewhat larger effect sizes could be expected if SM interventions were longer. Common sense and clinical experience, however, suggest that the dose–response curve will flatten at some point, and that the ultimate cost-benefit may then also decrease, likely due to the fact that participant fatigue will set in and adherence will drop.

Action Plan

The purpose of this book was not only to present a critical analysis of the literature on stress management but also to propose changes and new ideas; hence, the reader will ask for a constructive solution (or at least a glimpse at one). Numerous recommendations and action plans are offered throughout this final chapter. At the end of Chapter 2, after a review of the relevant experimental research and pertinent theories, a compilation of what a broad-based SM program should look like was presented. I have developed a program like this that is currently being evaluated as one of three active treatment conditions in a randomized controlled trial of psychological treatment for high blood pressure. It is manualized, planned as a 10-week program, represents a category 2 protocol—that is, the proposed skill-building, preventive type of SM—and contains the following:

1. A brief description of what stress is in lay terms and how it can be recognized is presented.

2. Stressor recognition (including use of diaries) is taught and includes a discussion of strategies for stressor manipulations.

3. An arousal reduction technique (i.e., Progressive Muscular Relaxation) is introduced early in the SM protocol so that participants can begin practicing and report on progress over many training sessions. An accompanying practice tape is offered as well.

4. Coping skills around time management, social skills, and problem solving are taught first in an instructional format, then paired with idiosyncratic homework assignments and reviewed in the following intervention sessions.

5. Some instruction about social support and buffer creation is provided, and participants are encouraged to choose and activate a number of the activities that are relevant to their lives and preferences.

6. Finally, participants are encouraged to review the success or failure of each step, and plan a lifestyle that maintains gains and that has reliable built-in buffers and recovery opportunities.

Given that this program is manualized and thus at least partly standardized, it meets the entrance criteria for testing as an empirically supported treatment. Whether this particular approach will ultimately qualify as an empirically supported treatment, and for what target problem or target population, remains to be demonstrated.

The review of treatment outcomes for stress management packages and for the effects of specific techniques allows some cautious optimism that treatment effect sizes are roughly similar to those of psychotherapy at large in that moderate to large effect sizes are often seen when either comparing pre/post test data or comparing SM techniques to wait-list or other passive controls. Whether SM is consistently inferior, equal, or superior to other active treatments remains to be determined because the literature cited above is confounded by widely varying definitions of SM; in its present, heterogeneous form, rather mixed results are obtained and cannot be reliably and meaningfully interpreted. Outcome data on the many techniques that can be subsumed under SM vary enormously in the quality and trustworthiness of their claimed benefits. On the whole, there is fairly strong support from randomized controlled trials that cognitive behavioral therapy directed at reducing anxiety and depression, physical exercise, and biofeedback and other self-regulation techniques are effective. In other areas, outcome data are scarce or nonexistent, although the rationales for these approaches often look promising. In some instances this can be attributed to the relative novelty of the research area (e.g., forgiveness interventions or use of pets); in other instances it is due to conceptual problems with the operationalization of what a given treatment actually consists of (e.g., social support interventions); and, finally, there are many areas of research where the sheer popularity and promising rationales for an intervention far outstrip the efficacy research base that is meant to support it; prime examples of these are humor therapy and time management. In these latter two cases there is a stunning absence of controlled trials to support their use. This lack of controlled research is particularly striking given that both interventions are widely practiced, inherently appealing, popular, and seemingly promising.

Action plans have been proposed here for multiple aspects of SM theorizing, research, and practice. With respect to communication, much can be achieved by adoption of and adherence to editorial policies regarding clear and sufficient descriptions of what SM procedures were used. Use of the proposed taxonomy of three SM types may facilitate comparisons of SM outcome studies. The goal has to be enhancement of replicability of a protocol by other researchers and practitioners, as well as maximizing transparency and comparability to aid future reviews, especially meta-analytic ones.

Researchers may want to tackle these critical questions:

- How is efficacy affected by standardization versus individual tailoring of protocols?
- Can a manual be sensitive to individual needs? Is comparability irrevocably lost if individual tailoring is brought in?
- What is the minimally needed length of treatment for clinically meaningful distress reduction?
- Is training as a psychotherapist required/beneficial, or can a layperson with common sense, good interpersonal skills, and some minimal training do the job?
- What is known about individual differences in the ability to learn SM techniques? How can protocols be adjusted for participant characteristics (like varying age groups, intelligence, insight orientation, cultural differences)?

The future is a wonderful country: You can do anything there.

—Hamilton Southam, 2000, Benefactor
(cited in Colombo, 2000)

Only by claiming our own future—and that of our immediate families and communities—will the human spirit prevail.

—Peter C. Newman, 1996,
Political Journalist and Author
(cited in Colombo, 2000)

References

Therapy Outcome Studies Reviewed by Ong, Linden, and Young (2004)

Aeschleman, S. R., & Imes, C. (1999). Stress inoculation training for impulsive behaviors in adults with traumatic brain injury. *Journal of Rational-Emotive and Cognitive-Behavior Therapy, 17*, 51–65.

Albright, G. L., Andreassi, J. L., & Brockwell, A. L. (1991). Effects of stress management on blood pressure and other cardiovascular variables. *International Journal of Psychophysiology, 11*, 213–217.

Alexander, C. N., Schneider, R. H., Staggers, F., Sheppard, W., Claybourne, B. M., Rainforth, M., Salerno, J., Kondwani, K., Smith, S., Walton, K. G., & Egan, B. (1996). Trial of stress reduction for hypertension in older African Americans II: Sex and risk subgroup analysis. *Hypertension, 28*, 228–237.

Alexander, C. N., Swanson, G. C., Rainforth, M. V., Carlisle, T. W., Todd, C. C., & Oates, R. M., Jr. (1993). Effects of the Transcendental Meditation program on stress reduction, health, and employee development: A prospective study in two occupational settings. *Anxiety, Stress, and Coping, 6*, 245–262.

Anshel, M. H., Gregory, W. L., & Kaczmarek, M. (1990). The effectiveness of a stress training program in coping with criticism in sport: A test of the COPE model. *Journal of Sport Behavior, 13*, 194–217.

Antoni, M. H., Baggett, L., Ironson, G., LaPerriere, A., August, S., Klimas, N., Schneiderman, N., & Fletcher, M. A. (1991). Cognitive-behavioral stress management intervention buffers distress responses and immunological changes following notification of HIV-1 seropositivity. *Journal of Consulting and Clinical Psychology, 59*, 906–915.

Arnetz, B. B. (1996). Techno-stress: A prospective psychophysiological study of the impact of a controlled stress-reduction program in advanced telecommunication systems design work. *Journal of Occupational & Environmental Medicine, 38*, 53–65.

Astin, J. A. (1997). Stress reduction through mindfulness meditation: Effects on psychological symptomatology, sense of control, and spiritual experiences. *Psychotherapy & Psychosomatics, 66*, 97–106.

Avants, S. K., Margolin, A., & Salovey, P. (1990). Stress management techniques: Anxiety reduction, appeal, and individual differences. *Imagination, Cognition and Personality, 10*, 3–23.

Barrios-Choplin, B., McCraty, R., & Cryer, B. (1997). An inner quality approach to reducing stress and improving physical and emotional wellbeing at work. *Stress Medicine, 13*, 193–201.

Barry, J., & von Baeyer, C. L. (1997). Brief cognitive-behavioral group treatment for children's headache. *Clinical Journal of Pain, 13*, 215–220.

Batey, D. M., Kaufmann, P. G., Raczynski, J. M., Hollis, J. F., Murphy, J. K., Rosner, B., Corrigan, S. A., Rappaport, N. B., Danielson, E. M., Lasser, N. L., & Kuhn, C. M. (2000). Stress management intervention for primary prevention of hypertension: Detailed results from Phase I of Trials of Hypertension Prevention (TOHP-I). *Annals of Epidemiology, 10*, 45–58.

Birk, T. J., McGrady, A., MacArthur, R. D., & Khuder, S. (2000). The effects of massage therapy alone and in combination with other complementary therapies on immune system measures and quality of life in human immunodeficiency virus. *Journal of Alternative and Complementary Medicine, 6*, 405–414.

Black, D. R., & Frauenknecht, M. (1997). Developing entry-level competencies in school health educators: Evaluation of a problem solving curriculum for stress management. *Education and Treatment of Children, 20*, 404–424.

Blumenthal, J. A., Jiang, W., Babyak, M. A., Krantz, D. S., Frid, D. J., Coleman, R. E., Waugh, R., Hanson, M., Appelbaum, M., O'Connor, C., & Morris, J. J. (1997). Stress management and exercise training in cardiac patients with myocardial ischemia: Effects on prognosis and evaluation of mechanisms. *Archives of Internal Medicine, 157*, 2213–2223.

Boardway, R. H., Delamater, A. M., Tomakowsky, J., & Gutai, J. P. (1993). Stress management training for adolescents with diabetes. *Journal of Pediatric Psychology, 18*, 29–45.

Bond, F. W., & Bunce, D. (2000). Mediators of change in emotion-focused and problem-focused worksite stress management interventions. *Journal of Occupational Health Psychology, 5*, 156–163.

Brand, E. F., Lakey, B., & Berman, S. (1995). A preventive, psychoeducational approach to increase perceived social support. *American Journal of Community Psychology, 23*, 117–135.

Bunce, D., & West, M. A. (1996). Stress management and innovation interventions at work. *Human Relations, 49*, 209–232.

Burnette, M. M., Koehn, K. A., Kenyon-Jump, R., Hutton, K., & Stark, C. (1991). Control of genital herpes recurrences using progressive muscle relaxation. *Behavior Therapy, 22*, 237–247.

Cady, S. H., & Jones, G. E. (1997). Massage therapy as a workplace intervention for reduction of stress. *Perceptual and Motor Skills, 84*, 157–158.

Cary, M., & Dua, J. (1999). Cognitive-behavioral and systematic desensitization procedures in reducing stress and anger in caregivers for the disabled. *International Journal of Stress Management, 6*, 75–87.

Castillo-Richmond, A., Schneider, R. H., Alexander, C. N., Cook, R., Myers, H., Nidich, S., Haney, C., Rainforth, M., & Salerno, J. (2000). Effects of stress reduction on carotid atherosclerosis in hypertensive African Americans. *Stroke, 31,* 568–573.

Cherbosque, J., & Italiane, F. L. (1999). The use of biofeedback as a tool in providing relaxation training in an employee assistance program setting. *Employee Assistance Quarterly, 15,* 63–79.

Clark, D. M., Salkovskis, P. M., Hackmann, A., Wells, A., Fennell, M., Ludgate, J., Ahmad, S., Richards, H. C., & Gelder, M. (1998). Two psychological treatments for hypochondriasis: A randomised controlled trial. *British Journal of Psychiatry, 173,* 218–225.

Cunningham, A. J., Edmonds, C. V. I., & Williams, D. (1999). Delivering a very brief psychoeducational program to cancer patients and family members in a large group format. *Psycho-Oncology, 8,* 177–182.

de Anda, D. (1998). The evaluation of a stress management program for middle school adolescents. *Child and Adolescent Social Work Journal, 15,* 73–85.

de Anda, D., Darroch, P., Davidson, M., Gilly, J., & Morejon, A. (1990). Stress management for pregnant adolescents and adolescent mothers: A pilot study. *Child and Adolescent Social Work, 7,* 53–67.

de Jong, G. M., & Emmelkamp, P. M. G. (2000). Implementing a stress management training: Comparative trainer effectiveness. *Journal of Occupational Health Psychology, 5,* 309–320.

De Wolfe, A. S., & Saunders, A. M. (1995). Stress reduction in sixth-grade students. *Journal of Experimental Education, 63,* 315–329.

Donnelly, J. W., Duncan, D. F., & Procaccino, A. T., Jr. (1993). Assessing anxiety within a weight-management setting: Impact of a stress management seminar. *Psychology, 30,* 16–21.

Ehlers, A., Stangier, U., & Gieler, U. (1995). Treatment of atopic dermatitis: A comparison of psychological and dermatological approaches to relapse prevention. *Journal of Consulting and Clinical Psychology, 63,* 624–635.

Eller, L. S. (1995). Effects of two cognitive-behavioral interventions on immunity and symptoms in persons with HIV. *Annals of Behavioral Medicine, 17,* 339–348.

Emery, C. F., Schein, R. L., Hauck, E. R., & MacIntyre, N. R. (1998). Psychological and cognitive outcomes of a randomized trial of exercise among patients with chronic obstructive pulmonary disease. *Health Psychology, 17,* 232–240.

Fawzy, F. I., Fawzy, N. W., Hyun, C. S., Elashoff, R., Guthrie, D., Fahey, J. L., & Morton, D. L. (1993). Malignant melanoma: Effects of an early structured psychiatric intervention, coping, and affective state on recurrence and survival 6 years later. *Archives of General Psychiatry, 50,* 681–689.

Fawzy, F. I., Fawzy, N. W., & Wheeler, J. G. (1996). A post-hoc comparison of the efficiency of a psychoeducational intervention for melanoma patients delivered in group versus individual formats: An analysis of data from two studies. *Psycho-Oncology, 5,* 81–89.

Faymonville, M. E., Mambourg, P. H., Joris, J., Vrigens, B., Fissette, J., Albert, A., & Lamy, M. (1997). Psychological approaches during conscious sedation. Hypnosis versus stress reducing strategies: A prospective randomized study. *Pain, 73,* 361–367.

Fontana, A. M., Hyra, D., Godfrey, L., & Cermak, L. (1999). Impact of a peer-led stress inoculation training intervention on state anxiety and heart rate in college students. *Journal of Applied Biobehavioral Research, 4,* 45–63.

Forbes, E. J., & Pekala, R. J. (1993). Psychophysiological effects of several stress management techniques. *Psychological Reports, 72,* 19–27.

Freedy, J. R., & Hobfoll, S. E. (1994). Stress inoculation for reduction of burnout: A conservation of resources approach. *Anxiety, Stress, and Coping, 6,* 311–325.

Friedman, E., & Berger, B. G. (1991). Influence of gender, masculinity, and femininity on the effectiveness of three stress reduction techniques: Jogging, relaxation response, and group interaction. *Journal of Applied Sport Psychology, 3,* 61–86.

Gallacher, J. E. J., Hopkinson, C. A., Bennett, P., Burr, M. L., & Elwood, P. C. (1997). Effect of stress management on angina. *Psychology and Health, 12,* 523–532.

Garcia-Vera, M. P., Labrador, F. J., & Sanz, J. (1997). Stress-management training for essential hypertension: A controlled study. *Applied Psychophysiology and Biofeedback, 22,* 261–283.

Germond, S., Schomer, H. H., Meyers, O. L., & Weight, L. (1993). Pain management in rheumatoid arthritis: A cognitive-behavioural intervention. *South African Journal of Psychology, 23,* 1–9.

Godbey, K. L., & Courage, M. M. (1994). Stress-management program: Intervention in nursing student performance anxiety. *Archives of Psychiatric Nursing, 8,* 190–199.

Goldenberg, D. L., Kaplan, K. H., Nadeau, M. G., Brodeur, C., Smith, S., & Schmid, C. H. (1994). A controlled study of a stress-reduction, cognitive behavioral treatment program in fibromyalgia. *Journal of Musculoskeletal Pain, 2,* 53–66.

Goodspeed, R. B., & DeLucia, A. G. (1990). Stress reduction at the worksite: An evaluation of two methods. *American Journal of Health Promotion, 4,* 333–337.

Greco, C. M., Rudy, T. E., Turk, D.C., Herlich, A., & Zaki, H. H. (1997). Traumatic onset of temporomandibular disorders: Positive effects of a standardized conservative treatment program. *Clinical Journal of Pain, 13,* 337–347.

Habib, S., & Morrissey, S. (1999). Stress management for atopic dermatitis. *Behaviour Change, 16,* 226–236.

Hahn, Y. B., Ro, Y. J., Song, H. H., Kim, N. C., Kim, H. S., & Yoo, Y. S. (1993). The effect of thermal biofeedback and progressive muscle relaxation training in reducing blood pressure of patients with essential hypertension. *Image: Journal of Nursing Scholarship, 25,* 204–207.

Hains, A. A. (1992). A stress inoculation training program for adolescents in a high school setting: A multiple baseline approach. *Journal of Adolescence, 15,* 163–175.

Hains, A. A. (1992). Comparison of cognitive-behavioral stress management techniques with adolescent boys. *Journal of Counselling and Development, 70,* 600–605.

Hains, A. A. (1994). The effectiveness of a school-based, cognitive-behavioral stress management program with adolescents reporting high and low levels of emotional arousal. *School Counselor, 42,* 114–125.

Hains, A. A., Davies, W. H., Parton, E., Totka, J., & Amoroso-Camarata, J. (2000). A stress management intervention for adolescents with type 1 diabetes. *Diabetes Educator, 26,* 417–424.

Hains, A. A., & Ellmann, S. W. (1994). Stress inoculation training as a preventative intervention for high school youths. *Journal of Cognitive Psychotherapy, 8,* 219–232.

Hains, A. A., & Szyjakowski, M. (1990). A cognitive stress-reduction intervention program for adolescents. *Journal of Counseling Psychology, 37,* 79–84.

Henry, J. L., Wilson, P. H., Bruce, D. G., Chisholm, D. J., & Rawling, P. J. (1997). Cognitive-behavioural stress management for patients with non-insulin dependent diabetes mellitus. *Psychology, Health and Medicine, 2,* 109–118.

Heron, R. J. L., McKeown, S., Tomenson, J. A., & Teasdale, E. L. (1999). Study to evaluate the effectiveness of stress management workshops on response to general and occupational measures of stress. *Occupational Medicine, 49,* 451–457.

Hostick, T., Newell, R., & Ward, T. (1997). Evaluation of stress prevention and management workshops in the community. *Journal of Clinical Nursing, 6,* 139–145.

Irvine, M. J., & Logan, A. G. (1991). Relaxation behavior therapy as sole treatment for mild hypertension. *Psychosomatic Medicine, 53,* 587–597.

Jay, S. M., & Elliot, C. H. (1990). A stress inoculation program for parents whose children are undergoing painful medical procedures. *Journal of Consulting and Clinical Psychology, 58,* 799–804.

Jin, P. (1992). Efficacy of tai chi, brisk walking, meditation, and reading in reducing mental and emotional stress. *Journal of Psychosomatic Research, 36,* 361–370.

Johansson, N. (1991). Effectiveness of a stress management program in reducing anxiety and depression in nursing students. *Journal of American College Health, 40,* 125–129.

Johnson, U. (2000). Short-term psychological intervention: A study of long-term–injured competitive athletes. *Journal of Sport Rehabilitation, 9,* 207–218.

Johnston, D. W., Gold, A., Kentish, J., Smith, D., Vallance, P., Shah, D., Leach, G., & Robinson, B. (1993). Effect of stress management on blood pressure in mild primary hypertension. *British Medical Journal, 306,* 963–966.

Jones, D. A., & West, R. R. (1996). Psychological rehabilitation after myocardial infarction: Multicentre randomized controlled trial. *British Medical Journal, 313,* 1517–1521.

Jones, M. C., & Johnston, D. W. (2000). Evaluating the impact of a worksite stress management programme for distressed student nurses: A randomised controlled trial. *Psychology and Health, 15,* 689–706.

Kabat-Zinn, J., Massion, A. O., Kristeller, J., Peterson, L. G., Fletcher, K. E., Pbert, L., Lenderking, W. R., & Santorelli, S. F. (1992). Effectiveness of a meditation-based stress reduction program in the treatment of anxiety disorders. *American Journal of Psychiatry, 149,* 936–943.

Kabat-Zinn, J., Wheeler, E., Light, T., Skillings, A., Scharf, M. J., Cropley, T. G., Hosmer, D., & Bernhard, J. D. (1998). Influence of a mindfulness meditation-based stress reduction intervention on rates of skin clearing in patients with moderate to severe psoriasis undergoing phototherapy (UVB) and photo-chemotherapy (PUVA). *Psychosomatic Medicine, 60,* 625–632.

Kagan, N. I., Kagan, H., & Watson, M. G. (1995). Stress reduction in the work-place: The effectiveness of psychoeducational programs. *Journal of Counseling Psychology, 42,* 71–78.

Kaluza, G. (2000). Changing unbalanced coping profiles—A prospective con-trolled intervention trial in worksite health promotion. *Psychology and Health, 15,* 423–433.

Kaplan, K. H., Goldberg, D. L., & Galvin-Nadeau, M. (1993). The impact of a meditation-based stress reduction program on fibromyalgia. *General Hospital Psychiatry, 15,* 284–289.

Kawakami, N., Araki, S., Kawashima, M., Masumoto, T., & Hayashi, T. (1997). Effects of work-related stress reduction on depressive symptoms among Japanese blue-collar workers. *Scandinavian Journal of Work, Environment and Health, 23,* 54–59.

Keinan, G., Segal, A., Ma, U. G., & Brenner, S. (1995). Stress management for psoriasis patients: The effectiveness of biofeedback and relaxation tech-niques. *Stress Medicine, 11,* 235–241.

Kiselica, M. S., Baker, S. B., Thomas, R. N., & Reedy, S. (1994). Effects of stress inoculation training on anxiety, stress, and academic performance among adolescents. *Journal of Counseling Psychology, 41,* 335–342.

Kolbell, R. M. (1995). When relaxation is not enough. In L. R. Murphy, J. J. Hurrell, Jr., S. L. Sauter, & G. P. Keita (Eds.), *Job stress interventions* (pp. 31–43). Washington, DC: American Psychological Association.

Leahy, A., Clayman, C., Mason, I., Lloyd, G., & Epstein, O. (1998). Computerised biofeedback games: A new method for teaching stress management and its use in irritable bowel syndrome. *Journal of the Royal College of Physicians of London, 32,* 552–556.

Lee, M. S., Ryu, H., & Chung, H. T. (2000). Stress management by psychosomatic training: Effects of Chun Do Sun Bup Qi-training on symptoms of stress: A cross-sectional study. *Stress Medicine, 16,* 161–166.

Lee, S., & Crockett, M. S. (1994). Effect of assertiveness training on levels of stress and assertiveness experienced by nurses in Taiwan, Republic of China. *Issues in Mental Health Nursing, 15,* 419–432.

Lin, M. L., Tsang, Y. M., & Hwang, S. L. (1998). Efficacy of a stress management program for patients with hepatocellular carcinoma receiving transcatheter arterial embolization. *Journal of the Formosan Medical Association, 97,* 113–117.

Linden, W., Lenz, J. W., & Con, A. H. (2001). Individualized stress management for primary hypertension: A randomized trial. *Archives of Internal Medicine, 161,* 1071–1080.

Lindop, E. (1993). A complementary therapy approach to the management of individual stress among student nurses. *Journal of Advanced Nursing, 18,* 1578–1585.

Littman, A. B., Fava, M., Halperin, P., Lamon-Fava, S., Drews, F. R., Oleshansky, M. A., Bielenda, C. C., & MacLaughlin, R. A. (1993). Physiologic benefits of a stress reduction program for healthy middle-aged Army officers. *Journal of Psychosomatic Research, 37,* 345–354.

Long, B. C. (1993). Aerobic conditioning (jogging) and stress inoculation interventions: An exploratory study of coping. *International Journal of Sport Psychology, 24,* 94–109.

Lopez, M. A., & Silber, S. (1991). Stress management for the elderly: A preventive approach. *Clinical Gerontologist, 10,* 73–76.

Lutgendorf, S. K., Antoni, M. H., Ironson, G. I., Klimas, N., Kumar, M., Starr, K., McCabe, P., Cleven, K., Fletcher, M. A., & Schneiderman, N. (1997). Cognitive-behavioral stress management decreases dysphoric mood and herpes simplex virus-type 2 antibody titres in symptomatic HIV-seropositive gay men. *Journal of Consulting & Clinical Psychology, 65,* 31–43.

Lutgendorf, S. K., Antoni, M. H., Ironson, G., Starr, K., Costello, N., Zuckerman, M., Klimas, N., Fletcher, M. A., & Schneiderman, N. (1998). Changes in cognitive coping skills and social support during cognitive behavioral stress management intervention and distress outcomes in symptomatic human immunodeficiency virus (HIV)-seropositive gay men. *Psychosomatic Medicine, 60,* 204–214.

MacLean, C. R. K., Walton, K. G., Wenneberg, S. R., Levitsky, D. K., Mandarino, J. V., Waziri, R., & Schneider, R. H. (1994). Altered response of cortisol, GH, TSH and testosterone to acute stress after four months' practice of Transcendental Meditation. *Annals of the New York Academy of Science, 746,* 381–384.

Maynard, I. W., & Cotton, P. C. J. (1993). An investigation of two stress management techniques in a field setting. *Sport Psychologist, 7,* 375–387.

Maysent, M., & Spera, S. (1995). Coping with job loss and career stress: Effectiveness of stress management training with outplaced employees. In L. R. Murphy, J. J. Hurrell, Jr., S. L. Sauter, & G. P. Keita (Eds.), *Job stress interventions* (pp. 159–170). Washington, DC: American Psychological Association.

McCain, N. L., Zeller, J. M., Cella, D. F., Urbanski, P. A., & Novak, R. M. (1996). The influence of stress management training in HIV disease. *Nursing Research, 45,* 246–253.

McCarberg, B., & Wolf, J. (1999). Chronic pain management in a health maintenance organization. *Clinical Journal of Pain, 15,* 50–57.

McCraty, R., Atkinson, M., Tomasino, D., Goelitz, J., & Mayrovitz, H. N. (1999). The impact of an emotional self-management skills course on psychosocial functioning and autonomic recovery to stress in middle school children. *Integrative Physiological and Behavioral Science, 34,* 246–268.

McCraty, R., Barrios-Choplin, B., Rozman, D., Atkinson, M., & Watkins, A. (1998). The impact of a new emotional self-management program on stress, emotions, heart rate variability, DHEA and cortisol. *Integrative Physiological and Behavioral Science, 33,* 151–170.

McCue, J. D., & Sachs, C. L. (1991). A stress management workshop improves residents' coping skills. *Archives of Internal Medicine, 151,* 2273–2277.

McGrady, A., Bailey, B. K., & Good, M. P. (1991). Controlled study of biofeedback-assisted relaxation in type 1 diabetes. *Diabetes Care, 14,* 360–365.

McGrady, A., Conran, P., Dickey, D., Garman, D., Farris, E., & Schumann-Brzezinski, C. (1992). The effects of biofeedback-assisted relaxation on cell-mediated immunity, cortisol, and white blood cell count in healthy adult subjects. *Journal of Behavioral Medicine, 15,* 343–354.

McNaughton-Cassill, M. E., Bostwick, M., Vanscoy, S. E., Arthur, N. J., Hickman, T. N., Robinson, R. D., & Neal, G. S. (2000). Development of brief stress management support groups for couples undergoing in vitro fertilization treatment. *Fertility and Sterility, 74,* 87–93.

Michie, S. (1992). Evaluation of a staff stress management service. *Health Manpower Management, 18,* 15–17.

Michie, S., & Sandhu, S. (1994). Stress management for clinical medical students. *Medical Education, 28,* 528–533.

Miller, J. J., Fletcher, K., & Kabat-Zinn, J. (1995). Three-year follow-up and clinical implications of a mindfulness meditation-based stress reduction intervention in the treatment of anxiety disorders. *General Hospital Psychiatry, 17,* 192–200.

Nelson, D. V., Baer, P. E., Cleveland, S. E., Revel, K. F., & Montero, A. C. (1994). Six-month follow-up of stress management training versus cardiac education during hospitalization for acute myocardial infarction. *Journal of Cardiopulmonary Rehabilitation, 14,* 384–390.

Nicholas, P. K., & Webster, A. (1996). A behavioral medicine intervention in persons with HIV. *Clinical Nursing Research, 5,* 391–406.

Orth-Gomer, K., Eriksson, I., Moser, V., Theorell, T., & Fredlund, P. (1994). Lipid lowering through work stress reduction. *International Journal of Behavioral Medicine, 1*(3), 204–214.

Parker, J. C., Smarr, K. L., Buckelew, S. P., Stucky-Ropp, R. C., Hewett, J. E., Johnson, J. C., Wright, G. E., Irvin, W. S., & Walker, S. E. (1995). Effects of stress management on clinical outcomes in rheumatoid arthritis. *Arthritis and Rheumatism, 38,* 1807–1818.

Peters, K. K., & Carlson, J. G. (1999). Worksite stress management with high-risk maintenance workers: A controlled study. *International Journal of Stress Management, 6,* 21–44.

Pistrang, N., & Barker, C. (1998). Partners and fellow patients: Two sources of emotional support for women with breast cancer. *American Journal of Community Psychology, 26,* 439–456.

Pruitt, R. H., Bernheim, C., & Tomlinson, J. P. (1991). Stress management in a military health promotion program: Effectiveness and cost efficiency. *Military Medicine, 156,* 51–53.

Reynolds, S. (1997). Psychological well-being at work: Is prevention better than cure? *Journal of Psychosomatic Research, 43,* 93–102.

Reynolds, S., Taylor, E., & Shapiro, D. (1993). Session impact and outcome in stress management training. *Journal of Community and Applied Social Psychology, 3,* 325–337.

Roger, D., & Hudson, C. (1995). The role of emotion control and emotional rumination in stress management training. *International Journal of Stress Management, 2,* 119–132.

Ross, M. J., & Berger, R. S. (1996). Effects of stress inoculation training on athletes' postsurgical pain and rehabilitation after orthopedic injury. *Journal of Consulting and Clinical Psychology, 64,* 406–410.

Roth, B., & Creaser, T. (1997). Mindfulness meditation-based stress reduction: Experience with a bilingual inner-city program. *Nurse Practitioner, 22,* 150–176.

Rowe, M. M. (2000). Skills training in the long-term management of stress and occupational burnout. *Current Psychology, 19,* 215–228.

Rudy, T. E., Turk, D. C., Kubinski, J. A., & Zaki, H. S. (1995). Differential treatment responses of TMD patients as a function of psychological characteristics. *Pain, 61,* 103–112.

Russler, M. F. (1991). Multidimensional stress management in nursing education. *Journal of Nursing Education, 30,* 341–346.

Rutledge, J. C., Hyson, D. A., Garduno, D., Cort, D. A., Paumer, L., & Kappagoda, C. T. (1999). Lifestyle modification program in management patients with coronary artery disease: The clinical experience in a tertiary care hospital. *Journal of Cardiopulmonary Rehabilitation, 19,* 226–234.

Rybarczyk, B. D., & Auerbach, S. M. (1990). Reminiscence interviews as stress management interventions for older patients undergoing surgery. *Gerontologist, 30,* 522–528.

Saam, R. H., Wodtke, K. H., & Hains, A. A. (1995). A cognitive stress reduction program for recently unemployed managers. *Career Development Quarterly, 44,* 43–51.

Sartory, G., Müller, B., Metsch, J., & Pothmann, R. (1998). A comparison of psychological and pharmacological treatment of pediatric migraine. *Behaviour Research and Therapy, 36,* 1155–1170.

Scharlach, A. E. (1988). Peer counselor training for nursing home residents. *The Gerontologist, 28,* 499–502.

Schaufeli, W. B. (1995). The evaluation of a burnout workshop for community nurses. *Journal of Health and Human Services Administration, 18,* 11–30.

Schneider, R. H., Staggers, F., Alexander, C. N., Sheppard, W., Rainforth, M., Kondwani, K., Smith, S., & King, C. G. (1995). A randomized controlled trial of stress reduction for hypertension in older African-Americans. *Hypertension, 26,* 820–827.

Schneider, W. J., & Nevid, J. S. (1993). Overcoming math anxiety: A comparison of stress inoculation training and systematic desensitization. *Journal of College Student Development, 34,* 283–288.

Schwartz, C. E. (1999). Teaching coping skills enhances quality of life more than peer support: Results of a randomized trial with multiple sclerosis patients. *Health Psychology, 18,* 211–220.

Schwartz, C. E., & Sendor, R. M. (1999). Helping others helps oneself: Response shift effects in peer support. *Social Science & Medicine, 48,* 1563–1575.

Shapiro, S. L., Schwartz, G. E., & Bonner, G. (1998). Effects of mindfulness-based stress reduction on medical and premedical students. *Journal of Behavioral Medicine, 21,* 581–599.

Shearn, M. A., & Fireman, B. H. (1985). Stress management and mutual support groups in rheumatoid arthritis. *American Journal of Medicine, 78,* 771–775.

Sheppard, W. D., II, Staggers, F. J., & John, L. (1997). The effects of a stress-management program in a high security government agency. *Anxiety, Stress, and Coping, 10*(4), 341–350.

Shulman, K. R., & Jones, G. E. (1996). The effectiveness of massage therapy intervention on reducing anxiety in the workplace. *Journal of Applied Behavioral Science, 32,* 160–173.

Smarr, K. L., Parker, J. C., Wright, G. E., Stucky-Ropp, R. C., Buckelew, S. P., Hoffman, R. W., O'Sullivan, F. X., & Hewett, J. E. (1997). The importance of enhancing self-efficacy in rheumatoid arthritis. *Arthritis Care and Research, 10,* 18–26.

Snodgrass, L. L., Yamamoto, J., Frederick, C., Ton-That, N., Foy, D. W., Chan, L., Wu, J., Hahn, P. H., Shinh, D. Y., Nguyen, L. H., de Jonge, J., &

Fairbanks, L. (1993). Vietnamese refugees with PTSD symptomatology: Intervention via a coping skills model. *Journal of Traumatic Stress, 6,* 569–575.

Sowa, C. J. (1992). Understanding clients' perceptions of stress. *Journal of Counseling and Development, 71,* 179–183.

Speca, M., Carlson, L. E., Goodey, E., & Angen, M. (2000). A randomized, wait-list controlled clinical trial: The effect of a mindfulness meditation-based stress reduction program on mood and symptoms of stress in cancer outpatients. *Psychosomatic Medicine, 62,* 613–622.

Speck, B. (1990). The effect of guided imagery upon first semester nursing students performing their first injections. *Journal of Nursing Education, 29,* 347–350.

Stachnik, T., Brown, B., Hinds, W., Mavis, B., Stoffelmayr, B., Thornton, D., & Van Egeren, L. (1990). Goal setting, social support, and financial incentives in stress management programs: A pilot study of their impact on adherence. *American Journal of Health Promotion, 5,* 24–29.

Stephens, R. L. (1992). Imagery: A treatment for student anxiety. *Journal of Nursing Education, 31,* 314–320.

Stetson, B. (1997). Holistic health stress management program: Nursing student and client health outcomes. *Journal of Holistic Nursing, 15,* 143–157.

Sullivan, C. M., Campbell, R., Angelique, H., Eby, K. K., & Davidson, W. S., II. (1994). An advocacy intervention program for women with abusive partners: Six-month follow-up. *American Journal of Community Psychology, 22,* 101–122.

Taylor, D. N. (1995). Effects of a behavioral stress-management program on anxiety, mood, self-esteem, and T-cell count in HIV-positive men. *Psychological Reports, 76,* 451–457.

Teasdale, E. L., & McKeown, S. (1994). Managing stress at work: The ICI-Zeneca Pharmaceuticals experience 1986–1993. In C. L. Cooper & S. Williams (Eds.), *Creating healthy work organizations* (pp. 134–165). London: Wiley.

Thomason, J. A., & Pond, S. B., III. (1995). Effects of instruction on stress management skills and self-management skills among blue-collar employees. In L. R. Murphy, J. J. Hurrell, Jr., S. L. Sauter, & G. P. Keita (Eds.), *Job stress interventions* (pp. 7–20). Washington, DC: American Psychological Association.

Timmerman, I. G. H., Emmelkamp, P. M. G., & Sanderman, R. (1998). The effects of a stress-management training program in individuals at risk in the community at large. *Behaviour Research and Therapy, 36,* 863–875.

Tolman, R. M., & Rose, S. D. (1990). Teaching clients to cope with stress: The effectiveness of structured group stress management training. *Journal of Social Service Research, 13,* 45–66.

Toobert, D. J., Glasgow, R. E., Nettekoven, L. A., & Brown, J. E. (1998). Behavioral and psychosocial effects of intensive lifestyle management for women with coronary heart disease. *Patient Education and Counseling, 35,* 177–188.

Toseland, R. W., Labrecque, M. S., Goebel, S. T., & Whitney, M. H. (1992). An evaluation of a group program for spouses of frail elderly veterans. *The Gerontologist, 32,* 382–390.

Trzcieniecka-Green, A., & Steptoe, A. (1994). Stress management in cardiac patients: A preliminary study of the predictors of improvement in quality of life. *Journal of Psychosomatic Research, 38,* 267–280.

Trzcieniecka-Green, A., & Steptoe, A. (1996). The effects of stress management on the quality of life of patients following acute myocardial infarction or coronary bypass surgery. *European Heart Journal, 17,* 1663–1670.

Tsai, S. L., & Crockett, M. S. (1993). Effects of relaxation training, combining imagery, and meditation on the stress level of Chinese nurses working in modern hospitals in Taiwan. *Issues in Mental Health Nursing, 14,* 51–66.

Turk, D. C., Rudy, T. E., Kubinski, J. A., Zaki, H. S., & Greco, C. M. (1996). Dysfunctional patients with temporomandibular disorders: Evaluating the efficacy of a tailored treatment protocol. *Journal of Consulting and Clinical Psychology, 64,* 139–146.

Turk, D. C., Zaki, H. S., & Rudy, T. E. (1993). Effects of intraoral appliance and biofeedback/stress management alone and in combination in treating pain and depression inpatients with temporomandibular disorders. *The Journal of Prosthetic Dentistry, 70,* 158–164.

Turner, L., Linden, W., van der Wal, R., & Schamberger, W. (1995). Stress management for patients with heart disease: A pilot study. *Heart and Lung, 24,* 145–153.

van Montfrans, G. A., Karemaker, J. M., Wieling, W., & Dunning, A. J. (1990). Relaxation therapy and continuous ambulatory blood pressure in mild hypertension: A controlled study. *British Medical Journal, 300,* 1368–1372.

White, J., & Keenan, M. (1990). Stress control: A pilot study of large group therapy for generalized anxiety disorder. *Behavioural Psychotherapy, 18,* 143–146.

Whitehouse, W. G., Dinges, D. F., Orne, E. C., Keller, S. E., Bates, B. L., Bauer, N. K., Morahan, P., Haupt, B. A., Carlin, M. M., Bloom, P. B., Zaugg, L., & Orne, M. T. (1996). Psychosocial and immune effects of self-hypnosis training for stress management throughout the first semester of medical school. *Psychosomatic Medicine, 58,* 249–263.

Whitney, D., & Rose, S. D. (1990). The effect of process and structured content on outcome in stress management groups. *Journal of Social Service Research, 13,* 89–104.

Wigers, S. H., Stiles, T. C., & Vogel, P. A. (1996). Effects of aerobic exercise versus stress management treatment in fibromyalgia: A 4.5 year prospective study. *Scandinavian Journal of Rheumatology, 25,* 77–86.

Wiholm, C., Arnetz, B., & Berg, M. (2000). The impact of stress management on computer-related skin problems. *Stress Medicine, 16,* 279–285.

Wing, R. R., & Jeffrey, R. W. (1999). Benefits of recruiting participants with friends and increasing social support for weight loss and maintenance. *Journal of Consulting and Clinical Psychology, 67,* 132–138.

Winzelberg, A. J., & Luskin, F. M. (1999). The effect of a meditation training in stress levels in secondary school teachers. *Stress Medicine, 15,* 69–77.

Wynd, C. A. (1992). Relaxation imagery used for stress reduction in the prevention of smoking relapse. *Journal of Advanced Nursing, 17,* 294–302.

References

Aamodt, M. G. (2004). *Applied industrial/organizational psychology* (4th ed.). Belmont, CA: Wadsworth.

Akerstedt, T., Knutsson, A., Westerholm, P., Theorell, T., Alfredsson, L., & Kecklund, G. (2004). Mental fatigue, work and sleep. *Journal of Psychosomatic Research, 56,* 1–7.

Alexander, C. N., Robinson, P., Orme-Johnson, D. W., Schneider, R. H., & Walton, K. G. (1994). The effects of Transcendental Meditation compared to other methods of relaxation and meditation in reducing risk factors, morbidity, and mortality. *Homeostasis in Health and Disease, 35,* 243–263.

Allen, K., & Blascovich, J. (1996). The value of service dogs for people with severe ambulatory disabilities. A randomized trial. *Journal of the American Medical Association, 275,* 1001–1006.

Allen, K., Blascovich, J., & Mendes, W. B. (2002). Cardiovascular reactivity, and the presence of pets, friends, and spouses: The truth about cats and dogs. *Psychosomatic Medicine, 64,* 727–739.

Allen, S. M., Shah, A. C., Nezu, A. M., Ciambrone, D., Hogan, J., & Mor, V. (2002). A problem-solving approach to stress reduction among younger women with breast carcinoma—A randomized controlled trial. *Cancer, 94,* 3089–3100.

American Psychiatric Association. (1994). *Diagnostic and statistical manual of mental disorders* (4th ed.). Washington, DC: Author.

Andrews, G., McMahon, S. W., Austin, A., & Byrne, D. G. (1984). Hypertension: Comparison of drug and non-drug treatments. *British Medical Journal, 284,* 1523–1526.

Antoni, M. H. (2003). Stress management effects on psychological, endocrinological, and immune functioning in men with HIV infection: Empirical support for a psychoneuroimmunological model. *Stress—The International Journal on the Biology of Stress, 6,* 173–188.

Antoni, M. H., Baggett, L., Ironson, G., LaPerriere, A., August, S., Klimas. N., Schneiderman, N., & Fletcher, M. A. (1991). Cognitive behavioral stress management intervention buffers. *Journal of Consulting and Clinical Psychology, 59,* 906–915.

Antonovsky, A. (1979). *Health, stress, and coping.* San Francisco: Jossey-Bass.

Antonucci, T. C. (1985). Personal characteristics, social support, and social behavior. In R. H. Binstock & E. Shanas (Eds.), *Handbook of aging and the social sciences* (pp. 94–128). New York: Van Nostrand Reinhold.

Arnetz, B. B. (2003). *Organizational efficiency: An important determinant of occupational stress.* Paper presented at the American Psychosomatic Society, Phoenix, AZ.

Astrand, P. O., & Rodahl, K. (1970). *Textbook of work physiology.* New York: McGraw-Hill.

Baker, B., Szalai, J. P., Paquette, M., & Tobe, S. (2003). Marital support, spousal contact and the course of mild hypertension. *Journal of Psychosomatic Research, 55,* 229–233.

Barlow, D. H., Raffa, S. D., & Cohen, E. M. (2002). Psychosocial treatments for panic disorders, phobias, and generalized anxiety disorder. In P. E. Nathan & J. M. Gorman (Eds.), *A guide to treatments that work* (2nd ed.). London: Oxford University Press.

Beck, A. T. (1993). Cognitive approaches to stress. In P. M. Lehrer & R. L. Woolfolk (Eds.), *Principles and practice of stress management* (2nd ed., pp. 333–372). New York: Guilford.

Beelman, A., Pfingsten, U., & Losel, F. (1994). Effects of training social competence in children: A meta-analysis of recent evaluation studies. *Journal of Clinical Child Psychology, 23,* 260–271.

Benson, H. (1975). *The relaxation response.* New York: William Morrow.

Berk, L. S., Felten, D. L., Tan, S. A., Bittman, B. B., & Westengard, J. (2001). Modulation of neuroimmune parameters during the eustress of humor-associated mirthful laughter. *Alternative Therapies in Health and Medicine, 7,* 62–76.

Berk, L. S., Tan, S. A., Fry, W. F., Napier, B. J., Lee, J. W., Hubbard, W. F., Lewis, J. E., & Eby, W. C. (1989). Neuroendocrine and stress hormone changes during mirthful laughter. *American Journal of Medical Science, 298,* 390–396.

Bernard, C. (1961). An introduction to the study of experimental medicine (H. C. Greene, Trans.). New York: Collier. (Original work published 1865)

Bernstein, D. A., & Borkovec, T. D. (1973). *Progressive relaxation training: A manual for the helping professions.* Champaign, IL: Research Press.

Biggam, F. H., & Power, K. G. (2002). A controlled, problem-solving, group-based intervention with vulnerable incarcerated young offenders. *International Journal of Offender Therapy and Comparative Criminology, 46,* 678–698.

Biggs, A. M., Aziz, Q., Tomenson, B., & Creed, F. (2003). Do childhood adversity and recent social stress predict health care use in patients presenting with upper abdominal or chest pain? *Psychosomatic Medicine, 65,* 1020–1028.

Black, P. H., & Garbutt, L. D. (2002). Stress, inflammation and cardiovascular disease. *Journal of Psychosomatic Research, 52,* 1–23.

Blagys, M. D., & Hilsenroth, M. J. (2002). Distinctive activities of cognitive-behavioral therapy: A review of the comparative psychotherapy process literature. *Clinical Psychology Review, 22,* 671–706.

Blumenthal, J. A., Babyak, M. A., Jiang, W., O'Connor, C., Waugh, R., Eisenstein, E., Mark, D., Sherwood, A., Woodley, P. S., Irwin, R. J., & Reed, G. (2002). Usefulness of psychosocial treatment of mental stress-induced myocardial ischemia in men. *American Journal of Cardiology, 89,* 164–168.

Blumenthal, J. A., Jiang, W., Babyak, M. A., Krantz, D. S., Frid, D. J., Coleman, R. E., Waugh, R., Hanson, M., Appelbaum, M., O'Connor, C., & Morris, J. J. (1997). Stress management and exercise training in cardiac patients with myocardial ischemia. *Archives of Internal Medicine, 157*, 2213–2223.

Bonnano, G. A. (2004). Loss, trauma, and human resilience: Have we underestimated the human capacity to thrive after extremely aversive events? *American Psychologist, 59*, 20–28.

Booth-Kewley, S., & Friedman, H. S. (1987). Psychological predictors of heart disease: A quantitative review. *Psychological Bulletin, 101*, 343–362.

Bottomley, A., Hunton, S., Roberts, G., Jones, L., & Bradley, C. (1996). A pilot study of cognitive behavioral therapy and social support group interventions with newly diagnosed cancer patients. *Journal of Psychosocial Oncology, 14*, 65–83.

Bower, J. E., & Segerstrom, S. C. (1994, January). Stress management, finding benefit, and immune function: Positive mechanisms for intervention effects on physiology. *Journal of Psychosomatic Research, 56*(1), 9–11.

Brand, E. F., Lakey, B., & Berman, S. (1995). A preventive, psychoeducational approach to increase perceived social support. *American Journal of Community Psychology, 23*, 117–135.

Brehm, B. A. (1998). *Stress management: Increasing your stress resistance.* New York: Longman.

Brody, H. (1973). The systems view of man: Implications of medicine, science, and ethics. In *Perspectives in biology and medicine* (Vol. 17, p. 77). Chicago: University of Chicago Press.

Bunker, S. J., Colquhoun, D. M., Esler, M. D., et al. (2003). Stress and coronary heart disease: Psychosocial risk factors. *Medical Journal of Australia, 178*, 272–276.

Burleson, M. H., Poehlmann, K. M., Ernst, J. M., Berntson, G. G., Malarjey, W. B., Kiecolt-Glaser, J. K., Glaser, R., & Cacioppo, J. T. (2003). Neuroendocrine and cardiovascular reactivity to stress in mid-aged and older women: Long-term temporal consistency of individual differences. *Psychophysiology, 40*, 358–369.

Burns, V. E., Drayson, M., Ring, C., Carroll, D. (2002). Perceived stress and psychological well-being are associated with antibody status after meningitis C conjugate vaccination. *Psychosomatic Medicine, 64*, 963–970.

Cacioppo, J. T., Hawkley, L. C., Crawford, L. E., Ernst, J. M., Burleson, M. H., Kowalewski, R. B., van Cauter, E., & Berntson, G. G. (2002). Loneliness and health: Potential mechanisms. *Psychosomatic Medicine, 64*, 407–417.

Caldji, C., Liu, D., Sharma, S., Diorio, J., Francis, D., Meaney, M. J., & Plotsky, P. M. (2001). Development of individual differences in behavioral and endocrine responses to stress: The role of post-natal environment. In B. S. McEwen (Ed.), *Handbook of physiology section 7* (Vol. 4, pp. 271–292). New York: Oxford University Press.

Cameron, J. I., Shin, J. L., Williams, D., & Stewart, D. (2004). A brief problem-solving intervention for family caregivers to individuals with advanced cancer. *Journal of Psychosomatic Research, 56*, 1–7.

Canadian Consensus Conference on Non-Pharmacological Approaches to the Management of High Blood Pressure. (1990). Recommendations of the Canadian Consensus Conference on Non-pharmacological Approaches to the Management of High Blood Pressure. *Canadian Medical Association Journal, 142,* 1397–1409.

Cann, A., Calhoun, L. G., & Nance, J. T. (2000). Exposure to humor before and after an unpleasant stimulus: Humor as a preventative or a cure. *Humor, 13,* 177–191.

Cann, A., Holt, K., & Calhoun, L. G. (1999). The roles of humor and sense of humor in responses to stressors. *Humor, 12,* 177–193.

Cannon, W. B. (1928). The mechanism of emotional disturbance of bodily functions. *New England Journal of Medicine, 198,* 165–172.

Cannon, W. B. (1935). Stresses and strains of homeostasis. *American Journal of the Medical Sciences, 189,* 1–14.

Caputo, J. L., Rudolph, D. L., & Morgan, D. W. (1998). Influence of positive life events on blood pressure in adolescents. *Journal of Behavioral Medicine, 21,* 115–129.

Carlson, J. G. (1999). Editorial: Trends in stress management. *International Journal of Stress Management, 6,* 1–3.

Cartwright, M., Wardle, J., Steggles, N., Simon, A. E., Croker, H., & Jarvis, M. J. (2003). Stress and dietary practices in adolescents. *Health Psychology, 22,* 362–369.

Carver, C. S., & Scheier, M. F. (1981). *Attention and self-regulation: A control-theory approach to human behavior.* New York: Springer.

Chambless, D. L., & Gillis, M. M. (1993). Cognitive therapy of anxiety disorders. *Journal of Consulting and Clinical Psychology, 61,* 248–260.

Chapman, R. F., Maier, G., Owen, A., Nousse, V., Park, J. H., & Enright, R. (2001). *Healing forgiveness: Group therapy for abused male forensic patients.* Paper presented at the World Conference of Cognitive and Behavioral Therapies, Vancouver, Canada.

Cohen, S., Frank, E., Doyle, W. J., Skoner, D. P., Rabin, B. S., & Gwaltney, J. M. (1998). Types of stressors that increase susceptibility to the common cold in healthy adults. *Health Psychology, 17,* 214–223.

Cohen, S., Miller, G. E., & Rabin, B. S. (2001). Psychological stress and antibody response to immunization: A critical review of the human literature. *Psychosomatic Medicine, 63,* 7–18.

Colombo, J. R. (2000). *John Robert Colombo's famous lasting words.* Vancouver, BC: Douglas & McIntyre.

Conn, V. S., Valentine, J. C., & Cooper, H. M. (2002). Interventions to increase physical activity among aging adults: A meta-analysis. *Annals of Behavioral Medicine, 24,* 190–200.

Corrigan, P. W. (1992). Social skills training in adult psychiatric populations: A meta-analysis. *Journal of Behavior Therapy and Experimental Psychiatry, 22,* 203–210.

Cossette, S., Frasure-Smith, N., & Lesperance, F. (2001). Clinical implications of a reduction in psychological distress on cardiac prognosis in patients participating in a psychosocial intervention program. *Psychosomatic Medicine, 63,* 257–266.

Cousins, N. (1976). *Anatomy of an illness.* New York: Norton.

Cox, T., & McKay, C. (1978). Stress at work. In T. Cox (Ed.), *Stress.* Baltimore, MD: University Park Press.

Coyne, J. C., & Racioppo, M. W. (2000). Never the twain shall meet? Closing the gap between coping research and clinical intervention research. *American Psychologist, 55,* 655–654.

Cremer, P. (2000). Defense mechanism in psychology today: Further processes for adaptation. *American Psychologist, 55,* 637–646.

Czeisler, C. A., Moore-Ede, M. C., & Coleman, R. M. (1982). Rotating shift work schedules that disrupt sleep are improved by applying circadian principles. *Science, 217,* 460–463.

Dakof, G. A., & Taylor, S. E. (1990). Victims' perception of social support: What is helpful for whom? *Journal of Personality and Social Psychology, 58,* 80–89.

Danner, D. D., Snowdon, D. A., & Friesen, W. V. (2001). Positive emotions in early life and longevity: Findings from the Nun Study. *Journal of Personality and Social Psychology, 80,* 804–813.

Danzer, A., Dale, J. A., & Klions, H. L. (1990). Effects of exposure to humorous stimuli on induced depression. *Psychological Reports, 66,* 1027–1036.

Davidson, R. J., & Kabat-Zinn, J. (2004). Response to Smith (2004). *Psychosomatic Medicine, 66,* 149–152.

Davidson, R. J., Kabat-Zinn, J., Schumacher, J., Rosenkrantz, M., Muller, D., Santorelli, S. F., Urbanowski, F., Harrington, A., Bonus, K., & Sheridan, J. F. (2003). Alterations in brain and immune function produced by mindfulness meditation. *Psychosomatic Medicine, 65,* 564–570.

Davison, K. P., Pennebaker, J. W., & Dickerson, S. S. (2000). Who talks? The social psychology of illness support groups. *American Psychologist, 55,* 205–217.

DeBellis, M. (2001). Developmental traumatology: The psychobiological development of maltreated children and its implications for research, treatment and policy. *Development and Psychopathology, 13,* 539–564.

DeLongis, A., Coyne, J. C., Dakof, G., Folkman, S., & Lazarus, R. S. (1982). Relationships of daily hassles, uplifts, and major life events to health. *Health Psychology, 1,* 119–136.

DeLongis, A., Folkman, S., & Lazarus, R. (1988). The impact of daily stress on health and mood: Psychological and social resources as mediators. *Journal of Personality and Social Psychology, 54,* 486–495.

Denollet, J., Sys, S. U., & Brutsaert, D. L. (1995). Personality and mortality after myocardial infarction. *Psychosomatic Medicine, 57,* 582–591.

Denollet, J., Sys, S. U., Stroobant, N., Rombouts, H., Gillebert, T. C., & Brutsaert, D. L. (1996). Personality as independent predictor of long-term mortality in patients with coronary heart disease. *Lancet, 347,* 417–421.

Dew, M. A., Hoch, C. C., Buysse, D. J., Monk, T. H., Begley, A. E., Houck, P. R., Hall, M., Kupfer, D. J., & Reynolds, C. F., III. (2003). Healthy older adults' sleep predicts all-cause mortality at 4 to 19 years of follow-up. *Psychosomatic Medicine, 65,* 63–73.

Dienstbier, R. A. (1989). Arousal and physiological toughness: Implications for mental and physical health. *Psychological Review, 96,* 84–100.

DiGiuseppe, R., & Tafrate, R. C. (2003). Anger treatments for adults: A meta-analytic review. *Clinical Psychology: Science & Practice, 10,* 70–84.

Dopp, J. M., Miller, G. E., Myers, H. F., & Fahey, J. L. (2000). Increased natural killer-cell mobilization and cytotoxity during marital conflict. *Brain, Behavior and Immunity, 14,* 10–26.

Dunkel-Schetter, C., & Bennett, T. L. (1990). Differentiating the cognitive and behavioral aspects of social support. In B. R. Sarason, I. G. Sarason, & G. R. Pearce (Eds.), *Social support: An interactional view* (pp. 267–296). New York: John Wiley.

Dusseldorp, E., Van Elderen, T., Maes, S., Meulman, J., & Kraail, V. (1999). A meta-analysis of psycho-educational programs for coronary heart disease patients. *Health Psychology, 18,* 506–519.

Dworkin, B. R., Filewich, R. J., Miller, N. E., & Craigmyle, N. (1979). Baroreceptor activation reduces reactivity to noxious stimulation: Implications for hypertension. *Science, 205,* 1299–1301.

D'Zurillia, T. J. (1998). Problem solving therapy. In K. S. Dobson & K. Craig (Eds.), *Empirically supported therapies: Best practice in professional psychology.* Thousand Oaks, CA: Sage.

D'Zurillia, T. J., & Goldfried, M. R. (1971). Problem solving and behavior modification. *Journal of Abnormal Psychology, 78,* 107–126.

Eaker, E. D., Pinsky, J., & Castelli, W. P. (1992). Myocardial infarction and coronary death among women: Psychosocial predictors from a 20-year follow-up in the Framingham study. *American Journal of Epidemiology, 135,* 854–864.

Earle, T. E., Linden, W., & Weinberg, J. (1999). Differential effects of harassment on cardiovascular and salivary cortisol reactivity and recovery in men and women. *Journal of Psychosomatic Research, 46,* 125–141.

Edelman, S., Bell, D. R., & Kidman, A. D. (1999). Group CBT versus supportive therapy with patients who have primary breast cancer. *Journal of Cognitive Psychotherapy: An International Quarterly, 13,* 189–202.

Edwards, D., Hannigan, B., Fothergill, A., & Burnard, P. (2002). Stress management for mental health professionals: A review of effective techniques. *Stress and Health, 18,* 203–215.

Elbert, T., Pietrowsky, R., Kessler, M., Lutzenberger, W., & Birbaumer, N. (1985). Stimulation of baroreceptors decreases cortical excitability and increases pain sensation threshold in borderline hypertension [Abstract]. *Psychophysiology, 22*, 588.

Ellis, A. (1962). *Reason and emotion in psychotherapy.* New York: Lyle Stuart.

Engel, G. L. (1971). Sudden and rapid death during psychological stress. *Annals of Internal Medicine, 74*, 771–782.

Eppley, K. R., Abrams, A. I., & Shear, J. (1989). Differential effects of relaxation techniques on trait anxiety—A meta-analysis. *Journal of Clinical Psychology, 45*, 957–974.

Ewart, C. K. (1991). Familial transmission of essential hypertension: Genes, environment, and chronic anger. *Annals of Behavioral Medicine, 13*, 40–47.

Fawzy, F. I., Fawzy, N. W., Hyun, C. S., Elashoff, R., Guthrie, D., Fahey, J. L., & Morton, D. L. (1993). Malignant melanoma: Effects of an early structured psychiatric intervention, coping, and affective state on recurrence and survival 6 years later. *Archives of General Psychiatry, 50*, 681–689.

Feuerstein, M., Labbe, E. E., & Kuczmierczyk, A. R. (1986). *Health psychology: A psychobiological perspective.* New York: Plenum.

Flood, K. R., & Long, B. C. (1996). Understanding exercise as a method of stress management: A constructionist framework. In J. Kerr, A. Griffiths, & T. Cox (Eds.), *Workplace health, employee fitness and exercise* (pp. 117–128). London: Taylor & Francis.

Folkman, S. (1984). Personal control and stress and coping processes: A theoretical analysis. *Journal of Personality and Social Psychology, 46*, 839–852.

Folkman, S., Lazarus, R. S., Dunkel-Schetter, C., DeLongis, A., & Gruen, R. J. (1986). Dynamics of a stressful encounter: Cognitive appraisal, coping, and encounter outcomes. *Journal of Personality and Social Psychology, 50*, 992–1003.

Folkman S., & Moskowitz, J. T. (2000). Positive affect and the other side of coping. *American Psychologist, 55*, 647–654.

Folkow, B. (1982). Physiological aspects of primary hypertension. *Physiological Reviews, 62*, 347–504.

Fournier, M., de Ridder, D., & Bensing, J. (1999). Optimism and adaptation to multiple sclerosis: What does optimism mean? *Journal of Behavioral Medicine, 22*, 303–326.

Fox, B., & Linden, W. (2002). Depressed cardiac patients: Does everybody have the same treatment needs? *Annals of Behavioral Medicine, 24*, S66.

Frankenhaeuser, M. (1989). A biopsychosocial approach to work life issues. *Journal of Health Services, 19*, 747–758.

Frankenhaeuser, M. (1991). The psychophysiology of workload, stress, and health: Comparison between the sexes. *Annals of Behavioral Medicine, 13*, 197–204.

Frankish, C. J., & Linden, W. (1996). Spouse pair risk factors and cardiovascular reactivity. *Journal of Psychosomatic Research, 40*, 37–51.

Franzini, L. R. (2000). Humor in behavior therapy. *Behavior Therapist, 23,* 25–26.

Franzini, L. R. (2001). Humor in therapy: The case for training therapists in its uses and risks. *Journal of General Psychology, 12,* 170–193.

Frasure-Smith, N., Lesperance, F., Prince, R. H., Verrier, P., Garber, R. A., Juneau, M., Wolfson, C., & Bourassa, M. G. (1997). Randomised trial of home-based psychosocial nursing intervention for patients recovering from myocardial infarction. *Lancet, 350,* 473–479.

Fukunaga, T., Mizoi, Y., Yamashita, A., Yamada, M., Yamamoto, Y., Tatsuno, Y., & Nishi, K. (1992). Thymus of abused neglected children. *Forensic Science International, 53,* 69–79.

Gallo, L. C., & Matthews, K. A. (2003). Understanding the association between socioeconomic status and physical health: Do negative emotions play a role? *Psychological Bulletin, 129,* 10–51.

Gardell, B. (1980). Work environment research and social change: Current developments in Scandinavia. *Journal of Occupational Behaviour, 1,* 3–17.

Ghiadoni, L., Donald, A. E., Cropley, M., Mullen, M. J., Oakley, G., Taylor, M., O'Connor, G., Betteridge, J., Klein, N., Steptoe, A., & Deanfield, J. E. (2000). Mental stress induces transient endothelial dysfunction in humans. *Circulation, 102,* 2473–2478.

Giga, S. I., Noblet, A. J., Faragher, B., & Cooper, C. L. (2003). The UK perspective: A review of research on organizational stress management interventions. *Australian Psychologist, 38,* 156–164.

Girdano, D. A., Everly, G. S., Jr., & Dusek, D. E. (1993). *Controlling stress and tension: A holistic approach* (4th ed.). Englewood Cliffs, NJ: Prentice Hall.

Glaser, R., Rabin, B. S., Chesney, M., & Cohen, S., & Natelson, B. (1999). Stress-induced immunomodulation: Are there implications for infectious disease? *Journal of the American Medical Association, 281,* 2268–2270.

Godfrey, K. J., Bonds, A. S., Kraus, M. E., Wiener, M. R., & Toth, C. S. (1990). Freedom from stress: A meta-analytic view of treatment and intervention programs. *Applied H.M.R. Research, 1,* 67–80.

Goodkin, K., Blaney, N. T., Feaster, D. J., Baldewicz, T., Burkhalter, J. E., & Leeds, B. (1999). A randomized controlled trial of a bereavement support group intervention in human immunodeficiency virus type I-seropositive and seronegative homosexual men. *Archives of General Psychiatry, 56,* 52–59.

Gould, R. A., Otto, M. W., Pollack, M. H., & Yap, L. (1997). Cognitive behavioral and pharmacological treatment of generalized anxiety disorder. *Behavior Therapy, 28,* 285–305.

Grignani, G., Pacchiarino, L., Zucchella, M., Tacconi, F., Canevari, A., Soffiantino, F., & Tavazzi, L. (1992). Effect of mental stress on platelet function in normal subjects and in patients with coronary artery disease. *Haemostasis, 22,* 138–146.

Grossi, G., Perski, A., Evengard, B., Blomkvist, V., & Orth-Gomer, K. (2003). Physiological correlates of burnout among women. *Journal of Psychosomatic Research, 55,* 309–316.

Grossman, R. J. (2000). Make ergonomics. *HR Magazine, 47,* 36–42.

Grossmann, P., Niemann, L., Schmidt, S., & Walach, H. (in press). Mindfulness-based stress reduction and health benefits: A meta-analysis. *Journal of Psychosomatic Research.*

Gump, B. B., & Matthews, K. A. (2000). Are vacations good for your health? The 9-year mortality experience after the multiple risk factor intervention trial. *Psychosomatic Medicine, 62,* 608–612.

Habib, S., & Morrissey, S. (1999). Stress management for atopic dermatitis. *Behaviour Change, 16,* 226–236.

Habra, M. E., Linden, W., Anderson, J. C., & Weinberg, J. (2003). Type D personality is related to cardiovascular and neuroendocrine reactivity to acute stress. *Journal of Psychosomatic Research, 55,* 235–245.

Hamilton, V. (1980). An information processing analysis of environmental stress and life crisis. In I. G. Sarason & C. D. Spielberger (Eds.), *Stress and anxiety* (Vol. 7). New York: Hemisphere.

Hansen, N. B., Lambert, M. J., & Forman, E. M. (2002). The psychotherapy dose-response effect and its implications for treatment delivery services. *Clinical Psychology: Science and Practice, 10,* 329–337.

Hanson, P. G. (1989). *Stress for success: Prescription for making stress work for you.* Garden City, NY: Doubleday.

Hartig, T. (in press). Restorative qualities of environment. In C. Spielberger et al. (Eds.), *Encyclopedia of applied psychology.* San Diego, CA: Academic Press.

Hartig, T., Evans, G. W., Jamner, L. D., Davis, D. S., & Gaerling, T. (2003). Tracking restoration in natural and urban field settings. *Journal of Environmental Psychology, 23,* 109–123.

Harvey, A. G., & Bryant, R. A. (2002). Acute stress disorder: A synthesis and critique. *Psychological Bulletin, 128,* 886–902.

Hawkins, J. D., Catalano, R. F., Jr., & Wells, E. A. (1986). Measuring effects of a skills training intervention for drug abusers. *Journal of Consulting and Clinical Psychology, 54,* 661–664.

Haynes, S. N., Gannon, L. R., Oromoto, L., O'Brien, W. H., & Brandt, M. (1991). Psychophysiological assessment of poststress recovery. *Psychological Assessment, 3,* 356–365.

Helgeson, V. S., Cohen, S., Schulz, R., & Yasko, J. (1999). Education and peer discussion group interventions and adjustment to breast cancer. *Archives of General Psychiatry, 56,* 340–347.

Hemphill, K. J. (1997). Supportive and unsupportive processes within the stress and coping context. *Dissertation Abstracts International, B: The Sciences and Engineering, 57,* 7775.

Henry, J. L., Wilson, P. H., Bruce, D. G., Chisholm, D. J., & Rawling, P. J. (1997). Cognitive-behavioural stress management for patients with non-insulin dependent diabetes mellitus. *Psychology, Health and Medicine, 2,* 109–118.

Herbert, T. B., & Cohen, S. (1993). Stress and immunity in humans—A meta-analytic review. *Psychosomatic Medicine, 55,* 364–379.

Hoff Macan, T. (1994). Time management: Test of a process model. *Journal of Applied Psychology, 79,* 381–391.

Hogan, B. E., Linden, W., & Najarian, B. (2002). Social support interventions: Do they work? *Clinical Psychology Review 22,* 381–440.

House, J. S., & Kahn, R. L. (1985). Measures and concepts of social support. In S. Cohen & S. L. Syme (Eds.), *Social support and health* (pp. 83–108). New York: Academic Press.

House, J. S., Landis, K. R., & Umberson, D. (1988). Social relationships and health. *Science, 241,* 540–545.

Hyman, R. B., Feldman, H. R., Harris, R. B., Levin, R. F., & Malloy, G. B. (1989). The effects of relaxation training on clinical symptoms: A meta-analysis. *Nursing Research, 38,* 216–220.

Ilfeld, F. W. (1980). Coping styles of Chicago adults: Description. *Journal of Human Stress, 6,* 2–10.

International Statistical Classification of Diseases (ICD) (9th rev.). (1975). World Health Organization, Geneva: Author.

Jacob, R. G., Chesney, M. A., Williams, D. M., Ding, Y., Shapiro, A. P. (1991). Relaxation therapy for hypertension: Design effects and treatment effects. *Annals of Behavioral Medicine, 13,* 5–17.

Jacobsen, P. B., Meade, C. D., Stein, K. D., Chirikos, T. N., Small, B. J., & Ruckdeschel, J. C. (2002). Efficacy and costs of two forms of stress management training for cancer patients undergoing chemotherapy. *Journal of Clinical Oncology, 20,* 2851–2862.

Jex, S. M., & Elacqua, T. C. (1999). Time management as a moderator of relations between stressors and employee strain. *Work & Stress, 13,* 182–191.

Jiang, W., Babyak, M., Krantz, D. S., Waugh, R. A., Coleman, R. E., Hanson, M. M., Frid, D. J., McNulty, S., Morris, J. J., O'Connor, C. M., & Blumenthal, J. A. (1996). Mental stress-induced myocardial ischemia and cardiac events. *Journal of the American Medical Association, 275,* 1651–1656.

Johnson, T. L. (1990). A meta-analytic review of absenteeism control methods. *Applied H.R.M. Research, 1,* 23–26.

The Joint National Committee on Detection, Evaluation, and Treatment of High Blood Pressure: The 1988 report of the Joint National Committee on Detection, Evaluation, and Treatment of High Blood Pressure. (1988). *Archives of Internal Medicine, 148,* 1023–1038.

Jones, D. A., & West, R. R. (1996). Psychological rehabilitation after myocardial infarction: Multicentre randomized controlled trial. *British Medical Journal, 313,* 1517–1521.

Jones, M. C., & Johnston, D. W. (2000). Reducing distress in first level and student nurses: A review of the applied stress management literature. *Journal of Advanced Nursing, 32,* 66–74.

Kabat-Zinn, J. (2003). Mindfulness-based interventions in context: Past, present, and future. *Clinical Psychology: Science and Practice, 10,* 144–156.

Kahn, R. L., & Antonucci, T. C. (1980). Convoys over the lifecourse: Attachment, roles, and social support. In P. B. Baltes & O. Brim (Eds.), *Lifespan development and behavior* (Vol. 3, pp. 253–286). New York: Academic Press.

Kamarck, T. W., & Jennings, J. R. (1991). Biobehavioral factors in sudden cardiac arrest. *Psychological Bulletin, 109,* 42–75.

Kamarck, T. W., & Lovallo, W. R. (2003). Cardiovascular reactivity to psychological challenge: Conceptual and measurement considerations. *Psychosomatic Medicine, 65,* 9–21.

Kaplan, K. H., Goldberg, D. L., & Galvin-Nadeau, M. (1993). The impact of a meditation-based stress reduction program on fibromyalgia. *General Hospital Psychiatry, 15,* 284–289.

Karasek, R. (1992). Stress prevention through work reorganization: A summary of 19 international case studies (Section 2). *Conditions of Work Digest, 11.*

Karasek, R. A., & Theorell, T. (1990). *Stress, productivity, and reconstruction of working life.* New York: Basic Books.

Kazantzis, N., Deane, F. P., & Ronan, K. R. (2002). Homework assignments in cognitive- and behavioral therapy: A meta-analysis. *Clinical Psychology: Science and Practice, 7,* 189–196.

Kelly, S., Hertzman, C., & Daniels, M. (1997). Searching for the biological pathways between stress and health. *Annual Review of Public Health, 18,* 437–462.

Kemeny, M. E., Cohen, F., Zegans, L. S., & Conant, M. A. (1989). Psychological and immunological predictors of genital herpes recurrence. *Psychosomatic Medicine, 51,* 195–208.

Kemeny, M. E., & Gruenewald, T. L. (2000). Affect, cognition, the immune system and health. In E. A. Mayer & C. Saper (Eds.), *The biological basis for mind-body interactions* (Progress in Brain Research Volume 122, pp. 291–308). Amsterdam: Elsevier/North Holland.

Kendler, K. S., Bulik, C. M., Silberg, J., Hettema, J. M., Myers, J., & Prescott, C. A. (2000). Childhood sexual abuse and adult psychiatric and substance use disorders in women—An epidemiological and cotwin control analysis. *Archives of General Psychiatry, 57,* 953–959.

Kessler, R. C., Mickelson, K. D., & Zhao, S. (1997). Patterns and correlates of self-help group membership in the United States. *Social Policy, 27,* 27–46.

Kivimaki, M., Leino-Arjas, P., Luukkonen, R., Riihimaki, H., Vahtera, J., & Kirjonen, J. (2002). Work stress and risk of cardiovascular mortality: Prospective cohort study of industrial employees. *British Medical Journal, 325,* 857–861.

Kop, W. (1999). Chronic and acute psychological risk factors for clinical manifestations of coronary artery disease. *Psychosomatic Medicine, 61,* 476–487.

Krantz, D. S., Santiago, H. T., Kop, W. J., Merz, C. N. B., Rozanski, A., & Gottdiener, J. S. (1999). Prognostic value of mental stress testing in coronary artery disease. *American Journal of Cardiology, 84,* 1292–1297.

Kugler, J., Seelbach, H., & Krueskemper, G. M. (1994). Effects of rehabilitation exercise programmes on anxiety and depression in coronary patients. *British Journal of Clinical Psychology, 33,* 401–410.

Kushnir, T., Malkinson, R., & Ribak, J. (1998). Rational thinking and stress management in health workers: A psychoeducational program. *International Journal of Stress Management, 5,* 169–178.

Lacks, P., & Morin, C. M. (1992). Recent advances in the assessment and treatment of insomnia. *Journal of Consulting and Clinical Psychology, 60,* 586–594.

Laessle, R. G., Tuschl, R. J., Kotthaus, B. C., & Pirke, K. M. (1989). Behavioral and biological correlates of dietary restraint in normal life. *Appetite, 12,* 83–94.

Lakey, B., & Lutz, C. J. (1996). Social and preventative and therapeutic interventions. In G. R. Pierce, B. R. Sarason, & I. G. Sarason (Eds.), *Handbook of social support and the family* (pp. 435–465). New York: Plenum.

Lange, A. J., & Jakubowski, P. (1976). *Responsible assertive behavior.* Champaign-Urbana, IL: Research Press.

Latack, J. (1986). Coping with stress: Measures and future directions for scale development. *Journal of Applied Psychology, 72,* 377–385.

Lazarus, R. S. (2000). Toward better research on stress and coping. *American Psychologist, 55,* 665–673.

Lazarus, R. S., & Folkman, S. (1984). *Stress, appraisal, and coping.* New York: Springer.

Lefcourt, H. M., Davidson-Katz, K., & Kueneman, K. (1990). Humor and immune system functioning. *Humor, 3,* 305–321.

Lehman, D. R., & Hemphill, K. J. (1990). Recipients' perceptions of support attempts and attributions for support attempts that fail. *Journal of Social and Personal Relationships, 7,* 563–574.

Lehrer, P. M., Carr, R., Sargunaraj, D., & Woolfolk, R. L. (1994). Stress management techniques—Are they all equivalent, or do they have specific effects? *Biofeedback and Self-Regulation, 19,* 353–401.

Lehrer, P. M., & Woolfolk, R. L. (1990). *Principles and practice of stress management* (2nd ed.). New York: Guilford.

Leor, J., Poole, W. K., & Kloner, R. A. (1996). Sudden cardiac death triggered by an earthquake. *New England Journal of Medicine, 334,* 413–419.

Levi, L. (1972). Introduction: Psychosocial stimuli, psychphysiological reactions, and disease. In L. Levi (Ed.), *Stress and distress in response to psychosocial stimuli* (pp. 11–27). Oxford, UK: Pergamon.

Lewis, M. H., Gluck, J. P., Petitto, J. M., Hensley, L. L., & Ozer, H. (2000). Early social deprivation in nonhuman primates: Long-term effects on survival and cell-mediated immunity. *Biological Psychiatry, 47,* 119–126.

Lichstein, K. L. (1988). *Clinical relaxation strategies.* New York: John Wiley.

Light, K. (1987). Psychosocial precursors of hypertension: Experimental evidence. *Circulation, 76*(Suppl. I), 67–76.

Light, K. C., Girdler, S. S., Sherwood, A., Bragdon, E. E., Brownley, K. A., West, S. G., & Hinderliter, A. L. (1999). High stress responsivity predicts later blood pressure only in combination with positive family history and high life stress. *Hypertension, 33,* 1458–1464.

Linden, W. (1987). A microanalysis of autonomic arousal during human speech. *Psychosomatic Medicine, 49,* 562–578.

Linden, W. (1990). *Autogenic Training: A practitioner's guide.* New York: Guilford.

Linden, W. (1994). Autogenic Training: A narrative and a meta-analytic review of clinical outcome. *Biofeedback and Self-Regulation, 19,* 227–264.

Linden, W. (2000). Psychological treatments in cardiac rehabilitation: A review of rationales and outcomes. *Journal of Psychosomatic Research, 48,* 443–454.

Linden, W. (2002). *A guided book for managing stress.* Unpublished manuscript, University of British Columbia, Vancouver, Canada.

Linden, W. (2003). Psychological treatment can be an effective treatment for hypertension. *Preventive Cardiology, 6,* 48–53.

Linden, W., & Chambers, L. A. (1994). Clinical effectiveness of non-drug therapies for hypertension: A meta-analysis. *Annals of Behavioral Medicine, 16,* 35–45.

Linden, W., Chambers, L. A., Maurice, J., & Lenz, J. W. (1993). Sex differences in social support, self-deception, hostility, and ambulatory blood pressure. *Health Psychology, 12,* 376–380.

Linden, W., Earle, T. L., Gerin, W., & Christenfeld, N. (1997). Physiological stress reactivity and recovery: Conceptual siblings separated at birth? *Journal of Psychosomatic Research, 42,* 117–135.

Linden, W., Gerin, W., & Davidson, K. (2003). Cardiovascular reactivity: Status quo and a research agenda for the new millennium. *Psychosomatic Medicine, 65,* 5–8.

Linden, W., Lenz, J. W., & Con, A. H. (2001). Individualized stress management for primary hypertension: A controlled trial. *Archives of Internal Medicine, 161,* 1071–1080.

Linden, W., Rutledge, T., & Con, A. (1998). A case for the ecological validity of social lab stressors. *Annals of Behavioral Medicine, 20,* 310–316.

Linden, W., Stossel, C., & Maurice, J. (1996). Psychosocial interventions for patients with coronary artery disease: A meta-analysis. *Archives of Internal Medicine, 156,* 745–752.

Linden, W., & Wen, F. K. (1990). Therapy outcome research, health care policy, and the continuing lack of accumulated knowledge. *Professional Psychology: Research and Practice, 21,* 482–488.

Long, B. C., & Van Stavel, R. (1995). Effects of exercise training on anxiety: A meta-analysis. *Journal of Applied Sport Psychology, 7,* 167–189.

Lovallo, W. R. (1997). *Stress and health: Biological and psychological interactions.* Thousand Oaks, CA: Sage.

Luebbert, K., Dahme, B., & Hasenbring, M. (2001). The effectiveness of relaxation training in reducing treatment-related symptoms and improving emotional adjustment in acute non-surgical cancer treatment: A meta-analytical review. *Psycho-Oncology, 10,* 490–502.

Lutgendorf, S. K., Antoni, M. H., Ironson, G. I., Klimas, N., Kumar, M., Starr, K., McCabe, P., Cleven, K., Fletcher, M. A., & Schneiderman, N. (1997). Cognitive-behavioral stress management decreases dysphoric mood and herpes simplex virus-type 2 antibody titres in symptomatic HIV-seropositive gay men. *Journal of Consulting & Clinical Psychology, 65,* 31–43.

Lutgendorf, S. K., Antoni, M. H., Ironson, G., Starr, K., Costello, N., Zuckerman, M., Klimas, N., Fletcher, M. A., & Schneiderman, N. (1998). Changes in cognitive coping skills and social support during cognitive behavioral stress management intervention and distress outcomes in symptomatic human immunodeficiency virus (HIV)-seropositive gay men. *Psychosomatic Medicine, 60,* 204–214.

Lutgendorf, S. K., Vitaliano, P. P., Tripp-Reimer, T., Harvey, J. H., & Lubaroff, D. M. (1999). Sense of coherence moderates the relationship between life stress and natural killer cell activity in healthy older adults. *Psychology and Aging, 14,* 552–563.

Luthe, W. (1970). *Autogenic therapy: Vol. 4. Research and theory.* New York: Grune & Stratton.

Maag, J. W., & Kotlash, J. (1994). Review of stress inoculation training with children and adolescents: Issues and recommendations. *Behavior Modification, 18,* 443–469.

Magee-Quinn, M., Kavale, K. A., Mathur, S. R., Rutherford, R. B., & Forness, R. (1999). A meta-analysis of social skills interventions for students with emotional or behavioral disorders. *Journal of Emotional and Behavioral Disorders, 7,* 54–64.

Mahoney, M. J. (1974). *Cognition and behavior modification.* Cambridge, MA: Ballinger.

Maier, S. F., & Watkins, L. R. (1998). Cytokines for psychologists: Implications for bi-directional immune-to-brain communication for understanding behavior, mood, and cognition. *Psychological Review, 105,* 83–107.

Martin, R. A. (2001). Humor, laughter, and physical health: Methodological issues and research findings. *Psychological Bulletin, 127,* 504–519.

Martin, R. A., & Dobbin, J. P. (1988). Sense of humor, hassles, and immunoglobulin A: Evidence for a stress-moderating effect of humor. *International Journal of Psychiatry in Medicine, 18,* 93–105.

Maton, K. I. (1987). Patterns and psychological correlates of material support within a religious setting: The bidirectional support hypothesis. *American Journal of Community Psychology, 15,* 185–207.

Maton, K. I. (1988). Social support, organizational characteristics, psychological well-being, and group appraisal in three self-help group populations. *American Journal of Community Psychology, 16,* 53–77.

McEwen, B. S. (1998). Protective and damaging effects of stress mediators. *New England Journal of Medicine, 338,* 171–179.

McEwen, B. S., & Stellar, E. (1993). Stress and the individual: Mechanisms leading to disease. *Archives of Internal Medicine, 153,* 2093–2101.

McGrady, A. V., Nadsady, P. A., & Schumann-Brzezinski, C. (1991). Sustained effects of biofeedback-assisted relaxation therapy in essential hypertension. *Biofeedback and Self-Regulation, 11,* 95–103.

McGregor, M. W., Davidson, K. W., Barksdale, C., Black, S., & MacLean, D. (2003). Adaptive defense use and resting blood pressure in a population-based sample. *Journal of Psychosomatic Research, 55,* 531–541.

McGuire, F. A., Boyd, R., & James, M. (1992). The Clemson Humor Project. *Activities, Adaptation, and Aging, 17,* 31–55.

Meaney, M. J., Diorio, J., Francis, D., Widdowson, J., LaPlante, P., Caldji, C., Sharma, S., Seckl, J. R., & Plotsky, P. M. (1996). Early environmental regulation of forebrain glucocorticoid receptor gene expression: Implications for adrenocortical responses to stress. *Developmental Neuroscience, 18,* 49–72.

Medalia, A., Revheim, N., & Casey, M. (2002). Remediation of problem-solving skills in schizophrenia: Evidence of a persistent effect. *Schizophrenia Research, 57,* 165–171.

Miller, G. E., & Cohen, S. (2001). Psychological interventions and the immune system: A meta-analytic review and critique. *Health Psychology, 20,* 47–63.

Miller, G. E., Cohen, S., Rabin, B. S., Skoner, D. P., & Doyle, W. J. (1999). Personality and tonic cardiovascular, neuroendocrine, and immune parameters. *Brain, Behavior, and Immunity, 13,* 109–123.

Mueller, C., & Donnerstein, E. (1977). The effects of humor-induced arousal upon aggressive behavior. *Journal of Research in Personality, 11,* 73–82.

Munz, D. C., Kohler, J. M., & Greenberg, C. I. (2001). Effectiveness of a comprehensive worksite stress management program: Combining organizational and individual interventions. *International Journal of Stress Management, 8,* 49–62.

Murphy, L. R. (1996). Stress management in work settings: A critical review of the health effects. *American Journal of Health Promotion, 11,* 112–135.

Murphy, S. A., Beaton, R. D., Pike, K. C., & Johnson, L. C. (1999). Occupational stressors. Stress responses, and alcohol consumption among professional firefighters: A prospective, longitudinal analysis. *International Journal of Stress Management, 6,* 179–196.

Newman, M. G., & Stone, A. A. (1996). Does humor moderate the effects of experimentally-induced stress? *Annals of Behavioral Medicine, 18,* 101–109.

Newton, T. (1995). *Managing stress: Emotion and power at work.* Thousand Oaks, CA: Sage.

Ng, D. M., & Jeffrey, R. W. (2003). Relationships between perceived stress and health behaviors in a sample of working adults. *Health Psychology, 22,* 638–642.

Nunes, E. V., Frank, K. A., & Kornfeld, D. S. (1987). Psychologic treatment for the type A behavior pattern and for coronary heart disease: A meta-analysis of the literature. *Psychosomatic Medicine, 48,* 159–173.

Oldridge, N. B., Guyatt, G. H., Fischer, M. E., & Rimm, A. A. (1988). Cardiac rehabilitation after myocardial infarction: Combined experience of randomized clinical trials. *Journal of the American Medical Association, 260,* 945–950.

Ong, L., Linden, W., & Young, S. B. (2004). Stress management: What is it? *Journal of Psychosomatic Research, 56,* 133–137.

Owen, N., & Steptoe, A. (2003). Natural killer cell and proinflammatory cytokine responses to mental stress: Associations with heart rate and heart rate variability. *Biological Psychology, 63,* 101–115.

Padgett, D. A., Sheridan, J. F., Berntson, G. G., Candelora, J., & Glaser, R. (1998). Social stress and the reactivation of latent herpes simplex virus type 1. *Proceedings of the National Academy of Science, 95,* 7231–7235.

Penley, J. A., Tomaka, J., & Wiebe, J. S. (2002). The association of coping to physical and psychological health outcomes. *Journal of Behavioral Medicine, 25,* 551–603.

Pennebaker, J. W. (1982). *The psychology of physical symptoms.* New York: Springer.

Perna, F. M., Antoni, M. H., Baum, A., Gordon, P., & Schneiderman, N. (2003). Cognitive behavioral stress management effects on injury and illness among competitive athletes: A randomized controlled trial. *Annals of Behavioral Medicine, 25,* 66–73.

Persons, J., Mennin, D. S., & Tucker, D. E. (2001). Common misconceptions about the nature and treatment of generalized anxiety disorder. *Psychiatric Annals, 31,* 501–507.

Pistrang, N., & Barker, C. (1998). Partners and fellow patients: Two sources of emotional support for women with breast cancer. *American Journal of Community Psychology, 26,* 439–456.

Polivy, J., & Herman, C. P. (1985). Dieting and bingeing: A causal analysis. *American Psychologist, 40,* 193–201.

Rasul, F., Stansfield, S. A., Hart, C. L., Gillis, C. R., & Smith, G. D. (2004). Psychological distress, physical illness and mortality risk. *Journal of Psychosomatic Research, 56,* 1–6.

Ray, O. (2004). How the mind hurts and heals the body. *American Psychologist, 59,* 29–40.

Ribordy, S. C., Holes, D. S., & Buchsbaum, H. K. (1980). Effects of affective and cognitive distractions on anxiety reduction. *Journal of Social Psychology, 112,* 121–127.

Rosenthal, R. (1984). *Meta-analytic procedures for social research.* Beverly Hills, CA: Sage.

Rostad, F. G., & Long, B. C. (1996). Exercise as a coping strategy for stress: A review. *International Journal of Sport Psychology, 27,* 197–222.

Roth, D. L., Bachtler, S. D., & Fillingim, R. B. (1990). Acute emotional and cardiovascular effects of stressful mental work during aerobic exercise. *Psychophysiology, 27,* 694–701.

Roth, D. L., & Holmes, D. S. (1985). Influence of physical-fitness in determining the impact of stressful life events on physical and psychologic health. *Psychosomatic Medicine, 47,* 164–173.

Roth, D. L., & Holmes, D. S. (1987). Influence of aerobic exercise training and relaxation training on physical and psychologic health following stressful life events. *Psychosomatic Medicine, 49,* 355–365.

Rothenbacher, D., Hoffmeister, A., Brenner, H., & Koenig, W. (2003). Physical activity, coronary heart disease, and inflammatory response. *Archives of Internal Medicine, 163,* 1200–1205.

Roy, M. P., Kirschbaum, C., & Steptoe, A. (2001). Psychological, cardiovascular, and metabolic correlates of individual differences in cortisol stress recovery in young men. *Psychoneuroendocrinology, 26,* 375–391.

Rozanski, A., Bairey, C. N., Krantz, D. S., Friedman, J., Resser, K. J., Morell, M., Hilton-Chalfen, S., Hestrin, L., Bietendorf, J., & Berman, D. S. (1988). Mental stress and the induction of silent myocardial ischemia in patients with coronary artery disease. *New England Journal of Medicine, 318,* 1005–1012.

Rozanski, A., Blumenthal, J. A., & Kaplan, J. (1999). Impact of psychological factors on the pathogenesis of cardiovascular disease and implications for therapy. *Circulation, 99,* 2192–2217.

Rutledge, T., & Hogan, B. E. (2002). A quantitative analysis of prospective evidence linking psychological factors with hypertension development. *Psychosomatic Medicine, 64,* 758–766.

Rutledge, T., & Linden, W. (2003). Defensiveness and 3-year blood pressure levels among young adults: The mediating effect of stress-reactivity. *Annals of Behavioral Medicine, 25,* 34–40.

Rutledge, T., Linden, W., & Paul, D. (2000). Cardiovascular recovery from acute laboratory stress: reliability and concurrent validity. *Psychosomatic Medicine, 62,* 648–654.

Sandlund, E. S., & Norlander, T. (2000). The effects of tai chi chuan relaxation and exercise on stress responses and well-being: An overview of research. *International Journal of Stress Management, 7,* 139–149.

Sarafino, E. P. (2002). *Health psychology* (4th ed.). New York: John Wiley.

Savelkoul, M., de Witte, L,, & Post, M. (2003). Stimulating active coping in patients with rheumatic diseases: A systematic review of controlled group intervention studies. *Patient Education and Counseling, 50,* 133–143.

Scharlach, A. E. (1988). Peer counselor training for nursing home residents. *The Gerontologist, 28,* 499–502.

Schneider, B. H. (1992). Didactic methods for enhancing social competence in children: A meta-analysis of recent evaluation studies. *Clinical Psychology Review, 12,* 363–382.

Schwartz, A. R., Gerin, W., Christenfeld, N., Glynn, L., Davidson, K., & Pickering, T. G. (2000). Effect of an anger-recall task on poststress rumination and blood pressure recovery in men and women. *Psychophysiology, 37,* S12–S13.

Schwartz, A. R., Gerin, W., Davidson, K., Pickering, T. G., Brosschot, J. F., Thayer, J. F., Christenfeld, N., & Linden, W. (2003). Towards a causal model of cardiovascular responses to stress and the development of cardiovascular disease. *Psychosomatic Medicine, 65,* 22–35.

Schwartz, C. E. (1999). Teaching coping skills enhances quality of life more than peer support: Results of a randomized trial with multiple sclerosis patients. *Health Psychology, 18,* 211–220.

Schwartz, M. D., Lerman, C., Audrain, J., Cella, D., Rimer, B., Stefanek, M., Garber, J., Lin, T. H., & Vogel, V. (1998). The impact of a brief problem-solving training intervention for relatives of recently diagnosed breast cancer patients. *Annals of Behavioral Medicine, 20,* 7–12.

Schwarzer, R., & Leppin, A. (1991). Social support and health: A theoretical and empirical overview. *Journal of Social and Personal Relationships, 8,* 99–127.

Segerstrom, S. C., & Miller, G. E. (2004). Psychological stress and the human immune system: A meta-analytic study of 30 years of inquiry. *Psychological Bulletin, 130,* 601–630.

Selye, H. (1936). A syndrome produced by diverse nocuous agents. *Nature, 138,* 32.

Selye, H. (1946). The general adaptation syndrome and the disease of adaptation. *Journal of Clinical Endocrinology, 6,* 117–230.

Selye, H. (1956). *The stress of life.* New York: McGraw-Hill.

Selye, H. (1976). *Stress in health and disease.* Reading, MA: Butterworth.

Siegrist, J. (1996). Adverse health effects of high effort/low reward conditions. *Journal of Occupational Health Psychology, 1,* 27–41.

Singer, D. L. (1968). Aggression arousal, hostile humor, catharsis. *Journal of Personality and Social Psychology, 8,* 1–14.

Shapiro, S., Shapiro, D. E., & Schwartz, G. E. R. (2000). Stress management in medical education: A review of the literature. *Academic Medicine, 75,* 748–759.

Shearn, M. A., & Fireman, B. H. (1985). Stress management and mutual support groups in rheumatoid arthritis. *American Journal of Medicine, 78,* 771–775.

Shen, B. J., McCreary, C. P., & Myers, H. F. (2004). Independent and mediated contributions of personality, coping, social support, and depressive symptoms to physical functioning outcome among patients in cardiac rehabilitation. *Journal of Behavioral Medicine, 27,* 39–62.

Sigmon, S. T., Stanton, A. L., & Snyder, C. R. (1995). Gender differences in coping: A further test of socialization and role constraint theories. *Sex Roles, 33,* 565–587.

Skinner, E. A., Edge, K., Altman, J., & Sherwood, H. (2003). Searching for the structure of coping: A review and critique of category systems for classifying ways of coping. *Psychological Bulletin, 129,* 216–269.

Sklar, L. S., & Anisman, H. (1981). Stress and cancer. *Psychological Bulletin, 89,* 369–406.

Smith, C. S., & Sulsky, L. M. (1995). Investigation of job-related coping strategies across multiple stressors and samples. In L. R. Murphy, J. J. Hurrell, Jr., S. L. Sauter, & G. P. Keita (Eds.), *Job stress interventions* (pp. 109–123). Washington, DC: American Psychological Association.

Smith, J. C. (2004). Alterations in brain and immune function produced by mindfulness meditation: Three caveats. *Psychosomatic Medicine, 66,* 148–149.

Somerfield, M. R., & McCrae, R. R. (2000). Stress and coping research: Methodological challenges, theoretical advances, and clinical applications. *American Psychologist, 55,* 620–625.

Speca, M., Carlson, L. E., Goodey, E., & Angen, M. (2000). A randomized, wait-list controlled clinical trial: The effect of a mindfulness meditation-based stress reduction program on mood and symptoms of stress in cancer outpatients. *Psychosomatic Medicine, 62,* 613–622.

Spence, J. D., Barnett, P. A., Linden, W., Ramsden, V., & Taenzer, P. (1999). Recommendations on stress management. *Canadian Medical Association Journal, 160,* S46–S50.

Stanton, A. L., Kirk, S. B., Cameron, C. L., & Danoff-Burg, S. (2000). Coping through emotional approach: Scale construction and validation. *Journal of Personality and Social Psychology, 78,* 1150–1169.

Steptoe, A., Kimbell, J., & Basford, P. (1998). Exercise and the experience and appraisal of daily stressors: A naturalistic study. *Journal of Behavioral Medicine, 21,* 363–371.

Steptoe, A., & Marmot, M. (2003). Burden of psychosocial adversity and vulnerability in middle age: Associations with biobehavioral risk factors and quality of life. *Psychosomatic Medicine, 65,* 1029–1037.

Sterling, P., & Eyer, J. (1988). Allostasis: A new paradigm to explain arousal pathology. In S. Fisher & J. Reason (Eds.), *Handbook of life stress, cognition and health* (pp. 629–649). Chichester, UK: Wiley.

Stetter, F., & Kupper, S. (2002). Autogenic training: A meta-analysis of clinical outcome studies. *Applied Psychophysiology and Biofeedback, 27,* 45–98.

Stewart, J. C., & France, C. R. (2001). Cardiovascular recovery from stress predicts longitudinal changes in blood pressure. *Biological Psychology, 58,* 105–120.

Story, L. B., & Bradbury, T. N. (2003). Understanding marriage and stress: Essential questions and challenges. *Clinical Psychology Review, 23,* 1139–1162.

Sullivan, C. M., Campbell, R., Angelique, H., Eby, K. K., & Davidson, W. S., II. (1994). An advocacy intervention program for women with abusive partners: Six-month follow-up. *American Journal of Community Psychology, 22,* 101–122.

Suls, J., & Wan, C. K. (1993). The relationship between trait hostility and cardiovascular reactivity: A quantitative review and analysis. *Psychophysiology, 30,* 615–626.

Surtees, P., Wainwright, N., Day, N., Brayne, C., Luben, R., & Khaw, K. T. (2003). Adverse experience in childhood as a developmental risk factor for altered immune status in adulthood. *International Journal of Behavioral Medicine, 10,* 251–268.

Taylor, S. (1996). Meta-analysis of cognitive behavioral treatment for social phobia. *Journal of Behavior Therapy and Experimental Psychiatry, 14,* 225–238.

Taylor, S. E., Lerner, J. S., Sherman, D. K., Sage, R. M., & McDowell, N. K. (2003). Are self-enhancing cognitions associated with healthy or unhealthy biological profiles? *Journal of Personality and Social Psychology, 85,* 605–615.

Tennen, H., Affleck, G., Armeli, S., & Carney, M. A. (2000). A daily process approach to coping: Linking theory, research and practice. *American Psychologist, 55,* 626–636.

Thayer, R. E., Newman, R., & McClain, T. M. (1994). Self-regulation of mood: Strategies for changing a bad mood, raising energy, and reducing tension. *Journal of Personality and Social Psychology, 67,* 910–925.

Thoresen, C. E., Luskin, F., & Harris, A. H. S. (1998). Science and forgiveness interventions: Reflections and recommendations. In E. Worthington (Ed.), *Dimensions of forgiveness* (pp. 163–192). Philadelphia: Templeton Foundation Press.

Treiber, F. A., Kamarck, T., Schneiderman, N., Sheffield, D., Kapuku, G., & Taylor, T. (2003). Cardiovascular reactivity and development of preclinical and clinical disease states. *Psychosomatic Medicine, 65,* 46–62.

Trice, A. D. (1985). Alleviation of helpless responding by a humorous experience. *Psychological Reports, 57,* 474.

Tummers, G. E. R., Landeweerd, J. A., & van Merode, G. G. (2002). Work organization, work characteristics, and their psychological effects on nurses in the Netherlands. *International Journal of Stress Management, 9,* 183–195.

Twisk, J. W. R., Snel, J., Kemper, H. C. G., & van Mechelen, W. (1999). Changes in daily hassles and life events and the relationship with coronary heart disease risk factors: A 2-year longitudinal study in 27–29-year-old males and females. *Journal of Psychosomatic Research, 46,* 229–240.

U.S. Department of Health and Human Services. (1986). *Positioning for prevention: Analytical framework and background document for chronic disease activities* (p. 17). Atlanta, GA: Centers for Disease Control.

Vaillant, G. E. (1977). *Adaptation to life.* Boston: Little, Brown.

Vaitl, D., & Petermann, F. (2000). *Handbuch der Entspannungsverfahren: Volumen I. Grundlagen und Methoden* (2nd ed.). Weinheim, Germany: Betz Verlag.

Van der Hek, H., & Plomp, H. N. (1997). Occupational stress management programmes: A practical overview of published effect studies. *Occupational Medicine, 47,* 133–141.

Van Diest, R., & Appels, R. (2002). Vital exhaustion: Behavioural and biological correlates. *Current Opinion in Psychiatry, 15,* 639–641.

Vance, C. M. (1987). A comparative study on the use of humor in the design of instruction. *Instructional Science, 16,* 79–100.

Ventis, W. L., Higbee, G., & Murdock, S. A. (2001). Using humor in systematic desensitization to reduce fear. *Journal of General Psychology, 28,* 241–253.

Vitaliano, P. P., Zhang, J., & Scanlan, J. (2003). Is caregiving hazardous to one's physical health? A meta-analysis. *Psychological Bulletin, 129,* 946–972.

Von Kaenel, R., Dimsdale, J. E., Patterson, M. L., & Grant, I. (2003). Association of negative life event stress with coagulation activity in elderly Alzheimer caregivers. *Psychosomatic Medicine, 65,* 145–150.

Ward, M. M., Swan, G. E., Chesney, M. A. (1987). Arousal reduction treatments for mild hypertension: A meta-analysis of recent studies. In S. Julius & D. R. Bassett (Eds.), *Behavioral factors in hypertension* (pp. 285–302). North Holland: Elsevier.

Webster's illustrated encyclopedic dictionary. (1990). Stress (p. 1639). Montreal, Canada: Tormont.

Webster-Stratton, C., Reid, J., & Hammond, M. (2001). Social skills and problem-solving training for children with early-onset problems: Who benefits? *Journal of Child Psychology and Psychiatry and Allied Disciplines, 42,* 943–952.

Weisenberg, M., Tepper, I., & Schwarzwald, J. (1995). Humor as a cognitive technique for increasing pain tolerance. *Pain, 63,* 207–212.

Weiss, J. M. (1971a). Effect of coping behavior with and without feedback signal on stress pathology in rats. *Journal of Comparative and Physiological Psychology, 77,* 22–30.

Weiss, J. M. (1971b). Effects of coping behavior in different warning-signal conditions on stress pathology in rats. *Journal of Comparative and Physiological Psychology, 77,* 1–13.

Weiss, J. M. (1972). Psychological factors in stress and disease. *Scientific American, 226,* 104–113.

Westen, D., & Morrison, K. (2001). A multidimensional meta analysis of treatments for depression, panic, and generalized anxiety disorder: An empirical examination of the status of empirically supported therapies. *Journal of Consulting and Clinical Psychology, 69,* 875–899.

Wheaton, B. (1996). The domains and boundaries of stress concepts. In H. B. Kaplan (Ed.), *Psychosocial stress: Perspectives on structure, theory, life-course, and methods* (pp. 29-70). San Diego, CA: Academic Press.

Wigers, S. H., Stiles, T. C., & Vogel, P. A. (1996). Effects of aerobic exercise versus stress management treatment in fibromyalgia: A 4.5 year prospective study. *Scandinavian Journal of Rheumatology, 25,* 77–86.

Williams, R. B., Barefoot, J. C., Blumenthal, J. A., Helms, M. J., Kuecken, L., Pieper, C. F., Siegler, I. C., & Suarez, E. C. (1997). Psychosocial correlates of job strain in a sample of working women. *Archives of General Psychiatry, 54,* 543–548.

Wing, R. R., & Jeffrey, R. W. (1999). Benefits of recruiting participants with friends and increasing social support for weight loss and maintenance. *Journal of Consulting and Clinical Psychology, 67,* 132–138.

Witztum, E., Briskin, S., & Lerner, V. (1999). The use of humor with chronic schizophrenic patients. *Journal of Contemporary Psychotherapy, 29,* 223–234.

The Writing Committee for the ENRICHD Investigators. (2003). Effects of treating depression and low perceived social support on clinical events after myocardial infarction: The enhancing recovery in coronary heart disease patients (ENRICHD) trial. *Journal of the American Medical Association, 289,* 3106–3116.

Yeung, A. C., Vekshtein, V. I., Krantz, D. S., Vita, J. A., Ryan, T. J., Ganz, P., & Selwyn, A. P. (1991). The effect of atherosclerosis on the vasomotor response of coronary arteries to mental stress. *New England Journal of Medicine, 325,* 1551–1556.

Yovetich, N. A., Dale, J. A., & Hudak, M. A. (1990). Benefits of humor in reduction of threat-induced anxiety. *Psychological Reports, 66,* 51–58.

Author Index

Subject Index